Child's body

PADDINGTON
PRESS LTD
NEW YORK & LONDON

A Parent's Manual

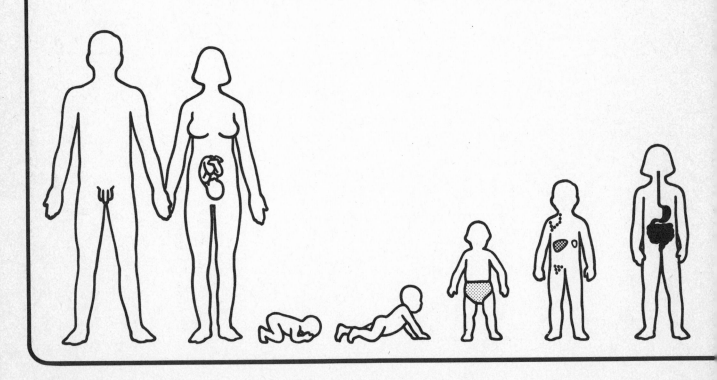

CHILD'S BODY

by the Diagram Group

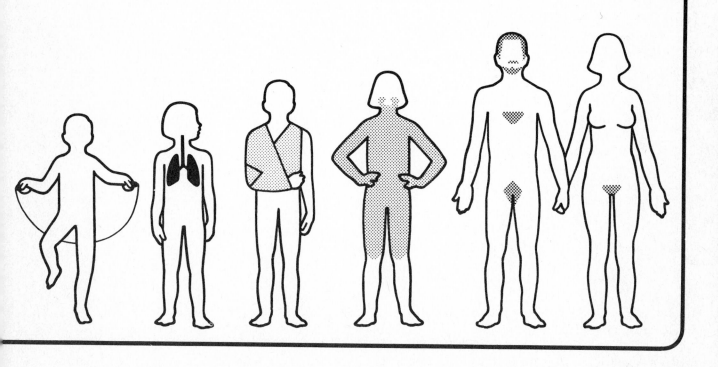

Library of Congress Cataloging in Publication Data

Diagram Group.
  Child's body.

  Bibliography: p.
  Includes index.
  1. Children–Care and hygiene.   2. Child development.
I. Title.
RJ61.D55   612.6'5   77-12566

ISBN 0-448-22187-X

Printed in England by Cox & Wyman Ltd.,
London, Fakenham & Reading

IN THE UNITED STATES
PADDINGTON PRESS LTD.
Distributed by
GROSSET & DUNLAP

IN THE UNITED KINGDOM
PADDINGTON PRESS LTD.

IN CANADA
Distributed by
RANDOM HOUSE OF CANADA LTD.

IN SOUTHERN AFRICA
Distributed by
ERNEST STANTON (PUBLISHERS) (PTY.) LTD.

The Diagram Group

© Diagram Visual Information Ltd 1977

Managing editor	Ruth Midgley
Research editor	Susan Sturrock
Contributors	Kati Boland, David Heidenstam, Ann Kramer, David Lambert, Mary Ling, Robert Royston, Judy Todd, Yvonne Wicken, Elizabeth Wilhide
Editorial assistants	Rosemary Chamberlain, Sue Leith
Art directors	Roger Kohn, Kathleen McDougall
Artists	Jeff Alger, Eileen Batterberry, Steven Clark, Robert Galvin, Richard Hummerstone, Susan Kinsey, Pavel Kostal, Jànos Màrffy, Graham Rosewarne, Diana Taylor
Art assistants	Carlton Facey, Brian Hewson

FOREWORD

Each child's growth and development, from conception through adolescence is obviously complex. The purpose of CHILD'S BODY is to clarify these complexities and help every parent to understand and appreciate more fully the variety of changes their child will inevitably experience.

The editors of CHILD'S BODY have brought together a wealth of information covering almost every aspect of child development and care. Medical jargon has been eliminated and all the facts are presented clearly and concisely with lively and informative illustrations to make every topic easy to comprehend. Carefully planned chapters, numbered subject panels, a full index, and cross-references where appropriate, enable each reader effectively to explore every subject area.

All the material included in CHILD'S BODY has been presented to a team of practicing pediatricians and child care experts for advice and approval. Because opinions and theories often vary and sometimes contradict each other, the editors have attempted to present as many points of view as possible.

Throughout the book we have referred to the child as "he" or "him"—obviously we do so only for convenience. Similarly we often refer to the "parent"—by which we mean either the mother or father, or any other person who may be acting, either temporarily or permanently, in a parental role.

There can be no fixed rules for bringing up and caring for children. Each one of us—parent or child—has individual strengths and weaknesses, talents and needs. In CHILD'S BODY we offer a great deal of practical advice, but considerable flexibility is called for on the part of every parent.

A prime aim of the editors has been to increase the reader's understanding of the fascinating processes of development that occur throughout the childhood years. By doing so, it is hoped that we may also help each parent to give and to gain as much as possible during the challenging and rewarding adventure of parenthood.

CONTENTS

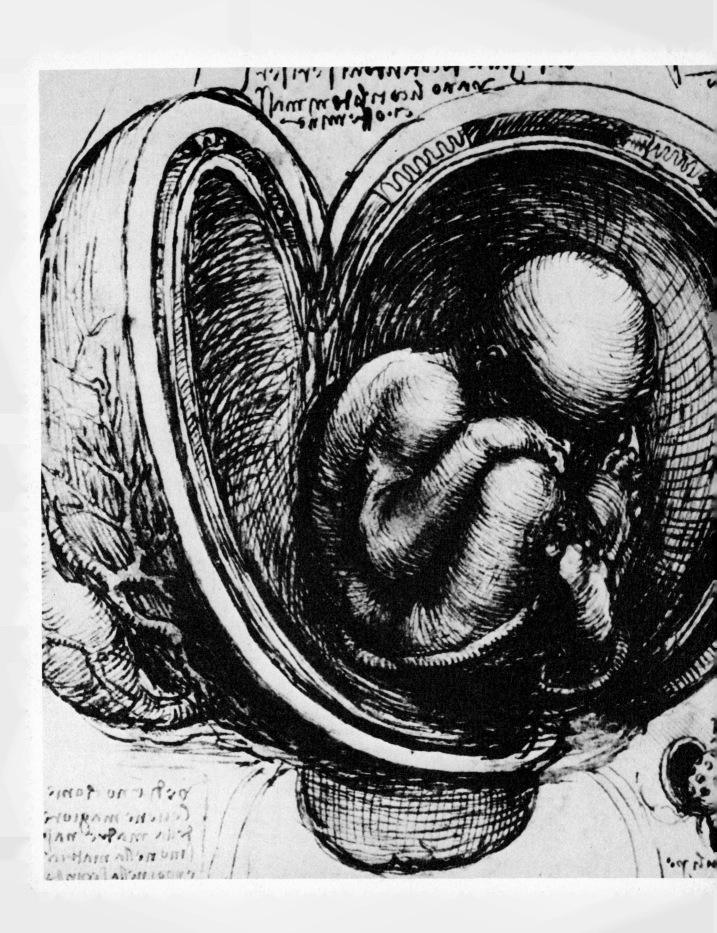

Before birth

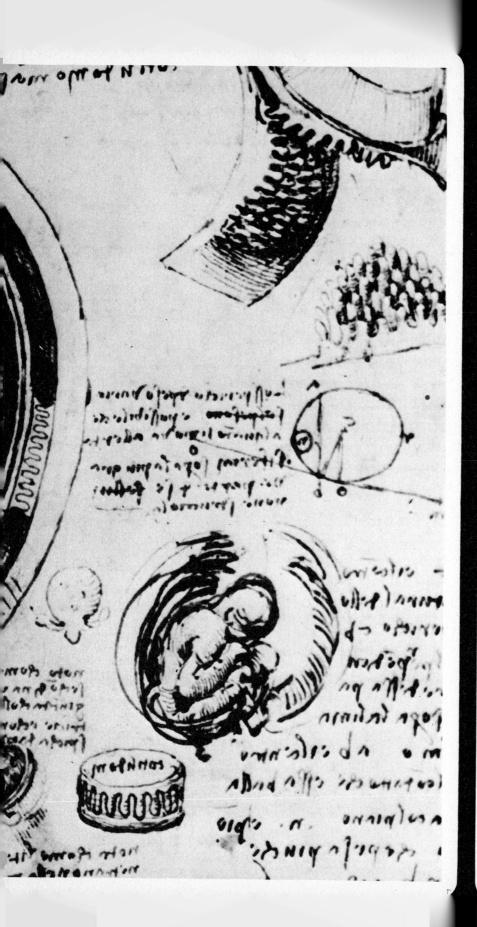

Never again does the human body develop and grow at such speed.

Left: Leonardo da Vinci drawings of the developing fetus (Reproduced by gracious permission of Her Majesty Queen Elizabeth II)

A NEW LIFE

A01 THE START OF LIFE

A new life begins at the moment of fertilization, when a male sperm unites with a female egg, or ovum. At fertilization the head (nucleus) of the sperm penetrates the ovum and fuses with its nucleus. The tail of the sperm drops off. Once the ovum has been fertilized its outer shell hardens to make it impenetrable to all other sperm.

Ova are present in the female ovaries from birth. Each month, from puberty to the menopause, one ovum (or more, see multiple pregnancies, A10) matures and is shed by its ovary for possible fertilization. This process is called ovulation.

A male is not born with a supply of sperm, but from puberty to old age sperm are formed continually in the testes.

A02 JOURNEY OF THE SPERM

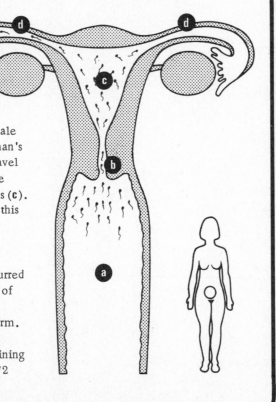

At intercourse, millions of male sperm are deposited in a woman's vagina by the penis. They travel up the vagina (a), through the cervix (b), and into the uterus (c). Many of them fail to survive this journey so that perhaps only 2000 to 3000 ever reach the Fallopian tubes (d).

If ovulation has recently occurred an ovum (e) is present in one of the Fallopian tubes awaiting possible fertilization by a sperm. If the ovum has not yet been released, however, the remaining sperm may survive for up to 72 hours to await its arrival.

A03 FERTILIZATION AND IMPLANTATION

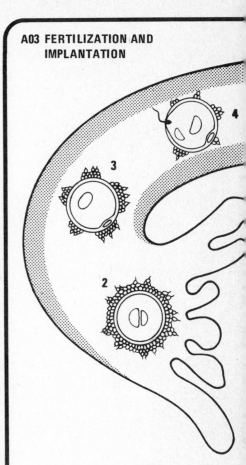

Illustrated here are the earliest stages in the development of a new life - release of the ovum, fertilization, cell division, and implantation in the uterus.

1 Hormones encourage the development of several ova in follicles within the ovary.

2 At ovulation, a mature ovum is released into the Fallopian tube and begins moving to the uterus. The nucleus of the ovum splits into two parts, each containing 23 chromosomes.

3 The larger part stays in the ovum and the smaller "polar body" moves to the shell of the ovum

4 After another split a second polar body moves to the shell of the ovum. Fertilization occurs when a sperm penetrates the ovum and fuses with the remaining part of the nucleus.

Before birth

A

5 The fertilized ovum continues
its journey to the uterus.
6 About 30 hours after
fertilization the ovum divides into
two cells.
7 About 20 hours later a second
division occurs, giving four cells.
These divisions continue, each
time doubling the number of cells.
8 About three to four days after
fertilization the ball of cells, or
morula, reaches the uterus.
9 Fluid begins to appear within
the ball of cells.
10 The fluid separates the cells
into two parts. The outer cells
will form the embryo and the
inner mass the placenta.
11 The ovum, properly called
the blastocyst at this stage, is now
the size of a pinhead. Its outer
shell breaks down and allows it to
be implanted in the uterine wall.

HEREDITY

A04 CHROMOSOMES

Each cell in the body contains 23 pairs of chromosomes that carry the "blueprint" of information on which the cell was built.
When a new cell is needed for growth or tissue replacement, an existing cell divides into two. Just before division, its chromosomes double up so that each new cell will have its own 23 pairs of chromosomes.
In sperm and ova there is no doubling up of the chromosomes before division. On division, therefore, each contains only 23 chromosomes - one from each pair. At fertilization, male and female chromosomes pair up to give the new cell its full 23 pairs. This new cell thus contains chromosomes bearing information to produce characteristics inherited from each parent.

Chromosomes during sexual reproduction

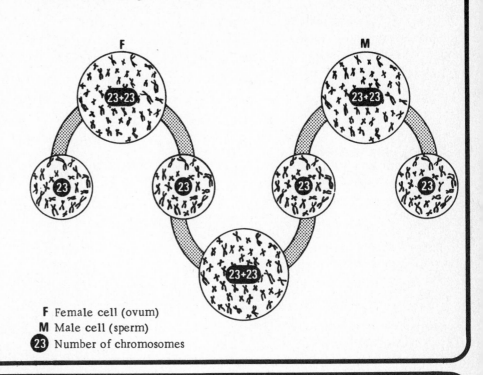

F Female cell (ovum)
M Male cell (sperm)
23 Number of chromosomes

A05 SEX DETERMINATION

Among the 23 chromosome pairs in every human cell, there is one pair of sex chromosomes. In a female the two chromosomes of the pair are identical, and because of their shape they are described as X chromosomes. In a male, however, the two sex chromosomes are different: one is an X chromosome, while the other is described as a Y chromosome. As outlined in A04, each partner contributes to his offspring only one chromosome from each of the chromosome pairs. Since a female has two X chromosomes she must always contribute an X chromosome. The male partner, however, may contribute either an X or a Y chromosome. If fertilization is by an X-bearing sperm, the offspring will be XX - female; if by a Y-bearing sperm, it will be XY - male.

Inheritance of X and Y chromosomes

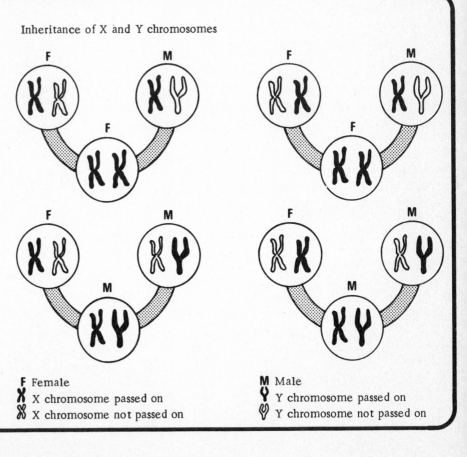

F Female
X X chromosome passed on
X X chromosome not passed on
M Male
Y Y chromosome passed on
Y Y chromosome not passed on

Before birth

A06 INHERITED TRAITS

All children inherit some of their characteristics of appearance and temperament from their parents. The information for these traits, such as color of eyes and hair, is carried in genes - chemical units in the chromosomes. Like chromosomes, genes occur in pairs, one inherited from each parent. In certain gene pairs, a "dominant" gene carrying a particular characteristic will always overpower a weaker, or "recessive," gene carrying a different characteristic. In the case of eye color, for instance, a gene for brown eyes dominates a gene for blue eyes. As the diagrams show, two brown-eyed parents usually produce a brown-eyed child (**1**,**2**,**3**, and **4**); they may produce a blue-eyed child (**5**), however, if each contributes a recessive gene for blue eyes.

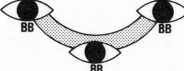

1 Brown-eye gene from each parent, producing brown-eyed child

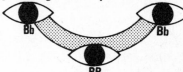

2 Brown-eye gene from each parent, producing brown-eyed child

3 Father's brown-eye gene dominates, producing brown-eyed child

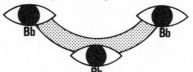

4 Mother's brown-eye gene dominates, producing brown-eyed child

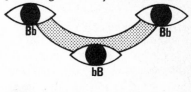

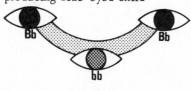

5 Recessive genes from each parent, producing blue-eyed child

Brown eyes
Blue eyes
BB Two brown-eye genes
Bb One brown-,one blue-eye gene
bB One blue-,one brown-eye gene
bb Two blue-eye genes

A07 SKIPPING GENERATIONS

Occasionally a child seems to bear very little resemblance to either of his parents, but shows strong similarities to a member of an earlier generation. This can also be explained genetically.

Red hair is a good example of a physical attribute that can skip several generations before reappearing. The gene for red hair is recessive, dominated by a gene for dark brown hair. It can thus be handed down unnoticed through generations of dark-haired people. If a recessive red-hair gene from one parent is matched by a similar gene from the other, a red-haired offspring will result - perhaps to the surprise of the parents if they were unaware of their red-haired ancestors!

Inheritance of a recessive characteristic

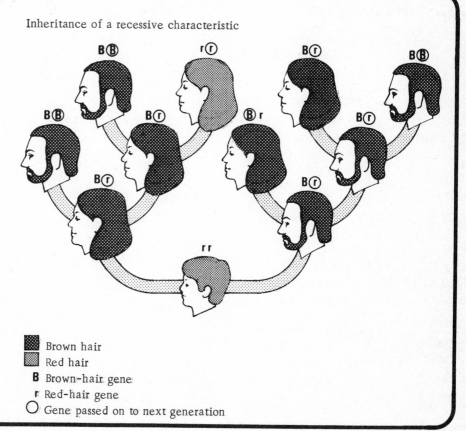

Brown hair
Red hair
B Brown-hair gene
r Red-hair gene
◯ Gene passed on to next generation

BLOOD GROUPS

A08 BLOOD GROUPS

Blood can be grouped in a variety of ways. The most common - and important because of its bearing on blood transfusions - is into groups A, B, AB, and O. This classification depends on the presence or absence of two factors - "A" and "B" - in the blood. A and B blood each contain one of these factors, AB contains both, while O contains neither.

A person's blood group is an inherited characteristic - and sometimes blood tests are used in paternity cases. It is not possible to prove that a certain individual fathered a child, but it is possible to show that someone could not have been the father. The diagram shows the possible blood groups of the father when a child and his mother have blood belonging to a particular group.

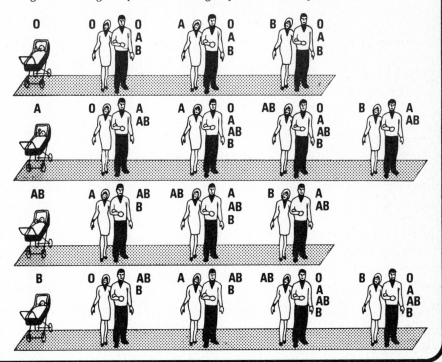

Diagram showing the possible blood groups of a child's parents

A09 THE RHESUS FACTOR

Blood is also grouped according to the presence or absence of a substance called the rhesus factor. The majority of the population (85%) have blood that contains this factor, and are denoted rhesus positive; people without this factor are denoted rhesus negative. Normally this has no significance, but problems can arise if a rhesus negative mother carries a rhesus positive baby. A blood test early in pregnancy is therefore essential. The first time a rhesus negative mother carries a rhesus positive baby, complications are unusual. But during delivery some of the baby's rhesus positive blood may enter the mother's bloodstream (a). This causes the mother to form antibodies to neutralize the "foreign" substance (b). In a subsequent pregnancy (if the fetus is again rhesus positive), these antibodies pass through the placenta

and attack the red blood cells in the fetal bloodstream (c). The effects on the fetus of rhesus incompatibility, or "rhesus disease," vary in severity. Anemia and jaundice may occur, and premature delivery may be necessary. Exchange blood transfusions are given in severe cases, either after birth, or sometimes while the baby is still in the uterus.

It is now routine, however, to give an injection of purified rhesus antibody (obtained from people with a high level of antibody) to a rhesus negative mother within 12 hours of her delivering a rhesus positive child. These antibodies react with the "foreign" cells before the mother has time to form antibodies, thus preventing problems in subsequent pregnancies.

Rhesus incompatibility in a first and subsequent pregnancy

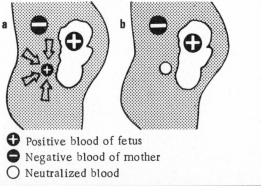

Positive blood of fetus
Negative blood of mother
Neutralized blood

Before birth

A10 MULTIPLE PREGNANCIES

A multiple pregnancy results from the splitting of a single ovum fertilized by one sperm (**a**), or the fertilization of two or more ova by different sperm (**b**). A twin pregnancy occurs once in about 87 pregnancies.
Triplet, quadruplet, and quintuplet pregnancies are successively less common. They may result from the multiple division of a single ovum into three, four, or five, or from the fertilization of three, four, or five separate ova. More commonly, there is a combination of these occurrences. Triplets, for instance, may be the product of a single ovum that has split into three (**c**), three separately fertilized ova (**d**), or one undivided ovum plus one that has divided (**e**).

Twin pregnancy

Triplet pregnancy

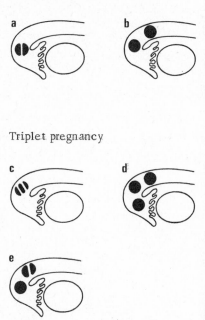

A11 INCIDENCE

Multiple pregnancies are most common in women in their thirties. Some races produce more multiple pregnancies than others; twin births, for instance, are less common in China than in Britain, and more common among some African peoples.
A multiple pregnancy seems to be more likely in some families than in others; this is partly because the tendency to shed more than one ovum at ovulation can be an inherited trait.
The use of fertility drugs has increased the incidence of multiple births. In rare cases, use of a fertility drug results in overstimulation of the ovaries and the production of more than one ovum.

A12 IDENTICAL OR NOT

Identical twins, formed from the splitting of a single ovum, account for 25% of all twin pregnancies. Each fetus has its own amniotic sac but the two share a single placenta. Because their genetic structure and chromosomes are the same, identical twins always are of the same sex and have the same characteristics.

Identical twins: one placenta

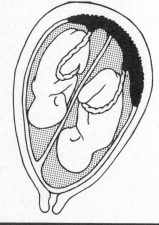

Non-identical twins, formed from two separate ova, have separate placentas as implantation occurs at two different sites in the uterus. They do not share the same genetic structure and so may be no more alike in appearance or in temperament than are any two children produced by the same parents.

Non-identical twins: two placentas

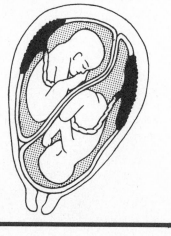

A13 DIAGNOSIS

The diagnosis of a multiple pregnancy is usually simple. The uterus is consistently larger than the dates would suggest.
As early as week 14 it may be possible, with the aid of sophisticated electronic equipment, to detect more than one fetal heartbeat.
From the 28th week, gentle palpation of the abdomen may reveal the presence of more than one fetus. If the diagnosis remains unchanged at this time, a multiple pregnancy can be confirmed by X-ray, or by the use of special scanning equipment on the mother's abdomen.
It is desirable to identify a multiple pregnancy in good time as its management requires a little extra care to ensure the safety of the babies.

FETAL DEVELOPMENT 1

A14 FETAL SUPPORT SYSTEM

Throughout pregnancy the growing baby is entirely dependent on its mother. Her diet, her general state of health, and even the amount of rest she takes all have their effect. For this reason it is essential that a pregnant woman should obtain proper antenatal care throughout her pregnancy.

The complex life support system on which the baby's development depends - the placenta, the umbilical cord and the amniotic sac - starts to form within hours of conception.

The placenta is a disk-shaped network of blood vessels attached to the lining of the uterus. It is connected with the fetus by the umbilical cord and through this system the baby obtains nourishment from the mother and is able to rid itself of waste products. The placenta is so important that during the first few weeks of pregnancy its growth far outstrips that of the baby.

The amniotic sac is a bag of fluid that encloses the fetus and protects it from jolts and knocks that might cause injury.

The neck of the uterus, or cervix, is plugged with mucus to seal it off from the vagina and prevent the entry of infection.

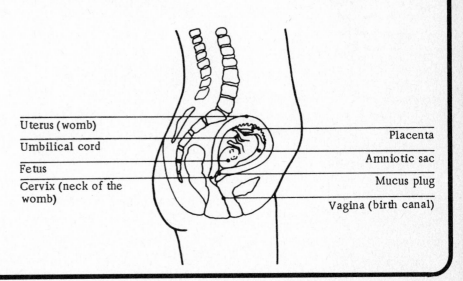

Uterus (womb)	Placenta
Umbilical cord	Amniotic sac
Fetus	Mucus plug
Cervix (neck of the womb)	Vagina (birth canal)

A16 THE FIRST WEEKS

An average pregnancy lasts 266 days from the fertilization of the ovum to the delivery of the baby. Since conception can seldom be dated accurately, however, most doctors regard pregnancy as lasting 280 days, or 40 weeks, counting the first day of the last menstrual period as day one.

During pregnancy the fertilized ovum grows astonishingly quickly. By the time the baby is born, that single egg cell has developed into a complex arrangement of no fewer than two billion cells.

Development in the first few weeks is particularly remarkable. Limbs and organs have formed, simple bodily processes are established, and the miniature being becomes recognizably human.

The development of the embryo during the vital first weeks of pregnancy is described here.

WEEKS 2-3

About 14 days after day 1 of the last menstrual period, ovulation occurs (see A01).

If intercourse takes place, conception may result. Following fertilization the ovum implants itself in the uterine wall (see A03).

WEEK 4

The embryo, well embedded in the uterus, continues to develop.

WEEK 5

The embryo is approximately 0.08in (2mm) long and just visible to the naked eye. It is clearly developing its main components, with a bulge for the head containing a rudimentary brain, a middle section containing a simple heart, and a tail. There is no skeleton, but a primitive spine is starting to form.

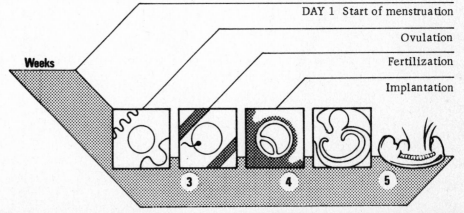

Weeks

DAY 1 Start of menstruation
Ovulation
Fertilization
Implantation

Before birth

A15 GROWTH IN THE UTERUS

Growth of the baby during pregnancy causes the uterus to expand, displacing some of the mother's internal organs.

WEEK 8
Growth of the embryo, though very rapid, is still not sufficient to enlarge the uterus.

WEEK 28
The uterus is considerably enlarged and extends to four finger-breadths above the mother's navel. Fetal movements are felt strongly by the mother, and the fetus often adopts a head-up position for long periods.

WEEK 40
The pregnancy is at full term and the baby has usually settled into a head-down position. The uterus occupies a large part of the abdominal cavity and may lead to shortness of breath, indigestion, or backache.

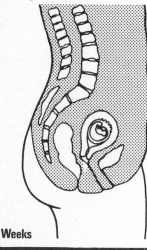 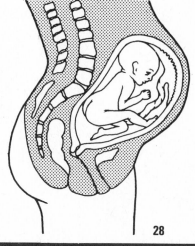 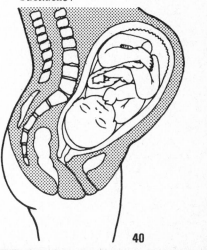

Weeks | 8 | 28 | 40

WEEK 6
The embryo is approximately 0.2in (6mm) long. Limb buds are discernible and chest and abdominal cavities are forming.

WEEK 7
The embryo is approximately 0.5in (1.3cm) long. Limbs are obvious, the lungs, liver, kidneys, and intestines are taking shape, and the brain and spinal column are growing quickly. Development of the eyes, ears, nostrils, and mouth begins.

WEEK 9
The embryo is approximately 1.2in (3cm) long and weighs 0.07oz (2gm). The internal organs are all formed but still simple in structure. The limbs are growing rapidly and rudimentary "webbed" fingers and toes can be seen. Eyes, ears, nostrils, and mouth continue to develop.

WEEK 11
The embryo is approximately 2in (5.5cm) long and weighs 0.35oz (10gm). The head is quite well rounded and facial features more clearly defined. Ovaries or testes have formed inside the body but the sex cannot yet be distinguished externally.

Development of embryo (not to scale)

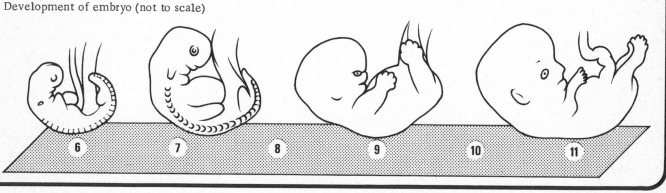

6 | 7 | 8 | 9 | 10 | 11

©DIAGRAM

FETAL DEVELOPMENT 2

A17 THE MIDDLE WEEKS

WEEK 12

The fetus is easily recognizable as human. The head is more rounded and less bent forward onto the chest. Development of the inner and middle ear is complete and the external ear is assuming its mature form. Development of the eyes is complete, though they are entirely covered by the eyelids. The limbs are longer, with muscles starting to develop. Ankles and wrists are obvious, and fingers and toes are easily distinguishable. Most of the major internal organs - liver, kidneys, intestines, and lungs - are fully formed and will continue to grow until the baby is ready to be born. The heart is complete and the blood is circulating in the body (J52). The fetus is now $3\frac{1}{2}$in (9cm) long and weighs $\frac{1}{2}$oz (14gm).

WEEK 16

The development period for the fetus is over and the remainder of the pregnancy is devoted to fetal growth.

The limbs are fully formed, many of the muscles are well developed, and the joints are in working order. The baby exercises his body within the uterus, stretching and flexing his limbs and spine, but the movements are usually too gentle to be felt by the mother. The body is bright red in color as the blood vessels show through the transparent skin. The heart beats very strongly and pumps up to $62\frac{1}{2}$ US pints (50 Imperial pints: 28.5 liters) of blood round the body each day. Hair follicles have begun to form and very fine hair may start to develop on the head. The primary sex characteristics are quite well developed and the sex of the baby is obvious. The two halves of the palate have fused and the vocal cords are complete. The baby can now swallow amniotic fluid, and urination has begun.

Development of fetus (not to scale)

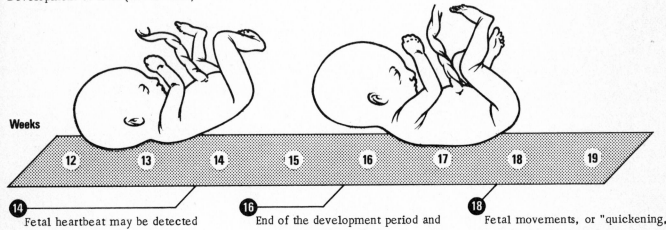

Weeks

12 13 14 15 16 17 18 19

14 Fetal heartbeat may be detected with sophisticated electronic equipment.

16 End of the development period and start of the growth phase. From this date, the risk of harm to the fetus resulting from drugs taken by the mother is reduced.
Length: 7in (18cm)
Weight: 4oz (113gm)

18 Fetal movements, or "quickening," may be felt by a mother carrying her first baby. They may be felt earlier than this in subsequent pregnancies.

Before birth

WEEK 20

Fetal movements are now felt as small "flutters" when the baby moves in the amniotic fluid. First noticed at about week 18 in women having their first baby, they are felt earlier in women carrying a second or subsequent child, and later in women who are overweight. The movements are intermittent and may cease to be felt for up to 48 hours. Some babies have hiccups, an experience also noted by their mothers! The heartbeat can be heard with the aid of a fetal stethoscope. Eyebrows begin to develop, nipples appear, and the nails harden.

WEEK 24

The body is still very thin and the skin red and wrinkled because of the absence of subcutaneous fat. Muscles in the arms and legs are strong and the fetal movements are very obvious to the mother. Many of the reflexes that can be elicited at birth are already present; the grasp reflex is particularly pronounced. Lanugo, a fine, downy growth of hair starts to

appear on the back, legs, and arms. The eyelids have separated but a membrane still covers the pupils. A baby born at this stage may survive briefly without assistance, but the lungs are too immature to sustain life. With sophisticated equipment and expert care, however, a very small percentage of 24 weekers do survive.

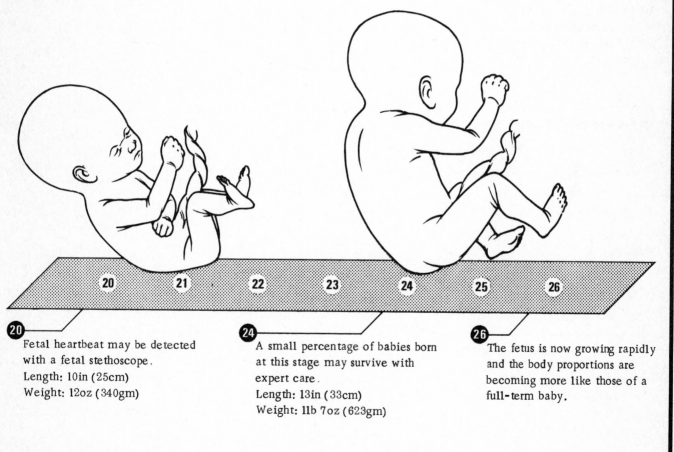

20 Fetal heartbeat may be detected with a fetal stethoscope.
Length: 10in (25cm)
Weight: 12oz (340gm)

24 A small percentage of babies born at this stage may survive with expert care.
Length: 13in (33cm)
Weight: 1lb 7oz (623gm)

26 The fetus is now growing rapidly and the body proportions are becoming more like those of a full-term baby.

FETAL DEVELOPMENT 3

A18 THE LAST WEEKS

WEEK 28
The body is now covered in vernix, a white, greasy substance that prevents the skin from becoming waterlogged in the amniotic fluid. The umbilical cord has reached its maximum length and the baby moves about energetically in the uterus. The torso has grown more rapidly than the head in the previous four weeks, so that the head now seems only slightly out of proportion to the overall body size. The baby can now open his eyes, and the membrane covering the pupils has gone.

WEEK 32
Proportions of head to body are closer to those at full term. The skin is still red and wrinkled but fat is being deposited to smooth it out. The baby is less active and now usually adopts a head-down position in the uterus (also see B06). The lungs are fairly well developed and chances of survival are quite good if expert care is available.

Development of fetus (not to scale)

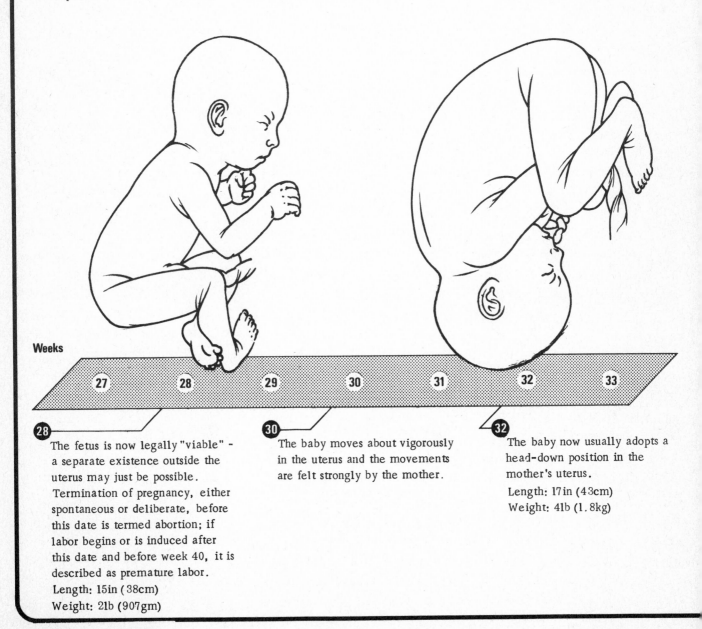

Weeks

27 28 29 30 31 32 33

28 The fetus is now legally "viable" - a separate existence outside the uterus may just be possible. Termination of pregnancy, either spontaneous or deliberate, before this date is termed abortion; if labor begins or is induced after this date and before week 40, it is described as premature labor.
Length: 15in (38cm)
Weight: 2lb (907gm)

30 The baby moves about vigorously in the uterus and the movements are felt strongly by the mother.

32 The baby now usually adopts a head-down position in the mother's uterus.
Length: 17in (43cm)
Weight: 4lb (1.8kg)

Before birth

WEEK 36
Up to 1½lb (680gm) of fat has been deposited beneath the skin in the preceding four weeks so the skin is less wrinkled and the body quite well rounded. The fingernails reach the fingertips and in a male infant the testes may have descended into the scrotum.

In the case of a first baby, the head may now settle low in the pelvis, or "engage" ready for delivery. (With subsequent babies the head usually engages later.) Chances of survival are as good as 90% if the baby is born at this stage.

WEEK 40
The pregnancy is at term, and the baby is fully grown and ready to be born. The skin is smooth, the body rounded, and the lanugo has usually disappeared. The eyes are bluish-gray in color, but may change later, often within minutes of birth.

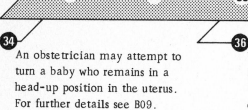

34   35   36   37   38   39   40

34
An obstetrician may attempt to turn a baby who remains in a head-up position in the uterus. For further details see B09.

36
With a first baby the head may sink low in the mother's pelvis. This "engagement" of the head occurs later in subsequent babies. A baby born at this stage stands a very good chance of survival.
Length: 18in (46cm)
Weight: 5lb 4oz (2.38kg)

40
In theory, the baby is born 280 days after the start of the last menstruation. In practice, the birth is commonly up to two weeks before or after this date.
Length: 20in (50.8cm)
Weight: 7lb (3.18kg)

(All lengths and weights included here are approximate. Infant boys may be heavier and longer, and infant girls lighter and shorter.)

Birth and the new baby

Eminent psychologists and obstetricians now claim that the experience of birth may have a lasting and fundamental effect on the child.

Left: Detail from "The Nativity of the Virgin Mary" by Pietro Lorenzetti (The Mansell Collection)

PREPARING FOR BIRTH

B01 HOME OR HOSPITAL

Forty years ago almost all babies were born at home. In Holland over half of all deliveries are still carried out at home, but in many other countries home deliveries are now unusual. (In the United States in 1975, 98.7% of all births were in a hospital.)

In countries where hospital delivery has become usual it is often difficult for a woman to have her baby at home, because local medical services are no longer organized to meet her needs. Provided that adequate care is available both during and after the birth, it may be possible in low-risk cases for a mother to choose to have her baby at home. Many doctors, however, believe that it is preferable for all babies to be born in a hospital.

Hospital delivery will generally be recommended:
1) if the mother is aged under 17 or over 35;
2) if the mother has certain medical conditions such as diabetes, heart trouble, or a kidney complaint;
3) if it is a first baby, or a fourth or subsequent baby;
4) if it is a multiple delivery;
5) if the mother suffers from severe anemia early in pregnancy;
6) if the mother develops toxemia or high blood pressure in pregnancy;
7) if there is rhesus incompatibility (see A09);
8) if there were any complications at a previous delivery;
9) if the mother's pelvis is small;
10) if the baby is not a cephalic presentation (B06);
11) if delivery is premature.

B02 HOSPITAL DELIVERY

A hospital delivery is generally recommended for most mothers. Facilities are available to cope with any difficulty or unforeseen complication that may arise during the birth and many women find this reassuring and comforting.

In addition, many mothers appreciate the constant presence of nurses in the few days after the birth to help and advise them, and also welcome the opportunity to get to know their new baby without the work and worry of running a home.

Some women, however, are anxious about leaving their family and prefer to return home as soon as possible; providing the birth was normal, some hospitals permit a 48-hour stay instead of the customary week or more.

B03 THE DELIVERY ROOM

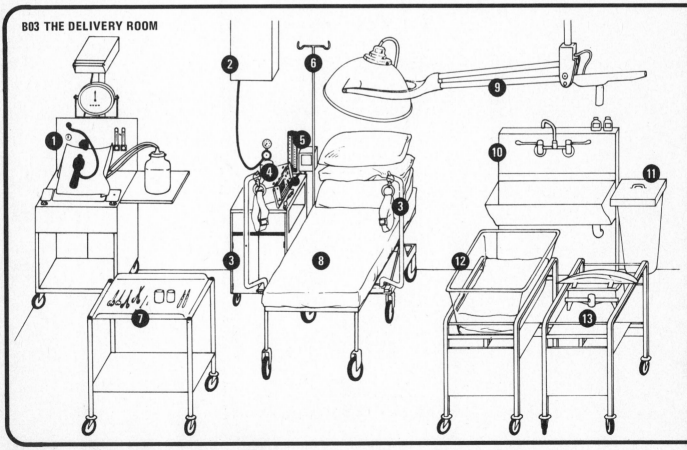

Birth and the new baby

B

B04 HOME DELIVERY

Some women prefer the relaxed atmosphere of a home birth, and welcome the degree of freedom that it allows. In addition, other children in the family may find it easier to accept the new arrival if he is born at home.

It is customary for the doctor or midwife to visit in advance the room in which the delivery will take place, in order to give advice on equipment needed and to suggest a possible rearrangement of furniture if necessary.

Essential items of furniture are a crib for the baby, a table for the doctor's instruments, and a bed for the mother. The mattress should be covered with a waterproof sheet and the bed linen should be old but newly washed. The floor around the bed should be covered with a protective sheet or layers of thick brown paper. Ideally, any carpet should be rolled back or removed.

The doctor or midwife needs ready access to a washbasin, a plentiful supply of boiled water, several small bowls, and a good light. Beneath the bed there should be a pail for used dressings. A sealed box containing important sterilized items such as towels, masks, and gowns for the doctor, pads and dressings for the mother, and tape for tying the umbilical cord, is prepared in advance and opened only when labor is well under way.

No solid food should be taken by a woman in labor, but clear liquids such as soup or fruit juice may be welcome.

A typical delivery room of the kind shown here contains all the equipment necessary to ensure that childbirth is as safe and comfortable as possible.

1 Baby resuscitation equipment
2 Pendant tanks containing oxygen and analgesic gases
3 Stirrups for lithotomy delivery
4 Fetal monitor
5 Blood pressure apparatus
6 Intravenous drip stand
7 Delivery table and instruments
8 Delivery bed
9 Light
10 Scrubbing sink
11 Container for soiled linens
12 Bassinette
13 Scales

B05 MANAGEMENT OF LABOR

The management of the process of birth depends on the facilities available, the wishes of the mother, and the condition of both mother and fetus.

Natural childbirth, pioneered by Grantly Dick-Read, is the process of giving birth without the help of drugs or obstetric techniques. Based on the assumption that the mother's fear causes tension and increases pain, preparation for natural childbirth includes the study of relaxation techniques.

Psychoprophylaxis, established by Fernand Lamaze, involves the application of pre-learned breathing and muscular exercises during the birth.

Drug-assisted childbirth is now very common. The drugs used are analgesics to relieve pain, and anesthetics to reduce sensation in a particular area. They are given by injection or inhalation.

B06 FETAL POSITIONS

By about week 32 of pregnancy, most babies are cephalic presentations: lying head-down in the pelvis ready for labor. If a baby remains head-up, an obstetrician may try to turn him (see B09).

CEPHALIC PRESENTATION (96%)
In most cephalic presentations, the back of the head, or vertex, is delivered first. Face-first deliveries are quite rare.

BREECH PRESENTATION (3.5%)
In a breech presentation, the baby's head lies at the top of the uterus and his bottom is delivered first.

TRANSVERSE LIE (0.5%)
A transverse lie can often be manipulated into another position. Uncorrected, it always requires a cesarian section (see B10).

B07 FIRST STAGE OF LABOR

Labor is divided into three stages. During the first stage, the uterus changes shape as the cervix effaces (thins out) and dilates (opens up). It lasts until the baby's head reaches the vagina, or birth canal. It is followed by the second stage, when the baby is delivered, and the third stage, expulsion of the placenta.

1 Before labor begins, the fetus is usually head-down in the uterus, facing one of the mother's hips.

2 The beginning of labor is marked by regular contractions of the uterus which, as labor progresses, increase in frequency and intensity. They are felt as a gradual tightening of the uterus. Tightening reaches a peak and then relaxes, after which nothing is felt until the next contraction. At the start of labor, contractions generally cause little discomfort. They occur every 15-30 minutes and last 45-60 seconds.

3 As the uterine muscles contract and retract they first cause effacement of the cervix. In effacement the thick walls of the cervix, which project slightly into the upper end of the vagina, are drawn up and become thinner. This process lasts, on average, 8-12 hours for a woman having her first child and 4-5 hours for a woman having subsequent babies. The rate of contractions speeds up gradually as effacement proceeds.

1

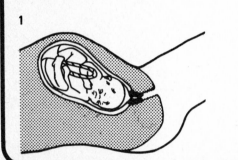

2

3

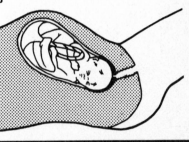

B08 SECOND AND THIRD STAGES OF LABOR

7 The second stage of labor - the delivery of the baby - begins once dilation is complete. This stage usually lasts 15-45 minutes for a first baby, and may be as short as 10 minutes at later births. Contractions are now less frequent and feel different from those in the first stage. The mother now can play an active part in her baby's birth, bearing down and using the controlled breathing techniques she has learned during pregnancy.

8 When the baby's head reaches the floor of the pelvis it usually rotates to a face-down position. The descent continues, bringing the baby's head to the perineum, the muscular outlet of the pelvis. Stretching of the perineal muscles to allow the baby to emerge from the vagina produces a burning sensation and a very strong urge to push. An episiotomy - an incision made in the perineum (see B13) - may be given at this stage to prevent tearing.

9 The top of the baby's head then appears at the entrance of the vagina. Once the head has completely emerged, the baby's shoulders rotate spontaneously to ease their way out of the vagina. This causes the head to return to its original side-facing position. The baby's eyes, nose, and mouth are now usually wiped with gauze, and the air passages of the nose and mouth may be cleared of mucus with the aid of a special extractor (see B15).

7

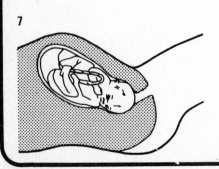

8

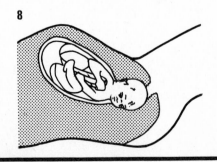

9

Birth and the new baby

4 By the time effacement nears completion, contractions are occurring every 3-5 minutes and last some 40-90 seconds. The cervix now begins to dilate as the uterine contractions pull open the circular muscles around the cervix. The mucus plug, which has kept the uterus free from infection during pregnancy, is now displaced and, if this has not happened earlier, the amniotic sac will probably rupture.

5 As dilation progresses contractions become more rapid and more intense. For the baby to pass through it, the cervix must dilate sufficiently to accommodate its head - about 4in (10cm). Dilation is sometimes measured in finger widths: full dilation equals five finger widths. For a woman having her first child dilation may take 3-5 hours; for subsequent children it takes less time.

6 Toward the end of dilation contractions are intense and occur every 2-3 minutes. The transition between the first and second stages of labor is a difficult time, often accompanied by feelings of nausea and irritability. Long, strong, and irregular contractions may now occur, and the woman feels a strong urge to bear down. It is important, however, not to bear down before the cervix is fully dilated.

4

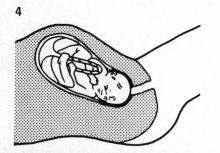

5

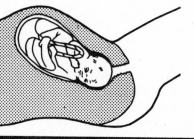

6

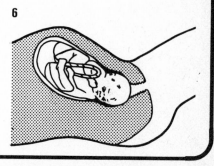

10 Contractions usually stop for a short while after the delivery of the head. When they resume, gentle pushing by the mother will deliver first one shoulder and then the other. The rest of the body then follows after comparatively little effort, with the doctor or nurse supporting the baby and drawing his head and shoulders up toward the mother's abdomen. This enables the mother to see her baby for the first time even before his delivery is complete.

11 On delivery most babies breathe and cry spontaneously. Sometimes the baby is held upside down to drain any remaining fluid from his air passages. The first cry is thought to be a reflex action to ensure that the lungs start operating efficiently. Once breathing is established the umbilical cord is clamped and cut. (A fuller account of the procedures after the baby's delivery is given in B15; the physical appearance of a newborn baby is described in B18.)

12 The third stage of labor - expulsion of the placenta and membranes - lasts 10-30 minutes after delivery of the baby. The placenta separates from the uterine wall and is expelled through the vagina by further contractions. It is usual for an injection to be given either during or after delivery of the placenta to encourage the uterus to contract back to its normal size. If needed - after an episiotomy or tearing - stitches are finally inserted in the perineum.

10

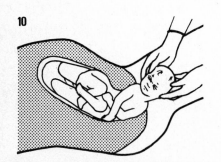

11

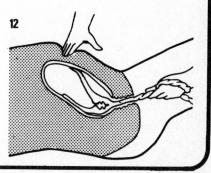

12

BIRTH 2

B09 BREECH DELIVERY

Between weeks 30 and 34 most babies adopt a head-down position in the uterus (see A18). If a baby remains bottom-down at week 34 it is usual for the doctor to attempt to turn him manually. If this fails the baby will be left as he is until delivery.

A breech delivery, with the baby born bottom first, need not cause any problems. An episiotomy

(B13) is given to speed delivery of the baby's head - so preventing lack of oxygen caused by the baby's head pressing for too long against the uterus during the second stage of labor.

However, if a breech baby is large or has a large head, or if the mother's pelvis is small, it is now usual practice to deliver by cesarian section (see B10).

Attempt by doctor to turn the fetus from a breech position

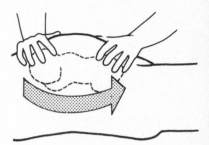

Emergence of the baby's buttocks

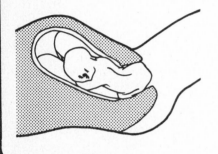

Legs and body follow the buttocks

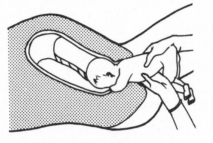

The head is gently eased out

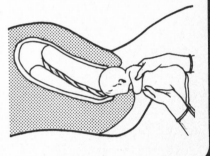

B10 CESARIAN SECTION

A baby is delivered by cesarian section - through incisions in the abdominal wall and uterus - in cases where vaginal delivery could be harmful to mother or baby. Reasons for it include: previous history of stillbirth or difficult delivery; difficult presentation, especially if the baby is large or the mother's pelvis small; prolapse

of the umbilical cord; displaced placenta; bleeding after 28th week. Since the early 1950s cesarian section has become a safe and straightforward operation. It is usually carried out under general anesthetic. An incision is made in the abdominal wall, and another in the uterus. The baby's head is delivered first, and the mouth and

nose are cleared before delivery is completed. An injection is then given to contract the uterus, the placenta is removed, and the incisions stitched or clamped. Vaginal delivery is sometimes possible for subsequent babies. If not, the scars from the first cesarian section are opened for further deliveries.

The doctor makes a curved incision in the lower uterus

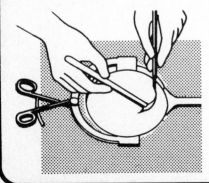

The incision is stretched with the fingers

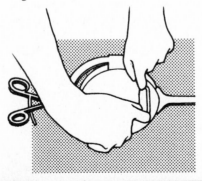

The baby's head is gently lifted out by hand

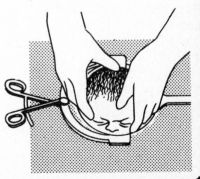

Birth and the new baby

B11 MULTIPLE BIRTHS

Most multiple births are easy and straightforward. The most serious possible complication, especially with more than three babies, is that labor may begin prematurely while the babies are still immature. Adequate rest after week 28 of the pregnancy may help delay the onset of labor.

When labor is established the first baby is usually in a head-down position and delivered normally. An episiotomy is generally performed (see B13). Contractions may cease briefly between deliveries, and the mother's abdomen is palpated to ascertain the position of the other babies. Head and breech presenting babies are delivered normally, but a baby lying in a transverse position (B06) will need to be turned, occasionally under a general anesthetic. The third stage of labor proceeds as that for a single birth.

B12 VACUUM EXTRACTION

Delivery by vacuum extraction - also called the ventouse - is sometimes used as an alternative to forceps delivery (B14). It is most popular in Scandinavia. A metal cup, attached to suction equipment, is inserted into the vagina and placed against the baby's head. Creation of a vacuum makes the cup stick to the baby's head, which is then drawn gently through the vagina. It is usual to wait until the cervix is fully dilated before inserting the cup, but vacuum extraction may be used before full dilation if labor is taking an undue length of time. A swelling on the baby's head, caused by tissues being drawn into the cup, disappears completely within a few hours of delivery.

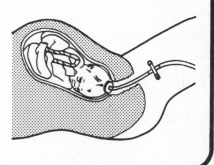

Delivery by vacuum extraction

B13 EPISIOTOMY

An episiotomy - cutting of the mother's perineum - is sometimes carried out during labor to ease the passage of the baby's head. It is a simple operation carried out under local anesthetic; the perineum is cut along the mid-line or slightly obliquely. The incision is stitched after the delivery. An episiotomy is needed during a breech delivery (B09), forceps delivery (B14), and if the baby is being delivered very quickly, as in a premature (B20) or multiple (B11) birth. It is also given if the tissues of the perineum are so rigid that they are delaying the second stage of labor, or if the entrance to the vagina is so tight that tearing is inevitable. Whether or not an episiotomy is desirable in all deliveries is a matter of dispute among doctors.

B14 FORCEPS DELIVERY

Forceps are used to assist the delivery of a baby if there is delay in the second stage of labor, or if there are signs of maternal or fetal distress. Before the application of forceps it is essential that the cervix is fully dilated, the baby's head engaged in the pelvis, uterine contractions occurring, and that there is no obvious obstruction to delivery. After giving a local or general anesthetic, the forceps are inserted one blade at a time. The handles are then fitted together, and the baby's head delivered very gently, little by little. Forceps cannot possibly damage the baby's head, and in fact help to protect it. An episiotomy is given. Once the head is delivered, the forceps are removed and delivery proceeds as usual.

The forcep blades are positioned on either side of the baby's head

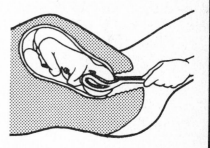

The forceps are used to draw the head gently through the vagina

©DIAGRAM

AFTER THE BIRTH

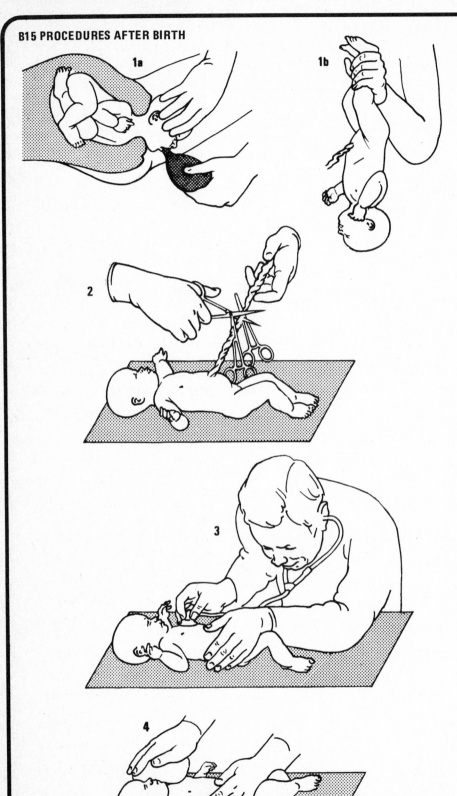

1 BREATHING
To aid breathing, air passages are cleared with a mucus extractor as the head emerges (**a**).
The baby may be held upside down to prevent inhalation of mucus (**b**). Oxygen may be given through a mask or, if necessary, through a tube passed into the trachea.

2 CUTTING THE CORD
The umbilical cord may be severed as soon as the baby's air passages are quite clear and regular breathing is established. One clamp is placed on the cord about 6in (15cm) from the baby and a second 3in (7.5cm) nearer the mother. The cord is then cut between these two points.

3 PRELIMINARY CHECKS
Immediately after birth, the baby's condition is briefly checked. This initial inspection includes a chest examination with a stethoscope to listen to the heartbeat and breathing rate.

4 WASHING
It is no longer usual to bathe a newborn baby immediately as it is thought that the vernix (B18) may give some protection against infection. Generally, only the hands and face are washed, either with warm water or with a very mild antiseptic.

Birth and the new baby

B

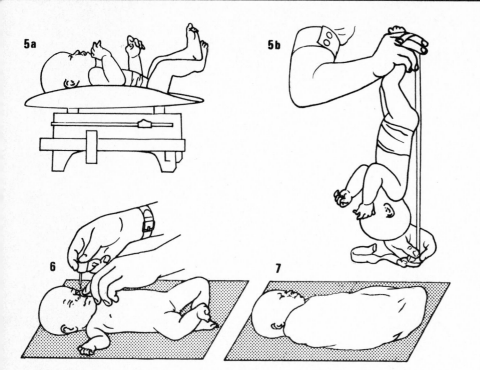

5a

5b

5 LABELING, WEIGHING, AND MEASURING
The baby is labeled with his family name, the time and date of birth, and any relevant details of the delivery. He is then weighed (**a**) and his body length (**b**) and head circumference are measured and recorded.

6

7

6 PREVENTING INFECTION
A drop of weak silver-nitrate solution may be put into each eye to eliminate any chance of serious infection.
7 KEEPING HIM WARM
A newborn baby's temperature can drop dramatically after birth, so it is essential that he is wrapped in a blanket or placed in a warm crib or incubator.

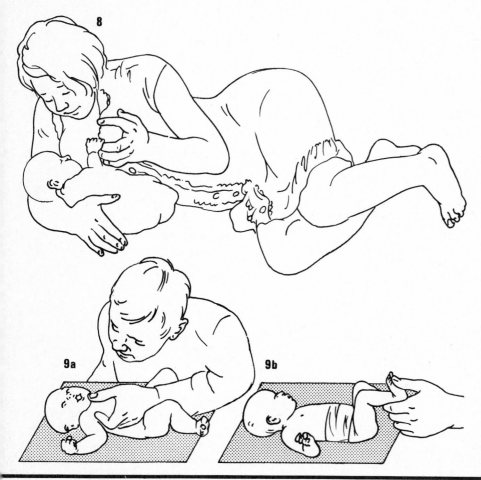

8

8 FEEDING
If the mother has decided to breast-feed and the condition of the baby is satisfactory, he may be given to his mother after delivery for a feeding. This is desirable as the baby's suckling stimulates milk production in the breasts, and also helps the uterus to contract.

9a

9b

9 MEDICAL EXAMINATION
Within 24 hours of delivery a baby is usually given a full medical examination. This includes a check for cleft palate (**a**) and club foot (**b**). Also checked are the head, spine, hips, and genitals. A blood test is performed to detect a rare but easily treated cause of mental handicap - phenylketonuria (PKU).

THE NEW BABY

B16 THE BIRTH EXPERIENCE

In recent years, obstetricians and psychologists have taken an increasing interest in the effect of the birth experience on a baby. Two in particular - R.D. Laing and Frederick Leboyer - have emphasized the importance of not severing the umbilical cord until the baby's own circulatory system is working fully. This, they argue, makes the birth process more natural and less traumatic.

In his book "Birth Without Violence," Leboyer suggests that lights and noise in the delivery room should be at a minimum, that the baby should be placed on the mother's abdomen before the cord is cut, and that after this the baby should be placed in a bath of warm water and allowed to "open up" in an unhurried way.

B17 CIRCUMCISION

Circumcision is the surgical removal of the foreskin covering the tip of the penis. It can be carried out for medical reasons, and is also commonly performed for religious reasons. Medical thinking in some countries used to favor circumcision for reasons of hygiene, but most doctors now argue that a normal foreskin is quite easy to keep clean and free from infection.

Circumcision involves a simple operation, usually carried out straight after the birth or about one week later. (The period between is avoided as the establishment of feeding may be interrupted.) For a few days after circumcision the penis requires special care, about which the doctor will give the necessary advice.

B18 THE NEWBORN BABY

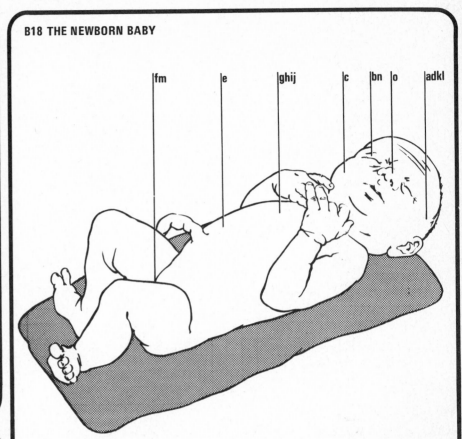

COMMON CHARACTERISTICS

Some aspects of a newborn baby's appearance may surprise or even alarm a new parent. All are quite normal and usually disappear within a day or so. They include:

a misshapen or swollen head due to pressure in labor;

b swollen, puffy eyes;

c tiny yellowish-white spots covering the face;

d throbbing fontanel (see J04);

e distended abdomen;

f swollen genitals;

g bright pink, purple, or even blue skin color due to temporary lack of oxygen during delivery;

h vernix - a greasy, white protective substance - on some parts of the body;

i lanugo - fine, downy hair - on some areas of the body;

j maternal blood smeared on the body due to tearing or cutting of vaginal tissues.

LESS COMMON CHARACTERISTICS

A newborn baby may display other characteristics. These features are less common but need not worry a parent as they are of no significance. They include:

k instrument marks on the head after a forceps delivery;

l a cephalhematoma - swelling caused by bruising during birth - on the head (sometimes the swelling hardens but it always remains harmless and subsides in a few months);

m vaginal discharge or bleeding in newborn girls, caused by the transfer of maternal hormones via the placenta before birth;

n crossed eyes; red spots or broken veins in the whites of the eyes caused by pressure on the neck during delivery;

o snuffly breathing and frequent sneezing caused by a shallow nose bridge.

Birth and the new baby

B19 PREMATURITY

Any baby who weighs less than
5½lb (2kg) at birth is generally
considered premature. Strictly,
however, premature babies fall
into two groups - those born
before week 35 of pregnancy (pre-
term) and those born at full term
but who weigh less than 5½lb
(low birth weight).

REASONS FOR PREMATURITY
Factors causing premature labor
can include: lack of adequate
antenatal care; poor maternal
health; maternal disease such as
diabetes; fetal congenital
abnormality; a multiple pregnancy;
and an accident or severe shock.
Low birth weight babies may
simply be the product of small
parents (genetically small), or
may have received insufficient
nourishment while developing in
the uterus.

BIRTH
Because of his smallness, a
premature baby is delivered very
quickly. As there is a slight risk
of brain damage if the soft bones
of the baby's head suddenly strike
the mother's hard perineum, an
episiotomy (B13) and forceps (B14)
are often used to ensure the baby's
safe delivery.

APPEARANCE
Apart from being small and light,
a premature baby's body seems
ill proportioned. His eyes are
widely spaced and usually shut,
and his nails very short. His skin
has no fat and is red and wrinkled.
His cry is feeble and his movements
weak.

DEVELOPMENT
Premature babies gradually catch
up both physically and mentally
with full-term babies. But a very
small premature baby - and some
with a birth weight of less than
2lb (0.9kg) now survive - may
take some time to do so.

B20 CARE OF THE PREMATURE

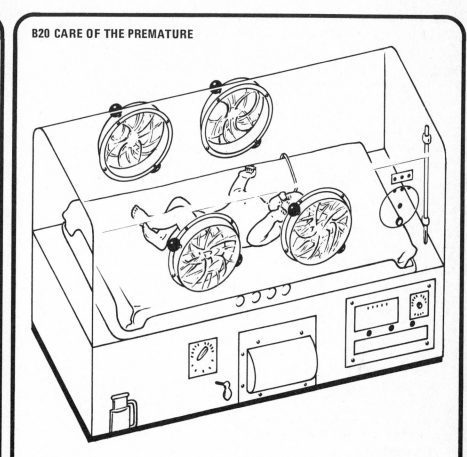

The body systems of a premature
baby are generally immature.
Breathing, feeding, keeping warm,
and resisting infection all present
problems to both pre-term and
low birth weight babies. The use of
an incubator improves the nursing
of a premature baby and greatly
increases his chances of growing
healthily and developing normally.
Temperature control is especially
difficult for a premature baby
who lacks the insulating layer of
fat beneath the skin. An
incubator provides extra warmth
and allows the careful control of
both humidity and air temperature.
The isolation of an incubator also
prevents the transfer of serious
infection.
An immature respiratory system
and poorly developed cough reflex
make breathing and clearing air

passages difficult and the baby may
need help from special apparatus
to maintain steady breathing.
Feeding can also be problematic
for a premature baby because his
ability to suck is poor. He is fed
on a strict three-hourly schedule
through a dropper or tube or, if
he is able to suck, from breast or
bottle. (Details of feeding a
premature baby are given in F26.)
The inevitable limitation of
physical contact between the
premature baby and his parents
can cause some distress in the
early days. The parent-child
bond, however, begins to be
established just as soon as the
baby no longer needs special
care - usually when he has
reached 5½lb (2kg) - and can be
freely handled by his parents.

REFLEXES

B21 REFLEXES OF A NEWBORN

Described on these pages are a variety of reflexes - automatic reactions to particular changes in surroundings - that are present in a newborn baby. These "primitive" reflexes are thought to be a legacy from man's earliest ancestors, when such actions were vital for an infant's survival.

Several important reflexes are usually tested soon after birth, as they give an indication of the baby's general condition and the normality of his central nervous system. Parents are warned of the potential dangers of testing some of these reflexes for themselves. By three months, a baby's

primitive reflexes have generally been replaced by voluntary movements. This can only happen when a baby learns to associate a particular action with the fulfillment of a certain need; he learns, for instance, that hunger is satisfied by food, which is obtained by sucking.

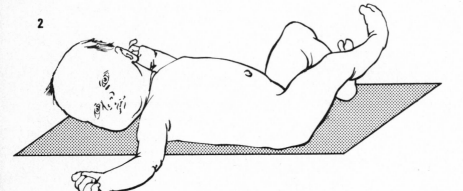

1 ROOTING REFLEX
If one side of a baby's cheek or mouth is gently touched, he will turn his head in the direction of the touch. This ensures that he will seek out the nipple when his cheek is brushed by his mother's breast. With the sucking and swallowing reflexes, the rooting reflex is essential for successful feeding in the newborn.

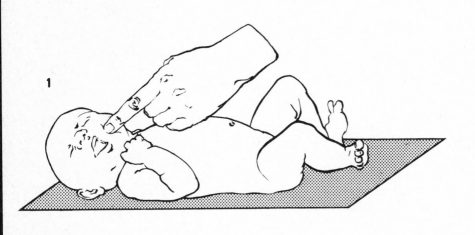

2 ASYMMETRIC TONIC NECK REFLEX
When on his back and not crying, a newborn baby lies with his head to one side, the arm on that side extended as shown, and the opposite leg bent at the knee.

3 GRASP REFLEX
This reflex makes a baby automatically clench his fist if an object is placed in his palm. If a finger is slipped into each of his palms, a baby will grasp them so tightly that he can support his own weight. The grasp reflex can also be evoked from the toes.

Birth and the new baby

B

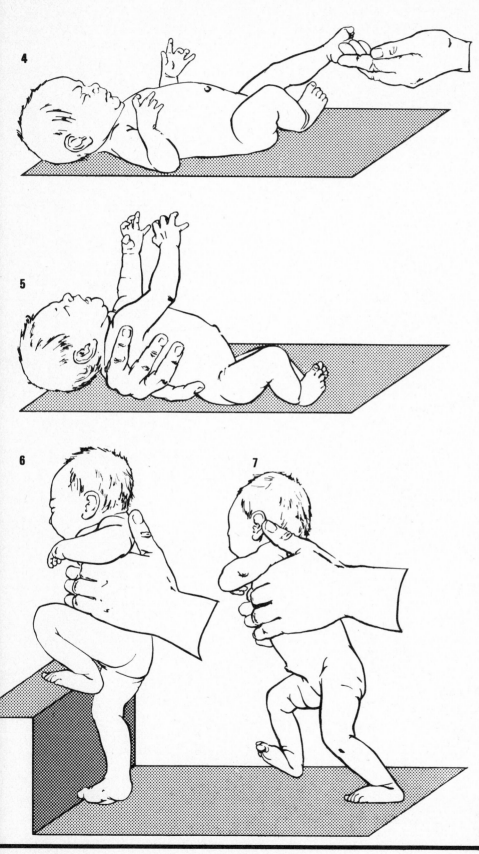

4 CROSSED EXTENSION REFLEX
If one of the baby's legs is held in an extended position and the sole of that foot stroked, the other leg flexes, draws toward the body, and then extends.

5 MORO REFLEX
This reflex is seen when the baby is startled. The arms and legs are outstretched and then drawn inward with the fingers curled as if ready to clutch at something. A baby's Moro reflex is tested to check muscle tone; if the limbs respond asymmetrically, there may be weakness or injury of a particular limb.

6 "STEPPING" REFLEX
If the front of his leg is gently brought into contact with the edge of a table, a baby will raise his leg and take a "step" up on to the table.

7 "WALKING" REFLEX
If a baby is held upright with the soles of his feet on a flat surface, and is then moved forward slowly, he will respond with "walking" steps.

BLINK REFLEX
A baby blinks in response to various stimuli - for instance, if the bridge of his nose is touched.

DOLL'S EYE REFLEX
If a baby's head is turned to the left or right, there is a delay in the following of the eyes.

©DIAGRAM

Development year by year

Based on the work of specialists in child development — Gesell, Ilg, Ames, Illingworth, Sheridan, Griffiths — this chapter describes milestones of development typically reached at different ages. Many normal variations occur, however, and professional investigation is needed only if a child's progress is significantly out of line.

Left: Peeping through the windows of a candy store in the country (The Mansell Collection)

NEWBORN / ONE MONTH

C01 NEWBORN: PROFILE

A newborn baby depends on others for almost every need. With his large head, tiny legs, soft bones, largely "unwired" nervous system, and flabby muscles, he appears unlikely ever to achieve an independent life. Yet at least he breathes, feeds, excretes waste, and cries when hungry, and his brain is richer in promise than that of any other infant animal.

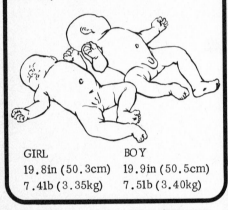

GIRL	BOY
19.8in (50.3cm)	19.9in (50.5cm)
7.4lb (3.35kg)	7.5lb (3.40kg)

C03 ONE MONTH: PROFILE

The month-old baby cannot yet hold up his head, let alone sit up, crawl, walk, or talk. He cannot even pick up an object or smile responsively. Yet his body has made tremendous progress in the first four weeks. Billions of nerve fibers effecting countless new interconnections produce much improved muscle tone, breathing, swallowing, and temperature control.

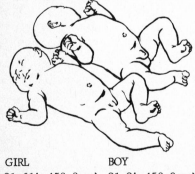

GIRL	BOY
21.01in (53.3cm)	21.2in (53.8cm)
8.5lb (3.86kg)	8.6lb (3.90kg)

C02 NEWBORN: DEVELOPMENT

MOTOR DEVELOPMENT

Head and limbs hang down when body held face down, horizontally. Placed face down, baby lies with knees drawn up, arms bent across chest, head turned sideways (**a**). Releasing head of supported baby evokes Moro reflex (see B21). Head lags if baby pulled to sit. Has grasp and walking reflexes.

a

EYE AND HAND DEVELOPMENT

Shuts eyes when suddenly dazzled by bright light.
Pupils respond to light.
Opens eyes if held erect.
Doll's eye reflex (B21) for first few days only - eyes lag as baby is swung in horizontal arc (**b**).
Turns toward diffused light after first week.

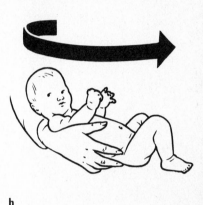

b

HEARING AND VOICE

Sudden sound produces blinking.
Visibly startled by sudden, loud sound.
"Freezes" in presence of steady, soft sounds.
Cries energetically (**c**), but stops in presence of fairly loud, steady adult voice.
Eyes may turn toward source of steady sound (but head does not).

c

PLAY AND SOCIAL DEVELOPMENT

Rooting (**d**) and sucking reflexes are present. (Also see B21.)

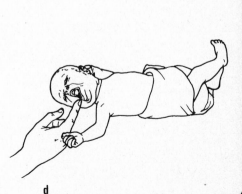

d

Development year by year

C04 ONE MONTH: DEVELOPMENT

MOTOR DEVELOPMENT
Lies on back with head and limbs
in positions illustrated (**a**).
Makes big, jerky movements.
Stretches limbs, fanning out toes
and fingers. Rests with hands shut
and thumbs turned in.
Head flops when body lifted.
Keeps head in line with body
when held face down horizontally.
Placed face down, lies with limbs
bent, elbows out from body, and
buttocks quite high.
Momentarily holds head upright
when pulled to sit.
Presses feet down and adopts
walking attitude if held standing.

a

EYE AND HAND DEVELOPMENT
Turns toward source of light.
Stares at window or bright wall.
Eyes briefly follow moving, nearby
light of small flashlamp.
Gazes at small, white ball moved
6-10in:15-25cm from face (**b**).
Alertly watches mother's face
when being fed by her.
Blinks defensively by six weeks.

b

HEARING AND VOICE
Sudden noise may cause stiffening,
blinking, quivering, stretching,
and crying.
Repeated, quiet, nearby sound
causes "freezing." Eyes and head
may turn toward source of sound.
Soothing voice stops whimpering.
Cries in hunger or discomfort.
Gurgles if contented (**c**).

c

PLAY AND SOCIAL DEVELOPMENT
Spends most of time sleeping.
Smiles socially and makes
responsive sounds by six weeks.
Grasps adult's finger when adult
opens hand (**d**).
Ceases crying if picked up and
talked to.
May turn to look at face of
nearby speaker.
Responsive awareness of bathing.

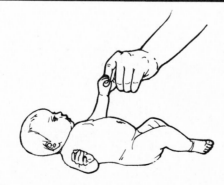

d

C05 THREE MONTHS: PROFILE

At three months a baby eyes his immediate world alertly and begins to respond in a lively way. Laid face down, he struggles futilely: on his back he brings his hands above his chest. He is becoming aware of the feel of his fingers and some objects.

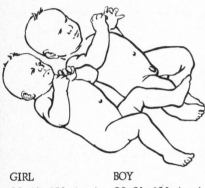

GIRL	BOY
23.4in (59.4cm)	23.8in (60.4cm)
12.4lb (5.46kg)	12.6lb (5.55kg)

C07 SIX MONTHS: PROFILE

Now learning the meaning of people's gestures and expressions, he reacts with two-syllabled and other sounds. His improved grasp encourages continual handling, mouthing, and banging which help him learn about objects within his reach. He still cannot sit or stand unaided but has begun to master parts of these operations.

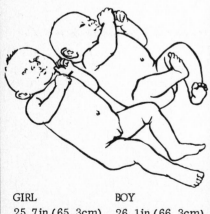

GIRL	BOY
25.7in (65.3cm)	26.1in (66.3cm)
16.0lb (7.26kg)	16.7lb (7.58kg)

C06 THREE MONTHS: DEVELOPMENT

MOTOR DEVELOPMENT
Lies on back, face upward (a).
Brings hands together above body.
Kicks, and waves arms.
Placed on stomach, uses forearms as props to lift head and chest.
Held horizontally, face down, raises head and extends hips and shoulders.
Little head lag if pulled to sit.

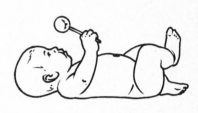

a

EYE AND HAND DEVELOPMENT
Moves head to gaze around.
Alertly watches any nearby face.
Watches own hands clasping and unclasping, and in finger play.
Briefly fixes eyes on small objects less than 1ft away.
Briefly holds rattle (b).
Visibly excited by arrival of feeding bottle.
Tries to focus on small ball approaching face.

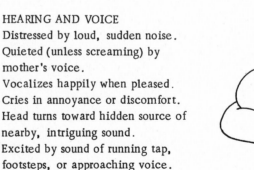

b

HEARING AND VOICE
Distressed by loud, sudden noise.
Quieted (unless screaming) by mother's voice.
Vocalizes happily when pleased.
Cries in annoyance or discomfort.
Head turns toward hidden source of nearby, intriguing sound.
Excited by sound of running tap, footsteps, or approaching voice.
Licks or sucks lips when hears food being prepared (c).

c

PLAY AND SOCIAL DEVELOPMENT
Gazes unblinkingly at face of person feeding him.
Baths and feeds evoke coos, smiles, and excited gestures.
Enjoys being bathed and cared for.
Responds happily to sympathetic handling, including tickling (d).

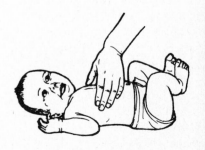

d

Development year by year

C08 SIX MONTHS: DEVELOPMENT

MOTOR DEVELOPMENT

Lying on back, lifts head to regard feet (**a**).
Lifts legs and grabs feet.
Kicks legs vigorously.
Rolls over.
Holds up arms to be lifted.
Pulls self to sit if hands grasped.
Sits supported, with head erect and back straight. Briefly sits unaided.
If laid on stomach, extends elbows to lift head and chest.
Bounces, when held standing.
Exhibits "downward parachute" (D10) when quickly lowered.

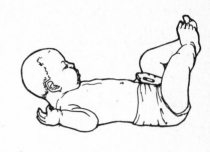

a

EYE AND HAND DEVELOPMENT

If someone attracts his attention, eagerly moves head and eyes in all directions.
Focuses without squinting.
Focuses on nearby, small objects and puts out both hands to grasp (**b**).
Grasps a toy with whole hand and passes to other hand (**c**).
Watches toys dropped from hand until they land, but ignores toys that land out of sight.

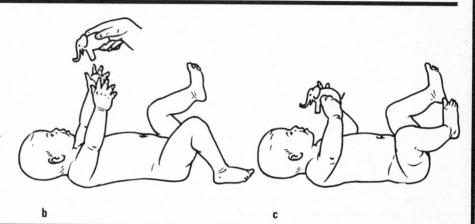

b

c

HEARING AND VOICE

Makes tuneful, sing-song, vowel and two-syllabled sounds ("goo," "adah," "a-a").
Turns at once toward sound of mother's voice heard across room.
Playfully squeals and chuckles (**d**).
Screams if annoyed.
Turns to very quiet sound from nearby, ear-level source.
Responds to varying emotional sounds in mother's voice.

d

PLAY AND SOCIAL DEVELOPMENT

Both hands reach out for and grab small toys.
Brings everything to his mouth (**e**).
Watches own feet moving.
Pats bottle when fed.
Shakes and watches rattle.
Passes objects from hand to hand.
Shy or anxious with strangers by about seven months.
Delighted if actively played with.

e

NINE MONTHS / ONE YEAR

C09 NINE MONTHS: PROFILE

He has now mastered sitting up, and may even pull himself to stand by holding on to the bars of his crib. Now, too, he can begin to roll or crawl along. Fingers are controlled with precision. He imitates simple actions, joins in some simple games, and babbles fluently.

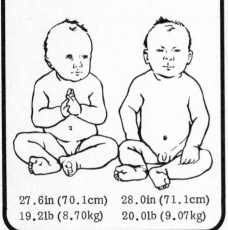

27.6in (70.1cm)   28.0in (71.1cm)
19.21b (8.70kg)   20.01b (9.07kg)

C11 ONE YEAR: PROFILE

Rates of growth and development are slowing. But agile crawling now gives real mobility, and he can nearly stand and walk unaided. He repeatedly lets an object fall, and handles several objects one by one. He loves to imitate actions, speaks his first words, enjoys an audience, and shows jealousy, sympathy, and other emotions.

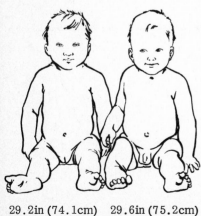

29.2in (74.1cm)   29.6in (75.2cm)
21.51b (9.75kg)   22.21b (10.06kg)

C10 NINE MONTHS: DEVELOPMENT

MOTOR DEVELOPMENT

Sits alone on floor (15 minutes).
Keeps balance while bending forward to grasp toy (**a**).
Can turn sideways to look, while stretching forward for toy.
Rolls or wriggles along on floor, and tries to crawl.
Pulls himself to stand, briefly.
Extremely lively in bath and cot.

a

EYE AND HAND DEVELOPMENT

Watches nearby people or animals for several minutes.
Handles objects with interest.
Puts out one hand to grasp toy, but stares at strange toy first.
Uses first finger to poke and point at objects.
Grips string or piece of candy between thumb and finger (**b**).
Drops toy but cannot put it down.
Looks for toy fallen out of sight.

b

HEARING AND VOICE

Fascinated by ordinary sounds.
Comprehends "no-no," "bye-bye."
Cannot yet localize sound produced directly above and behind him (**c**).
Babbles loudly and repetitively ("ma-ma," "da-da," etc).
Shouts for attention.
Makes "friendly" and "annoyed" sounds at other people.
Copies cough, and playful vocal sounds made by adults.

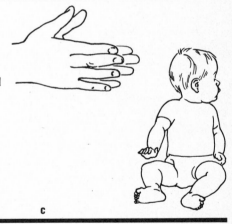

c

PLAY AND SOCIAL DEVELOPMENT

When feeding, uses both hands to grasp cup or bottle.
Can hold, bite, and chew cookie.
Hides face against familiar adult in the presence of strangers.
When annoyed, protests and stiffens body.
Holds bell in one hand and rings.

Offers toy to adult but still cannot release it.
Clasps hands and plays peek-a-boo in imitation of adult.
Retrieves a toy he has watched being partly or wholly hidden under a cover, or cannot discover it and cries.

Development year by year

C12 ONE YEAR: DEVELOPMENT

MOTOR DEVELOPMENT

Can rise from lying to sitting, and sits well for a long time.
Crawls or shuffles quickly (**a**).
Perhaps crawls upstairs.
Grasps furniture to pull self up to stand (**b**), to lower self, and to walk sideways.
Walks forward, possibly unaided.
Briefly stands unaided.

a

b

EYE AND HAND DEVELOPMENT

Gazes at moving people, animals, and vehicles out of doors.
Recognizes known people approaching 20ft (6.1m) away.
Begins to notice pictures.
Takes crumbs precisely between thumb and tip of first finger.
May favor use of one hand.
Clicks cubes together (**c**).
Deliberately drops and throws toys, watching them fall.
Can find a ball that has rolled out of sight.

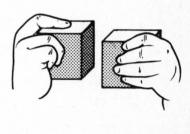

c

HEARING AND VOICE

Turns when called by name.
Soon ignores sound of hidden rattle after locating its source.
Understands some words in context.
Understands simple commands accompanied by gestures.
When requested, hands to an adult objects such as a cup or spoon (**d**).
Converses loudly in jargon.
Copies playfully made vocal sounds, and repeats some words.

d

PLAY AND SOCIAL DEVELOPMENT

Uses cup almost unaided (**e**).
Holds but cannot use spoon.
Offers arm and foot for dressing.
Bangs spoon in cup.
Rings bell with assurance.
Enjoys working sound-making toys.
Copying adult, inserts wooden blocks into cup and removes them.
Soon finds toys that he has watched being hidden.
Enjoys playing pat-a-cake.
Waves "bye-bye."
Shows affection to known adults.
Seeks their constant company.

e

EIGHTEEN MONTHS

C13 EIGHTEEN MONTHS: PROFILE

Immensely active, the eighteen-month-old child manipulates his body like a brash young driver trying out an automobile. Feet and arms somewhat apart, he runs about, exploring corners and clambering upstairs. He stops and starts but cannot turn corners easily or properly coordinate hands and feet. But he lugs big toys and even furniture around, learning what different places are. Lacking wrist control, he plays ball with movements of the whole arm. His world is one of here and now. His use of words is very limited. Self-willed, he takes but cannot give; and, unable to see other children as people like himself, he cannot share in their play.

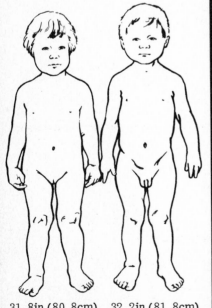

31.8in (80.8cm)   32.2in (81.8cm)
24.5lb (11.11kg)   25.2lb (11.43kg)

C14 EIGHTEEN MONTHS: DEVELOPMENT

MOTOR DEVELOPMENT

Kneels upright, unsupported (a).
Squats to reach toy and stands up using hands as aids (b).
Enjoys pulling and pushing boxes and wheeled toys around (c).
Walks easily, with controlled starting and stopping, and feet fairly close together (d). No longer needs to stretch his arms to keep balance when walking.
Can run, but stares at ground just ahead (e), and stops for obstacles.
Likes clutching a big teddy bear or doll while walking.
Walks upstairs if hand is held,

EYE AND HAND DEVELOPMENT

Points to intriguing objects in the distance.
Absorbed by picture books; turns groups of pages (f), and points to brightly colored illustrations.
Becoming noticeably right-handed or left-handed.
Using precise pincer grip, swiftly picks up small objects such as beads.
Piles three cubes to build a tower when first shown how (g).
Grips middle of pencil in palm, and scribbles (h).

HEARING AND VOICE

Pays attention when spoken to.
Obeys requests to pass familiar named items to an adult; also understands and performs simple tasks like shutting a door.
Points to hair, nose, shoes (i), etc.
In play, jabbers continually.
Says 6-20 words and knows many more than that.
When spoken to, repeats last word of a short sentence.
Urgently vocalizes and points to an object that he wants (j).
Likes nursery rhymes and attempts to say them with an adult.
Tries singing.

PLAY AND SOCIAL DEVELOPMENT

Conveys food to mouth by spoon (k).
Drinks from cup, spilling little.
May control bowels but not bladder.
Fidgets and makes agitated sounds when urgently in need of toilet.
Removes own hat, socks, and shoes but usually cannot put them on.
Tries to open doors while energetically probing environment.
Plays alone on floor with toys.
Likes putting small articles into containers (l), and then taking them out again.
Remembers where familiar household objects are kept.
Copies everyday actions such as sweeping floor and reading.
Still needs much emotional support from mother or other familiar adult, but often resists authority.

Development year by year

and comes downstairs crawling
backward or bumping forward on
his buttocks.
Seats himself by backing or
slipping sideways into a child's
low chair, but climbs head-first
into a big chair before he turns
and sits.

a   b   c   d   e

f

g

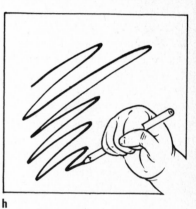

h

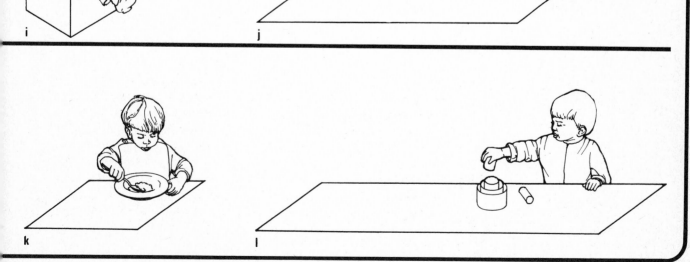

i

j

k   l

TWO YEARS

C15 TWO YEARS: PROFILE

No more an infant, the two-year-old gains control over bowels and bladder, cuts his last primary teeth, and rapidly builds up his vocabulary.

Surer now upon his feet, he loves to romp, chase, and be pursued. He seldom falls but walks with hunched shoulders and slightly bent knees and elbows, and, as he runs, leans forward. Rising and bending down are still done somewhat awkwardly.

Hand movements are now more varied and assured. A twist of the wrist and he can turn a door knob. He loves exploring objects: taking things apart; fitting things together; pushing in and pulling out; filling and emptying. He tests everything to hand by taste and touch. Daily chores intrigue him and he enjoys copying them.

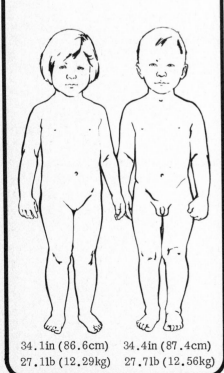

34.1in (86.6cm)   34.4in (87.4cm)
27.1lb (12.29kg) 27.7lb (12.56kg)

C16 TWO YEARS: DEVELOPMENT

MOTOR DEVELOPMENT

Squats steadily and stands without using hands as props (a).
Runs easily (b), controlling stops and starts, and dodging obstacles.
Climbs on furniture to reach windows and door handles, and gets down unaided.
Increasingly aware of own size compared with objects around him.
Can throw a small ball forward while standing (c).
Walks up against a big ball in a bid to kick it (d).
Holding handrail or wall, walks up and down stairs, placing both feet on each step.
Steers tricycle, sitting astride, pushing along with his feet (e).

EYE AND HAND DEVELOPMENT

Identifies photographs of adults well known to him (but not of self) after one showing.
Identifies miniature toys of familiar objects.
Turns picture-book pages one at a time, and recognizes tiny details in the pictures.
Now definitely right-handed or left-handed.
Swiftly picks up tiny objects like crumbs and puts down carefully.
Can unwrap a small candy (f).
Uses six cubes to build a tower (g).
Grips pencil near point, between first two fingers and thumb, makes circular and to-and-fro scribbles and dots, and can copy a vertical line (h).

HEARING AND VOICE

Shows interest in conversation between other people (i).
Talks to self continually and largely unintelligibly as he plays.
Uses own name to refer to himself.
Says at least 50 words and knows many more.
Can say short sentences.
Asks the names of various people and things.
Names (after adult) and shows hand, eyes, mouth, shoes, etc.
Participates in songs and nursery rhymes.
Names and hands over familiar pictures and objects when asked.
Obeys simple commands, eg telling father a meal is ready.
Begins correctly assembling a miniature doll's house setting when asked to do so (j).

PLAY AND SOCIAL DEVELOPMENT

Competently spoon feeds and drinks from a cup.
Requests food, drink, and toilet. May be dry by day.
Can put on shoes and hat (k).
Opens doors and runs outside, oblivious of danger.
Imitates mother as she performs household chores.
Demands her attention and often clings to her (l).
Resists authority and throws tantrums if frustrated.
Fiercely possessive over toys (m).
Does not play with other children and resents attention shown them by his parents.

Development year by year

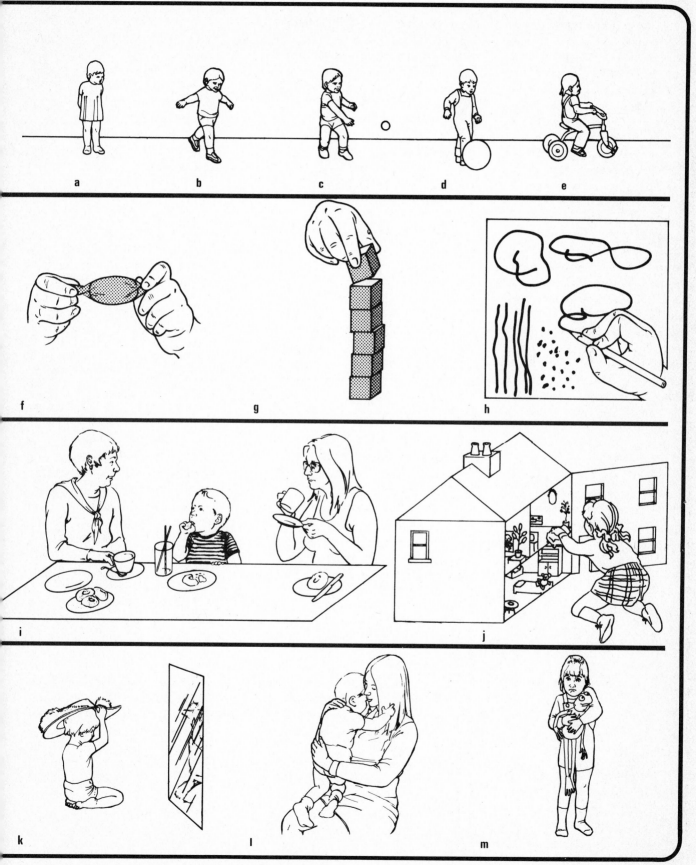

a   b   c   d   e

f   g   h

i   j

k   l   m

C

THREE YEARS

C17 THREE YEARS: PROFILE

The three-year-old has made great strides toward physical and psychological maturity and we glimpse in him the adult of the future. His motor mechanisms now mesh effectively; he walks erect, swings his arms in adult fashion, maneuvers around corners, and manages stairs with ease. He is also toilet trained. Hand-eye coordination are good enough for him to draw a recognizable copy of some simple shapes.

Increasing interest in words and numbers marches hand in hand with a growth of simple, verbal logic - comparing one object with another, for example.

Willingness to please, to share in play and wait his turn are major pointers to the psychological progress he has made.

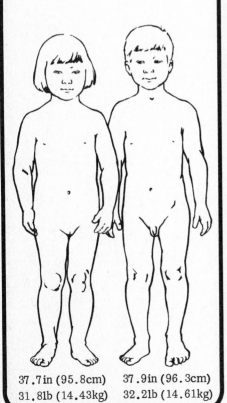

37.7in (95.8cm)   37.9in (96.3cm)
31.8lb (14.43kg)   32.2lb (14.61kg)

C18 THREE YEARS: DEVELOPMENT

MOTOR DEVELOPMENT
Sits on chair, ankles crossed.
Stands briefly on one leg (a).
Can stand and walk on tiptoe.
Runs and hauls and shoves big toys around obstacles.
Walks forward, sideways or backward, pulling big toys.
Kicks ball hard (b), and catches a big ball between outstretched arms.
Places one foot on each step when walking upstairs, but both feet on each step when walking down.
May jump off bottom step.
Nimbly mounts children's furniture.
Pedals and steers a tricycle (c).
Now well aware of own size and movements in relation to objects around him.

EYE AND HAND DEVELOPMENT
Readily picks up crumbs, with one eye covered.
Cuts paper with scissors (d).
Builds a nine-brick tower, and a three-brick bridge (e).
Controls pencil well between thumb and first two fingers; copies circle and letters HTV; draws a man, showing head and maybe two other parts of body (f).
May name colors and match three primary colors.
Paints color wash all over paper; makes and names "pictures."
Matches up to seven letters with test letters 10ft (3m) away.

HEARING AND VOICE
Loves hearing favorite stories (g).
Cooperates in hearing test by carrying out required action.
Speaks with modulated pitch and volume.
Says many intelligible words, with childish mispronunciations and mangled grammar.
Accurately uses plurals and personal pronouns. Gives own name, sex, and maybe age.
Talks to self about actions during play (h).
Can briefly say what he is doing now and describe past experiences.
Asks countless questions starting "what," "where," "who."
Can repeat some nursery rhymes.
May count to 10 but is unlikely to understand quantities greater than three.

PLAY AND SOCIAL DEVELOPMENT
Uses spoon and fork at table (i).
Washes and dries hands with help.
Pulls panties up and down and can put on or take off some clothes with simple fastenings.
May now be dry day and night.
Affectionate and less rebellious.
Helps to shop, garden, etc, and tries to tidy own toys.
Imaginary people and things figure in make-believe games.
Plays with other children, sharing toys and candies (j).
Now affectionate toward sisters and brothers.
Begins to grasp differences between past, present, future.
No longer insists on instant gratification of desires.

Development year by year

a

b

c

d

e

f

g

h

i

j

© DIAGRAM

FOUR YEARS

C19 FOUR YEARS: PROFILE

Exuberant of mind and body, the four-year-old breaks through constraints that held the three-year-old in check.

Well controlled motor muscles help him energetically climb, jump, hop, skip, and ride a tricycle. But he is also becoming good at tasks demanding careful hand-eye control, for instance sawing, lacing shoes, and scissoring along a line.

Boastful, bossy, and a smart aleck, he talks incessantly, trying out new words - inventing some, and often using adult terms incongruously out of proper context. Word play reflects the darting movements of his thoughts, which spawn inventive games and drawings. His mental life is blossoming.

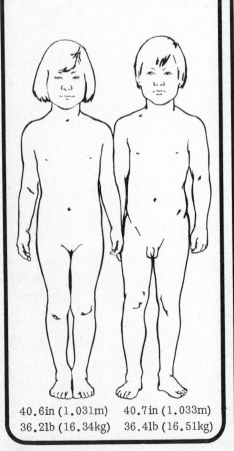

40.6in (1.031m)   40.7in (1.033m)
36.2lb (16.34kg)   36.4lb (16.51kg)

C20 FOUR YEARS: DEVELOPMENT

MOTOR DEVELOPMENT

Sits on chair with knees crossed.
Can stand, walk, run on tiptoe.
Keeping legs straight, can bend at waist in order to pick up objects from the floor (a).
Can climb trees and ladders.
Turns sharp corners, running.
Walks or runs both upstairs and downstairs, placing only one foot on each step.
Can kick, catch, throw, and bounce a ball, and strike it with a bat (b).
Hops on favored foot and balances upon it for 3-5 seconds (c).
Can make sharp turns on a tricycle.

EYE AND HAND DEVELOPMENT

Names and matches colors.
Matches seven test-card letters with specimens 10ft (3m) away.
Readily picks up and replaces crumbs or other small objects with one eye covered.
Can thread beads (d), but still cannot thread a needle.
Builds a tower 10 cubes high (e).
When shown how, arranges six cubes to build three steps.
Shown how, presses thumb against each finger in turn.
Grasps pencil maturely; copies cross and letters HOTV; draws a man, showing head and legs plus probably arms and trunk (f).

HEARING AND VOICE

Can talk intelligibly, using correct grammar and few childish mispronunciations.
Can give own name in full as well as address and age.
Perpetually asks questions starting "why," "when," "how."
Asks what different words mean.
Loves hearing and telling long tales, often mixing up fantasy and fact.
Counts to 20 by rote, and counts actual objects up to five.
Likes jokes (g).
Accurately says or sings a few nursery rhymes.

PLAY AND SOCIAL DEVELOPMENT

Handles fork and spoon well.
Cleans teeth (h). Washes hands and dries them capably.
Can dress and undress except for managing difficult fastenings.
Sense of humor developing.
Independent - answers back.
Plays theatrical games involving dressing up.
Plays complex floor games (i).
Less tidy than at age three.
Builds things outdoors.
Argues with other children, but needs their companionship and learns to take turns.
Concerned for younger brothers and sisters, and sympathetic toward distressed playmates.
Understands differences between past, present, and future.

Development year by year

C

a

b

c

d

e

f

g

h

i

FIVE YEARS

C21 FIVE YEARS: PROFILE

Scatterbrained four develops into maturer five, whose mind works more precisely - less ruled by the mouth, as it were. He is more self-critical, and inclined to finish some project he has started. Well balanced and unflappable, the five-year-old has gained a clearer concept of himself and his role in the family and in a somewhat broader environment. He can now cope with most daily personal duties and some household tasks, and is ready for the wider world of school. But coordination of hand, eye, and brain are still developing and he is unlikely to be ready yet to learn to read and write with ease. He also remains unaware of many simple facts we take for granted.

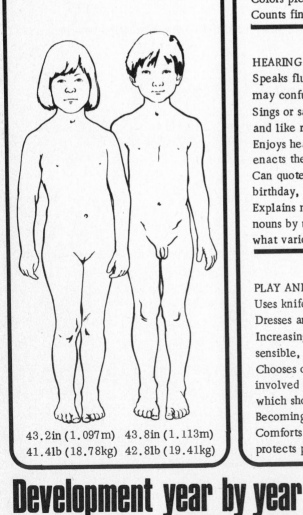

43.2in (1.097m)   43.8in (1.113m)
41.4lb (18.78kg)   42.8lb (19.41kg)

C22 FIVE YEARS: DEVELOPMENT

MOTOR DEVELOPMENT

Stands on one foot 8-10 seconds. Touches toes with legs straight. Hops 2-3yd (2-3m) forward on either foot; skips on alternate feet. Runs on toes (**a**), and moves to music. Can walk along a thin line. Climbs, digs, slides, and swings. Plays ball games quite well.

a

EYE AND HAND DEVELOPMENT

Matches 10-12 colors. Threads needle. Sews stitches. Builds 3-4 steps from cubes. Copies square (later triangle) and letters ACHLOTUVXY; writes some letters unprompted; draws man with trunk, head, arms, legs, and features (**b**); also house with roof, windows, door, chimney. Colors pictures carefully. Counts fingers of one hand.

b

HEARING AND VOICE

Speaks fluently and correctly but may confuse sounds f, s, and th. Sings or says jingles and rhymes, and like riddles and jokes. Enjoys hearing stories and later enacts them with friends (**c**). Can quote full name, age, birthday, and address. Explains meaning of concrete nouns by usage and often asks what various abstract words mean.

c

PLAY AND SOCIAL DEVELOPMENT

Uses knife and fork well (**d**). Dresses and undresses self. Increasingly independent and sensible, but rather untidy. Chooses own friends and invents involved make-believe games in which shows sense of fair play. Becoming aware of clock time. Comforts distressed playmates and protects pets and young children.

d

Development year by year

C23 SIX YEARS: PROFILE

Lively, expansive, eager to try out something new, the six-year-old has an insatiable appetite for fresh experiences. But he must succeed in everything he tackles; win every game he plays; have the most of anything that's going. Otherwise there will be tears and tantrums. Six is a demanding, stubborn, and unruly age.

By six years old the first adult tooth is pushing through. At school the child takes early steps along the paths that lead to an ability to read, write, and use numbers. But what he learns must still be firmly based on things that he can see and do. He cannot reason in an abstract adult way.

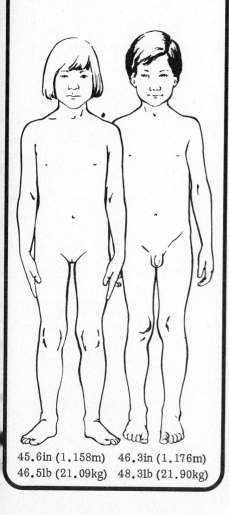

45.6in (1.158m) 46.3in (1.176m)
46.5lb (21.09kg) 48.3lb (21.90kg)

C24 SIX YEARS: DEVELOPMENT

MOTOR DEVELOPMENT

Jumps over rope 10in:25cm high (**a**).
Hops 1-3 times on one foot so that it nudges a toy brick along.
Trots around a sizable open space such as a playground.
Skips at least 12 times indoors (more outdoors).
Holding a rope, skips three or more times.

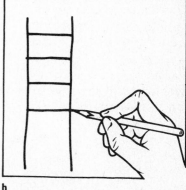

a

EYE AND HAND DEVELOPMENT

Copies a square accurately.
Neatly copies a ladder (**b**).
Attempts to produce a copy of a diamond.
Draws a triangle more precisely than when aged five.
Can say in two cases how one object differs from another that in some way resembles it.

b

HEARING AND VOICE

Accurately repeats a sentence containing 16 syllables.
Uses at least three sentences to describe a test picture.
Names and recognizes at least 20 capital letters (**c**).
In a verbal test can say how one object resembles another.

c

PLAY AND SOCIAL DEVELOPMENT

Cuts own meat when using knife and fork at table (**d**).
Can now be expected to behave reasonably well at table.
Ties own shoelaces.

d

SEVEN YEARS

C25 SEVEN YEARS: PROFILE

Physical and mental progress march ahead. But broadening the mind's horizons predominates over physical activity. Many a seven-year-old prefers to watch instead of do. He reads and watches television, and often likes to do so on his own partly because he feels at odds with everyone around him. Moodiness is frequent.

Spells of intensive learning alternate with spasms of forgetfulness. He loves drawing and other tasks requiring precise hand-eye coordination. But he tends to overreach himself, and attempts tasks that he becomes too tired to finish.

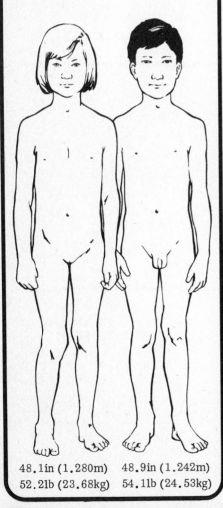

48.1in (1.280m)   48.9in (1.242m)
52.2lb (23.68kg)   54.1lb (24.53kg)

C26 SEVEN YEARS: DEVELOPMENT

MOTOR DEVELOPMENT

Can jump off the bottom four steps of a staircase.
Rides a two-wheeled bicycle, but not very far.
Hops four times on one foot, so that it nudges a toy brick along (a).
Skips 12 times or more.

a

EYE AND HAND MOVEMENT

Writes 24-26 letters (b).
Fairly accurately draws a "window" (a cross inscribed in a square).
Draws a man with originality, eg clothed, side-face, seated.
Draws a diamond neatly.

A B C D E F G
H I J K L M N
O P Q R S T U V
W X Y Z

b

HEARING AND VOICE

Can use at least four sentences to describe a test picture.
Correctly answers six questions from a comprehension test list.
Says in three cases how one object resembles a similar object.
Says in three cases how one object differs from another that in some way resembles it (c).
Gives the opposite meanings for four terms in a test list.

c

PLAY AND SOCIAL DEVELOPMENT

Has a special friend at school.
Sets a table, given some help.
Brushes own hair regularly (d).
Dresses and undresses unaided, managing fastenings well.

d

Development year by year

EIGHT YEARS

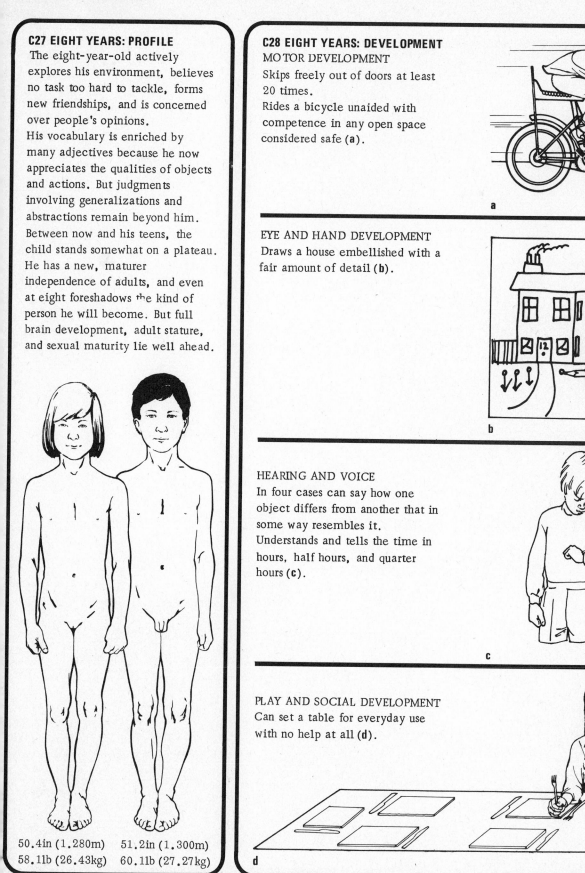

C27 EIGHT YEARS: PROFILE

The eight-year-old actively explores his environment, believes no task too hard to tackle, forms new friendships, and is concerned over people's opinions.

His vocabulary is enriched by many adjectives because he now appreciates the qualities of objects and actions. But judgments involving generalizations and abstractions remain beyond him. Between now and his teens, the child stands somewhat on a plateau. He has a new, maturer independence of adults, and even at eight foreshadows the kind of person he will become. But full brain development, adult stature, and sexual maturity lie well ahead.

50.4in (1.280m) 51.2in (1.300m)
58.1lb (26.43kg) 60.1lb (27.27kg)

C28 EIGHT YEARS: DEVELOPMENT

MOTOR DEVELOPMENT
Skips freely out of doors at least 20 times.
Rides a bicycle unaided with competence in any open space considered safe (a).

EYE AND HAND DEVELOPMENT
Draws a house embellished with a fair amount of detail (b).

HEARING AND VOICE
In four cases can say how one object differs from another that in some way resembles it.
Understands and tells the time in hours, half hours, and quarter hours (c).

PLAY AND SOCIAL DEVELOPMENT
Can set a table for everyday use with no help at all (d).

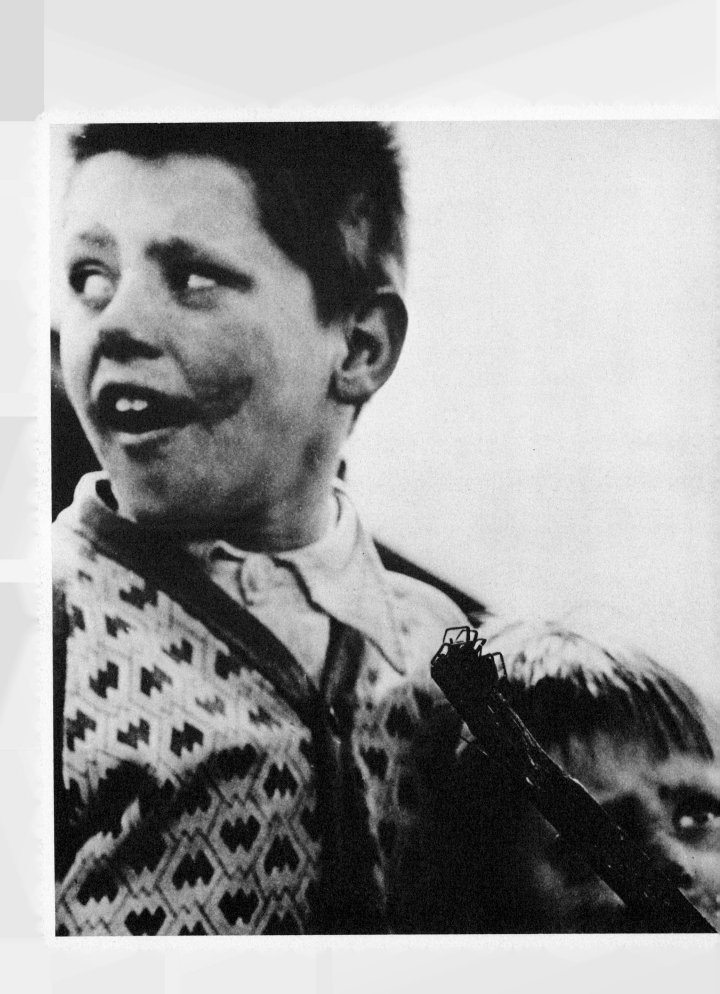

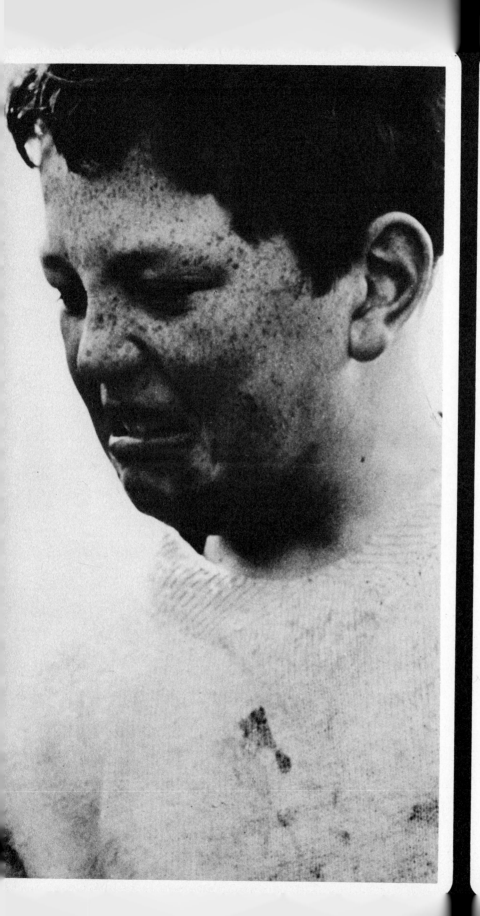

Aspects in development

The development of acquired abilities and characteristics — from standing up to solving complex problems — depends on the interaction of biological maturation and learning.

Left: Discovering the delights of wildlife (Photo Ron Chapman)

GROWTH 1

D01 GROWTH TO THREE YEARS

A child grows rapidly in the first three years, but successive measurements within this period show that the rate of growth is slowing down. (Fastest growth in fact occurs in the three months before birth, see A18.)

WEIGHT In the first few days a new baby loses weight. Subsequent weight gain reduces individual differences: in the first six months a 5lb (2.3kg) baby trebles his birthweight while a 9lb (4.1kg) baby only doubles his. In the second six months weight gain is halved. Weight gain from one to two years equals that from six to 12 months. There is a further slowing down from two to three.

LENGTH Growth is fastest in the first year, but slowing down. From two to three years it is the same as in the first three months.

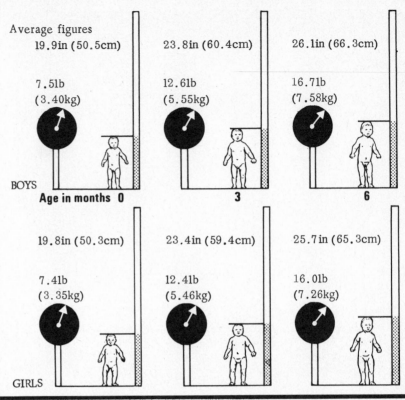

Average figures

BOYS
Age in months 0	3	6
19.9in (50.5cm)	23.8in (60.4cm)	26.1in (66.3cm)
7.5lb (3.40kg)	12.6lb (5.55kg)	16.7lb (7.58kg)

GIRLS
| 19.8in (50.3cm) | 23.4in (59.4cm) | 25.7in (65.3cm) |
| 7.4lb (3.35kg) | 12.4lb (5.46kg) | 16.0lb (7.26kg) |

D02 BIRTHWEIGHT AND LENGTH

Birthweight and length vary greatly among healthy newborn infants. The graphs here show the percentage of full-term babies born with different crown-to-rump lengths and different weights. Most babies are born close to the middle length and weight figures. But some are a lot shorter than and weigh only half as much as others. Major factors that determine weight and length at birth are:
a) term of development inside the mother's uterus;
b) mother's health in pregnancy;
c) baby's nutrition before birth;
d) heredity;
e) race;
f) siblings (twins tend to be smaller than singletons, and first-born babies smaller than ones born subsequently).

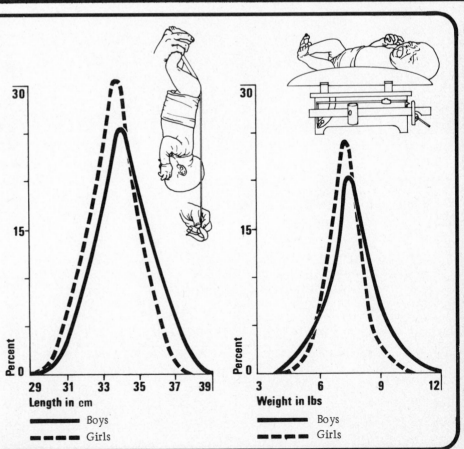

Length in cm
Weight in lbs

——— Boys
- - - - Girls

Aspects in development

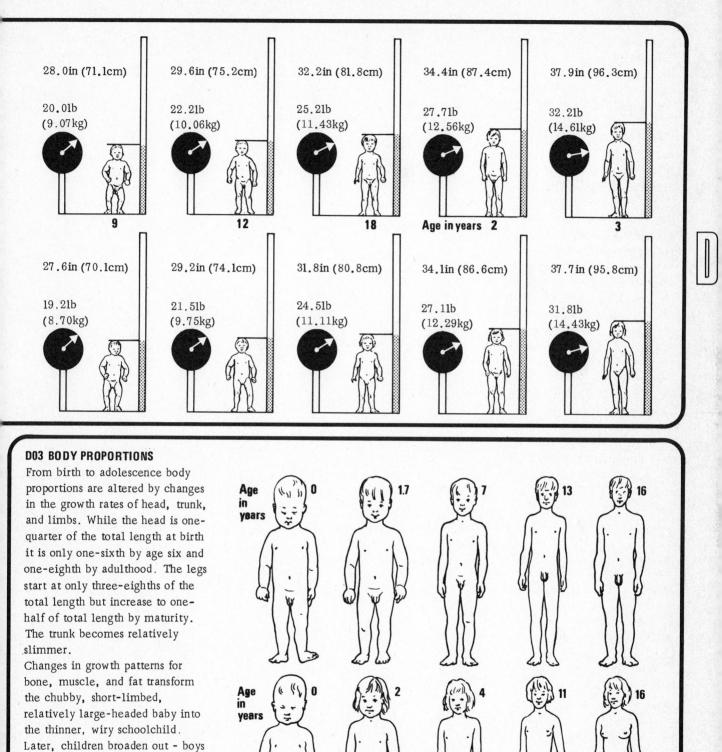

28.0in (71.1cm)

20.0lb
(9.07kg)

29.6in (75.2cm)

22.2lb
(10.06kg)

32.2in (81.8cm)

25.2lb
(11.43kg)

34.4in (87.4cm)

27.7lb
(12.56kg)

37.9in (96.3cm)

32.2lb
(14.61kg)

9

12

18

Age in years 2

3

27.6in (70.1cm)

19.2lb
(8.70kg)

29.2in (74.1cm)

21.5lb
(9.75kg)

31.8in (80.8cm)

24.5lb
(11.11kg)

34.1in (86.6cm)

27.1lb
(12.29kg)

37.7in (95.8cm)

31.8lb
(14.43kg)

D03 BODY PROPORTIONS

From birth to adolescence body proportions are altered by changes in the growth rates of head, trunk, and limbs. While the head is one-quarter of the total length at birth it is only one-sixth by age six and one-eighth by adulthood. The legs start at only three-eighths of the total length but increase to one-half of total length by maturity. The trunk becomes relatively slimmer.

Changes in growth patterns for bone, muscle, and fat transform the chubby, short-limbed, relatively large-headed baby into the thinner, wiry schoolchild. Later, children broaden out - boys especially at the shoulders, girls at the hips. But eventual physique varies with individuals and may be detected early on, in some cases by the age of two.

Age in years 0 1.7 7 13 16

Age in years 0 2 4 11 16

© DIAGRAM

GROWTH 2

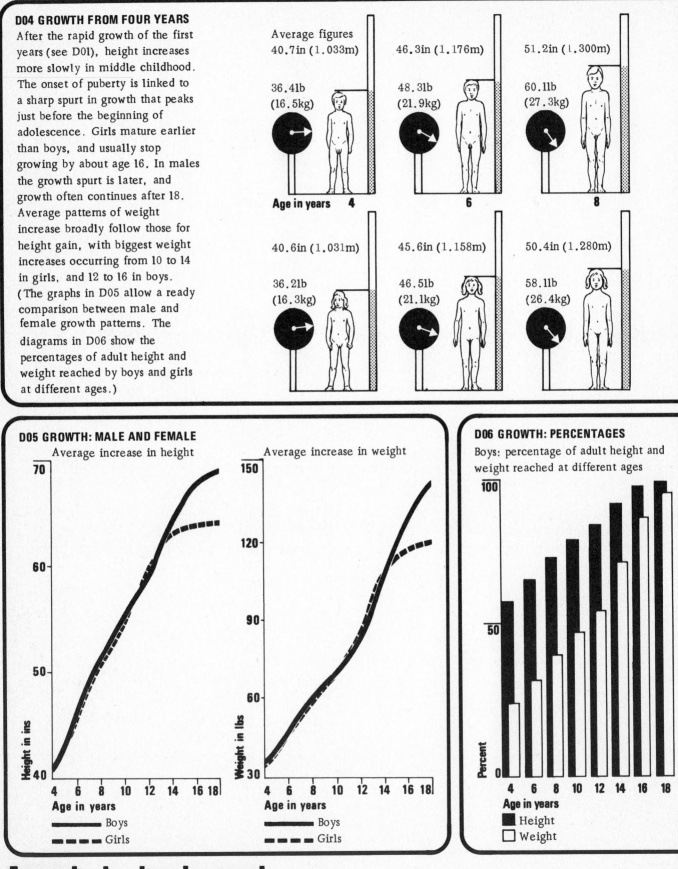

D04 GROWTH FROM FOUR YEARS

After the rapid growth of the first
years (see D01), height increases
more slowly in middle childhood.
The onset of puberty is linked to
a sharp spurt in growth that peaks
just before the beginning of
adolescence. Girls mature earlier
than boys, and usually stop
growing by about age 16. In males
the growth spurt is later, and
growth often continues after 18.
Average patterns of weight
increase broadly follow those for
height gain, with biggest weight
increases occurring from 10 to 14
in girls, and 12 to 16 in boys.
(The graphs in D05 allow a ready
comparison between male and
female growth patterns. The
diagrams in D06 show the
percentages of adult height and
weight reached by boys and girls
at different ages.)

Average figures
40.7in (1.033m)   46.3in (1.176m)   51.2in (1.300m)

36.4lb
(16.5kg)   48.3lb (21.9kg)   60.1lb (27.3kg)

Age in years   4   6   8

40.6in (1.031m)   45.6in (1.158m)   50.4in (1.280m)

36.2lb
(16.3kg)   46.5lb (21.1kg)   58.1lb (26.4kg)

D05 GROWTH: MALE AND FEMALE

Average increase in height

70

60

50

Height in ins
40

4 6 8 10 12 14 16 18
Age in years

——— Boys
- - - Girls

Average increase in weight

150

120

90

60

Weight in lbs
30

4 6 8 10 12 14 16 18
Age in years

——— Boys
- - - Girls

D06 GROWTH: PERCENTAGES

Boys: percentage of adult height and
weight reached at different ages

100

50

Percent
0

4   6   8   10 12 14 16 18
Age in years
■ Height
□ Weight

Aspects in development

D

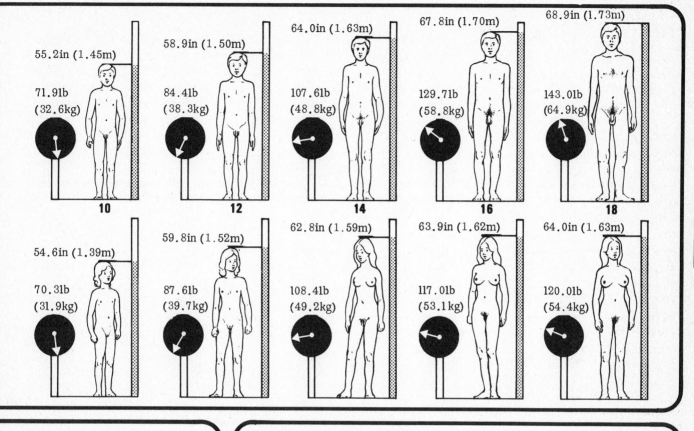

55.2in (1.45m)

71.9lb (32.6kg)

58.9in (1.50m)

84.4lb (38.3kg)

64.0in (1.63m)

107.6lb (48.8kg)

67.8in (1.70m)

129.7lb (58.8kg)

68.9in (1.73m)

143.0lb (64.9kg)

10 **12** **14** **16** **18**

54.6in (1.39m)

70.3lb (31.9kg)

59.8in (1.52m)

87.6lb (39.7kg)

62.8in (1.59m)

108.4lb (49.2kg)

63.9in (1.62m)

117.0lb (53.1kg)

64.0in (1.63m)

120.0lb (54.4kg)

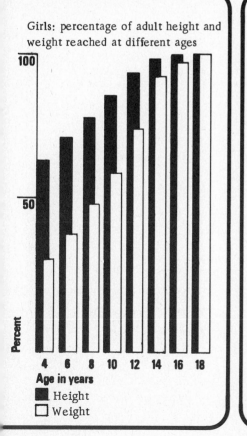

Girls: percentage of adult height and weight reached at different ages

Percent

4 6 8 10 12 14 16 18

Age in years

■ Height
□ Weight

D07 GROWTH OF BODY PARTS

Different parts of the body have different types of growth. This graph shows the percentage increase for each type from birth to adulthood.

a General type (affecting most of the body including muscles, lungs, blood volume, intestines) spurts in infancy, slows in childhood, spurts toward adolescence, then decelerates.

b Neural type (affecting brain, eyes, skull, spinal cord) spurts dramatically from birth to six years. By then 90% of neural growth is over.

c Genital type (testes, ovaries, etc) stays minimal, then spurts at puberty and during adolescence.

d Lymphoid type (thymus and lymph nodes) peaks from 10 to 12 years, then lymph and thymus tissue shrinks. Hence the graph shows lymphoid type reaching 200% before diminishing.

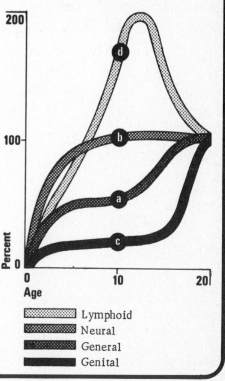

Percentage of different types of growth at different ages

Percent

Age

▨ Lymphoid
▨ Neural
▨ General
■ Genital

MOTOR DEVELOPMENT 1

D08 GENERAL TRENDS

There are three broad trends in motor development.
1) Outward: central body areas function before outer areas. Children control upper legs and upper arms earlier than lower legs, forearms, and hands.
2) Head to foot: head control comes before hauling the body along with the hands. Creeping on hands and knees follows. Walking comes last of all.
3) Big to small muscles: early movements are wild jerks of the whole body, trunk, or entire limbs. Control of small muscles is needed before a child can pick up a crumb with thumb and forefinger, and walk with an economical action. Each trend reflects increasing maturation of the nervous system. Walking practice is useless until the nervous system is ready. Moreover voluntary movements can come only after the newborn's primitive reflexes (B21) have gone.

D09 HELD HORIZONTALLY

A newborn baby's head droops – he lacks the coordination and strength required to raise it.

At six weeks he can raise his head in line with his body, but can do so only for a moment.

By 12 weeks he can lift his head well above the general body line and hold it there for a time.

D11 CRAWLING

Placed in a prone position, the newborn baby draws his knees up beneath his abdomen and lies with his pelvis high and his head directed to one side.

By six weeks old he tends to lie less tucked up. His pelvis is lower. Legs are more extended. Sometimes he kicks out. Now and then he lifts his chin well up.

By 12 weeks the baby lies with legs fully extended and pelvis flat upon the bed or couch. He raises chin and shoulders and may hold his head almost upright.

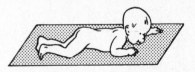

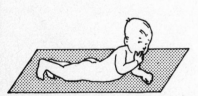

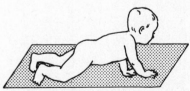

By 28 weeks he lies with the upper part of his body supported only on one hand. (By this time he is also able to roll over from abdomen to back and vice versa.)

The 36-week-old child learns that by thrusting down and forward on a surface he can move his body backward. He is well on the way to true crawling.

At 40 weeks he crawls forward on his belly, pulling himself along with his hands. At this stage his legs do no more than trail along unhelpfully behind.

Aspects in development

D10 SECONDARY RESPONSES

So-called secondary responses begin appearing at about four months when primitive reflexes decline. Some secondary responses may be absent in normal babies before one year. Vital in later life, secondary responses concern balancing, rolling, and protection of the falling body.

ROLLING RESPONSE From the fourth month, rolling the body over by the legs evokes a complex response involving the baby's head and unimpeded arm.

DOWNWARD PARACHUTE If someone holds a baby upright then swiftly lowers him, the legs stretch and move apart as though anticipating a hard landing.

FORWARD PARACHUTE If someone holds a baby upright and swiftly tilts him forward toward the ground, arms and fingers outstretch and spread protectively.

SIDEWAYS PROPPING REACTION This time a child sitting upright is tilted sideways. He extends an arm and hand, pressing on the ground to stop his body falling.

At 16 weeks he can press down with his forearms to lift his head and front part of the chest. He also stretches all his limbs, and "swims" on his abdomen.

By 20 weeks the infant has had some weeks of practice and uses forearms in an even surer manner than before to help him lift up head and upper chest.

By 24 weeks he can lift his entire head, chest, and upper abdomen. Thrusting down with outstretched arms, he bears the weight of his upper body on his hands.

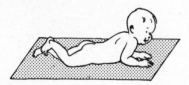

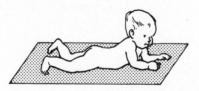

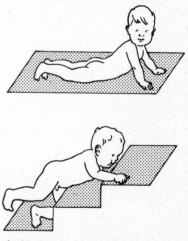

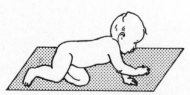

By 44 weeks he has learned a more agile mode of crawling. Arms and legs all work together as he now creeps along on hands and knees, with belly held up off the ground.

At one year old he rests some weight upon his soles and ambles bear-like on his hands and feet. He has reached the final stage before unaided walking.

At 15 months he sometimes still feels safest on all fours, for instance when he starts tackling that formidable stepped cliff known to adults as a staircase.

MOTOR DEVELOPMENT 2

D12 SITTING

The newborn baby cannot sit, and his head lags flaccidly if he is pulled into a sitting position.

At four weeks his head still lags but lifts briefly if he is held to sit. His back is rounded.

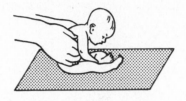

By 12 weeks a baby supported to sit holds his head up, but the head may still bob forward.

At 28 weeks he can sit alone on the floor, but uses arms and hands as props for his unsteady body.

By 32 weeks he is already able to sit on the floor, briefly unsupported by his arms.

At 36 weeks he can sit for 10 minutes, regaining balance if he bends his body forward.

D13 STANDING AND WALKING

A newborn baby held with the sole of the foot on a table moves his legs in a reflex walking action.

At eight weeks the baby briefly keeps his head up if he is held in a standing posture.

By 36 weeks he can pull himself up and remains standing by grasping hold of furniture.

At 18 months he can go up and down stairs without assistance.

By two he runs, walks backward, and picks things up without overbalancing.

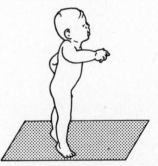

At 2½ he can balance on tiptoe, and jump with both feet.

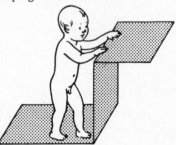

Aspects in development

At 16 weeks only the lower back of the supported baby is curved. The head wobbles if the body sways.

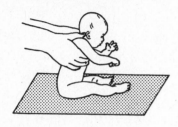

By 40 weeks the sitting child can lie down on his stomach and return to a sitting position.

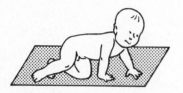

By 20 weeks there is no head lag or wobble and the baby pulled to sit keeps his back straight.

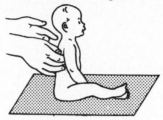

By 48 weeks the sitting child can twist around to pick up something, yet keep his balance.

At 24 weeks he lifts his head to be pulled up, and sits supported in a high chair or baby carriage.

About 15 months he sits down in a low chair, climbing forward into it and then turning around.

By 48 weeks he can walk forward if both hands are held (or sideways, gripping furniture).

At three he can balance for some seconds while standing on one foot.

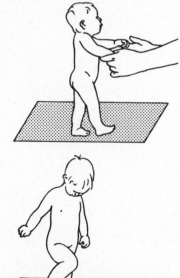

At one year the child walks forward if someone holds one of his hands.

At four he walks downstairs by placing only one foot on each step.

By 13 months the child has become capable of walking without help.

At five he skips on both feet.

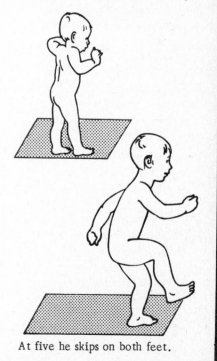

EYE AND HAND DEVELOPMENT

D14 FIELD OF VISION

At birth a baby's eyes move independently. At this early stage he finds it hard to fix on any object with his eyes.

Soon after birth (**a**) he can watch a dangling ball swung through a 45° arc - one-quarter of an adult's field of vision.

By six weeks (**b**) he moves his eyes to watch a ball through 90°. (This coincides with the development of binocular vision: visual fields now overlap so that most of the image formed on one retina duplicates most of the image on the other.)

By three months (**c**) he can watch a ball swung through 180° - the full adult field of vision.

This progress partly reflects the baby's increasing mastery of the six muscles attaching each eyeball to its socket.

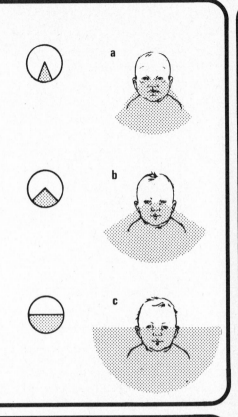

D15 VISUAL PERCEPTION

Adults check their visual impressions against a memory bank stored in the brain. This helps instant recognition of the shapes, sizes, colors, positions, and other qualities of the objects that are seen.

To the newborn infant with no experience to draw upon, the visible world may seem no more than a muddle of blotches.

Perception dawns gradually. Tests devised by psychologists give an indication of the times at which visual perception of shape, size, and color appear.

By six months old, tested infants could perceive simple forms. When one of three test blocks - a circle, triangle, and square - was sweetened, the infants learned to recognize and suck it.

At six months children reached for a small nearby rattle rather than a larger one farther away, although they appeared to be similar. (But a child is 10 years old before he can discount distance in a fully adult way to judge the size of an object.)

Color vision dawns at about three months, when the cones in the eye's retina become sufficiently developed (J34). Tested children of that age gazed longer at colored paper than at gray paper of equal brightness.

D16 DEPTH OF VISION

Depth of vision improves during the first year. A month-old baby gazes at a small white ball moved 6-10in (15-25cm) from his face, but not at one across the room. Tests with rolling balls of different diameters help to show the rate at which depth of vision improves. By six months old (**a**) a baby watches a ball $\frac{1}{4}$in (6mm) in diameter 10ft (3m) away. This suggests a visual acuity as measured by a standard eye-test card of 20/120: i.e. the baby can clearly focus an object 20ft away that someone with normal 20/20 vision would clearly see from 120ft away. By nine months (**b**) a baby watches a ball 1/8in (3mm) in diameter 10ft (3m) away, implying 20/60 vision. Such tests suggest 20/20 or normal visual acuity by one year old (**c**).

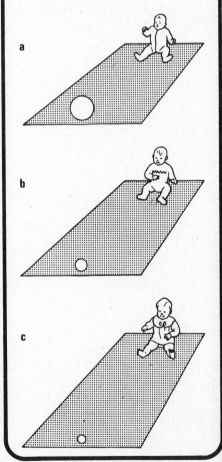

Aspects in development

D17 MANIPULATION

At birth the hands are closed; the reflex grasp action (B21) is present. The hands are still closed at one month, but are often opened by two months. Grasp reflex has gone by three months and a baby can hold a rattle. At four months the hands meet in play. By six months he can deliberately, but awkwardly, grasp a cube (a). By this time he passes it from hand to hand and bangs it on a table. By eight months he begins to grip the cube with his thumb opposite his fingers (b). By nine months thumb and finger grip is good enough to pick up a candy. By one year he holds a cube in a mature pincer grip of thumb and fingers (c). By two years he can turn a doorknob and unscrew lids. He is now clearly left- or right-handed. By 2½ he holds a pencil in his hand, no longer in his fist, and starts to scribble and draw.

a

b

c

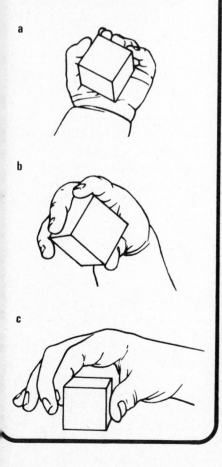

D18 DRAWING

As hand-eye coordination and wrist control improves, children become capable of drawing an increasing number of shapes, always in the same sequence though sometimes earlier or later than the dates given below.

At two a child usually learns to copy a vertical line. At 2½ he can copy a horizontal line. At three he can copy a circle. By then he is also drawing a man, but shows no more than the head and maybe two other parts of the body.

Only at age four does he manage to copy a cross by combining the vertical and horizontal strokes that he had mastered earlier. Another year may pass before he learns to rearrange these lines into a square. He can now draw a rather basic box-like type of house but quite likely cannot achieve the oblique strokes needed for showing a sloping roof. By five his man is more obviously human and may possess recognizable head, trunk, arms, and legs.

Between five and six the child becomes proficient at making oblique strokes and can now draw triangles. By seven he copies a diamond well, and fairly accurately inscribes a cross inside a square to make a "window."

He has now built up a repertory of vertical, horizontal, oblique, and curved strokes. Thus armed, he draws increasingly complex houses and people, often with some touches of originality. For instance his people wear distinctive clothes and may appear in profile. His house may have a smoking chimney and a garden containing flowers and bordered by a fence.

The illustrations included here show how a child's drawing of a man becomes increasingly developed between the ages of three and seven.

Development of drawing ability

Age two

Age three

Age three

Age five

Age seven

HEARING AND SPEECH DEVELOPMENT

D19 DEVELOPMENT OF HEARING

The hearing mechanism is fully formed at birth, but amniotic fluid in the eustachian tubes causes a few hours' deafness. Then a newborn reacts to harsh, sharp sounds. By 10 days he responds to a loudly ticking watch or voice, and soon responds to sounds of different pitch and loudness.

Sound localization improves over the first year. At three months a child turns his head vaguely toward a sound and his eyes seek it (**a**). At five months he turns his head, then inclines it, to locate a sound below ear level (**b**). At seven to eight months turning and inclination begin to merge (**c**). By nine to ten months the child swivels his head diagonally in a direct searching movement (**d**). By one year he localizes sound as well as any adult.

Localization of sound

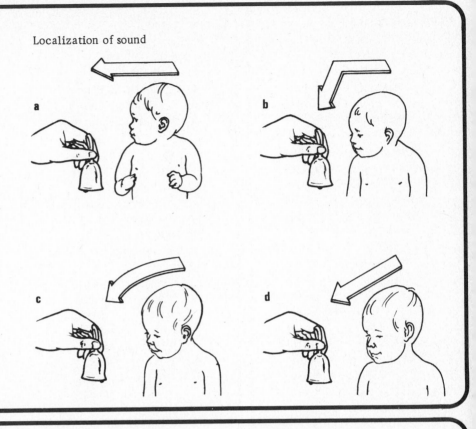

D20 SOUNDS OF SPEECH

Speaking English involves mastering over 40 speech sounds, or phonemes. Children gain this skill in two ways. First, they learn to babble, and so find out how to make a wide variety of sounds. Second, adult responses to their babbling teach them to select for use the sounds they hear most often. Not all children learn phonemes in the same order. But phonemes do tend to appear in a pattern. Children usually say easily pronounced phonemes such as "a" before harder ones like "s." But the frequency with which people around them utter certain sounds also affects the learning sequence. A typical order for the emergence of sounds is described here. By eight weeks the child utters "a" and some other vowel sounds. By 16 weeks he mouths "m" as well as "b," "g," "k," "p." By 32 weeks he masters "t," "d," "w." But only later will he get his tongue around "s," "f," "h," "r," "th." Some sounds give trouble for considerable time – it may take three years to learn all 20 vowel sounds. The phonemic system is usually well established when a child is aged five to seven years.

Formation of speech sounds

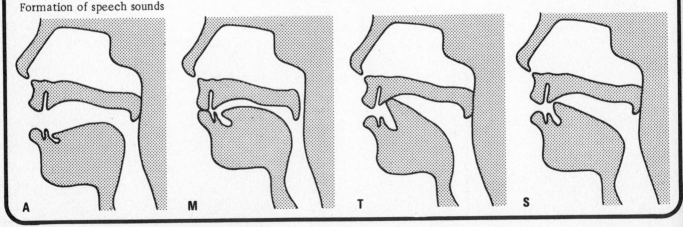

A   M   T   S

Aspects in development

D21 LEARNING TO SPEAK

Learning to speak involves making and monitoring sounds.
Speech occurs when motor nerves bearing signals from the brain operate the larynx and its vocal cords, also the pharynx, soft palate, tongue, and lips. Monitoring speech involves feedback to the brain. Sensory nerves bring the brain signals from the speech muscles and from the ears which have picked up sound waves pushed out by the voice. Thanks to this feedback system a child learns to modify the sounds he makes to match words that he has heard others speaking. It becomes markedly more difficult to learn to speak after age three. Thus deafness must be diagnosed and treated as soon as possible (see L05).

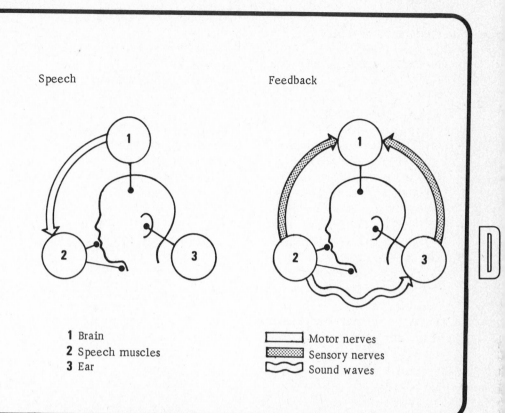

Speech   Feedback

1 Brain
2 Speech muscles
3 Ear

▭ Motor nerves
▨ Sensory nerves
〰 Sound waves

D22 SPEECH DEVELOPMENT

Rates of vocabulary growth vary with a child's aptitude, parents, presence or absence of brothers and sisters, and general living patterns.
Speech development usually starts with vocalized vowels at about seven weeks. By 16 weeks a child utters some consonants, and produces syllables by 20 weeks. The first meaningful word appears at 44-48 weeks. By one year he says two or three words, and by 21-24 months is using two-word phrases. By three years he talks incessantly.
Included here are two graphs showing speech development in tested groups of normal children. The first shows the percentage of children uttering words, phrases, and intelligible speech by different ages. The second shows the average number of words understood at ages up to six.

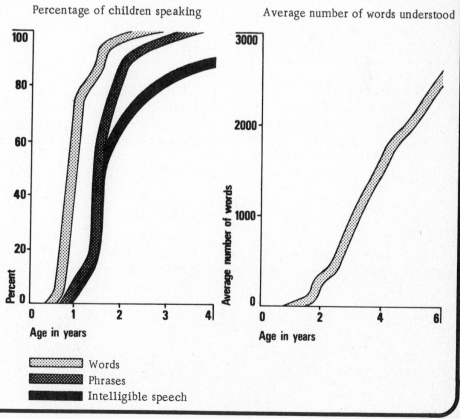

Percentage of children speaking

Average number of words understood

Age in years

Age in years

▨ Words
▨ Phrases
■ Intelligible speech

CONCEPTUAL DEVELOPMENT

D23 PIAGET'S THEORIES

Theories evolved by the influential Swiss psychologist Jean Piaget hold that a child's intellectual development moves through regular stages, where cognitive and emotional factors interact.

1) Sensorimotor stage (0-2 years). Intelligence is empirical, and largely non-verbal. Muscles and senses help children deal with external objects and events. They experiment with objects and graft new experiences onto old. They grasp that objects persist out of sight and touch. They start symbolizing - representing by words and gestures.

2) Pre-operational stage (2-7 years). Children use words for perceived objects and inner feelings, and experimentally manipulate them in the mind as they physically handled objects earlier. They act by trial and error, intuition, and experience.

3) Concrete-operational stage (7-12 years). Logical operations begin. Objects classified by similarities and differences.

4) Formal (adult) operations (12 years onward). Children use thought more flexibly, to handle hypothetical issues.

Grasping the idea of conservation of amount and number is a major advance in mental development as assessed by Piaget. In the test shown below a child under seven watching equal amounts of water poured into containers of unequal height may say that a tall, narrow container (**a**) receives more than a short, broad container (**b**).

D25 STAGES IN MENTAL DEVELOPMENT

6 mth Recognizes familiar faces. May perceive differences between some shapes.

1 Says first words. Defines some common objects by use.

0-2 Manipulates objects in trial and error fashion. May use observation of cause and effect to solve some simple, practical problems by action.

2 Gives own first name. Knows difference between "one" and "many." Understands simple language.

2½ Knows many more words than he uses. Knows own sex.

2-4 Believes that changing an object's shape also alters its size, weight, and volume. Imagination developing: uses signs and symbols (words) to stand for absent objects and events but often confuses the sign or symbol with the thing signified or symbolized.

3 Knows own age in years. Now gaining accurate visual judgment of depth. Knows difference between "big" and "little."

4 Speaks fully intelligibly and now uses many words. Knows "yesterday," "today," and "tomorrow." Attempts to reason often involve confusing cause and effect. Understands "higher," "longer," and "heavier."

4-7 Intelligent behavior largely limit to actions and intuitive thought based on incomplete perceptions.

5 Perceives relative sizes of object well by now. Counts up to 15 bricks. May be learning to read. Can write some letters.

Aspects in development

D24 HOW CHILDREN LEARN

At age two a child given a form-board puzzle tries to force a block into the hole opposite irrespective of their shapes (a).

At 2½ years, if the block does not fit one hole the child tries to push it into another (b).

By age three the child matches shapes by eye before placing a block in a hole (c).

Such tests suggest that a child's early steps in learning are based on simple trial and error association. The puzzle is a stimulus evoking a response of effort pleasurably rewarded by solving the puzzle. Thus effort and reward become associated in the child's brain, and next time the puzzle is presented he will complete it

faster.

By age three he solves some problems in the mind. Language facilitates this process.

Some psychologists discount cognition ("the act of knowing") and consider that throughout life learning consists of mental habits formed by stimulus-response relationships.

5-8 Intersensory perception developing rapidly.

6 May be learning to write joined-up letters by now.
Can say days of the week.
Counts up to 30 by rote.
Knows "right" and "left."

7 Tells time from clock.
Knows own birthday.
Realizes that changing an object's shape need not mean changing the amount of the substance.

8 Now reasons well about data he can see and touch.
Solves simple mathematical problems.
Enjoys reading children's books with more text than pictures.

8-11 Becomes able to group objects in classes and series. Hence concepts of space, time, number, and realization of an ordered material world first fully emerge.

9 Abstract response to the concept of weight is developing.

10 Mental problem solving improves as he draws conclusions from less concrete situations than before.

11 Begins to reason logically about statements instead of just about concrete objects and events.
Perception of physical volume well developed by now.

12 Historical time sense developing. Well able to formulate hypotheses and theories, make assumptions, and draw conclusions. Ability to reason increases through teens.

SOCIAL DEVELOPMENT

D26 UP TO EIGHTEEN MONTHS

By three months a child recognizes his mother (**a**). By eight months he is shy with strangers. By one year he is developing a deeper relationship with his father (**b**). Close, continuous physical and emotional contact with one person in this period is vital for developing a stable personality in adulthood.

D27 EIGHTEEN MONTHS TO FIVE YEARS

At first children closely identify with their parents, copying household actions (**a**). Parents discourage overdependency and outbursts of aggression. At two children cannot yet join in games with others, but at three do so (**b**) and show affection for younger brothers and sisters. Speech increasingly helps the promotion of new social relationships.

D30 CHANGES IN BEHAVIOR

Sometimes a child gets on well with those around him. At other times he seems at odds with everyone. Psychologists have shown that, through childhood, phases when a child seems in balance with his world alternate with phases when he is unhappy and difficult. A child's personality pendulum swings between equilibrium and disequilibrium so regularly that psychologists have compiled timetables indicating when each swing is likely to occur. Behavior fluctuating from "focal" (eg clinging to the mother) to "peripheral" (eg expansive and exploratory) creates another rhythm. Growth usually strikes a balance, yielding a stable, socially well adjusted adult.

Diagrammatic representation of typical swings in behavior

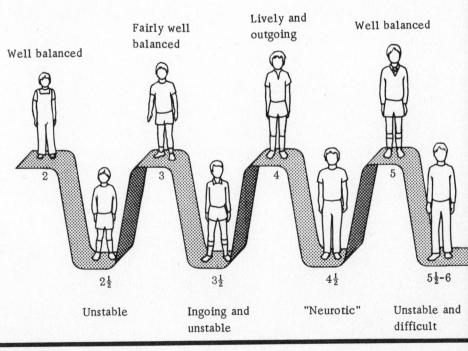

Well balanced

Fairly well balanced

Lively and outgoing

Well balanced

2   3   4   5

2½   3½   4½   5½-6

Unstable   Ingoing and unstable   "Neurotic"   Unstable and difficult

Aspects in development

D28 FIVE TO TWELVE YEARS

A five-year-old has a best friend (**a**), but group games and sports (**b**) gain in importance. He seeks to identify with his contemporaries and to conform with his own school, class, and friends. Less under his parents' influence than formerly, he questions parental values that he once unthinkingly accepted.

D29 ADOLESCENCE

Young teenagers are disoriented by rapid growth and sexual development. They often gain reassurance from a stable home and from conforming with their age group in fads of fashion and behavior (**a**). By 16, adolescents are adjusting to their future role as adults. They begin heterosexual activity (**b**) and may develop a more mature relationship with their parents.

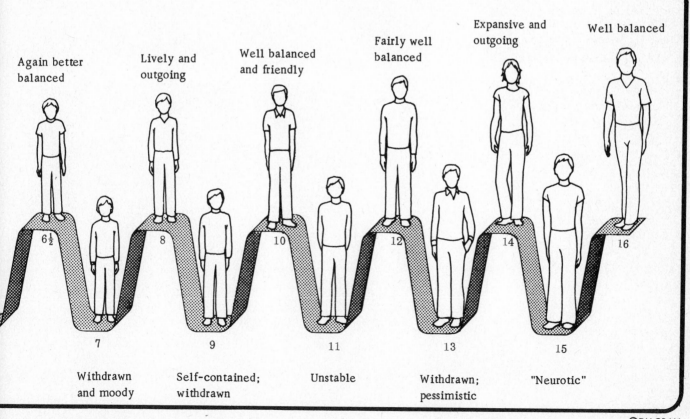

Again better balanced · 6½

Withdrawn and moody · 7

Lively and outgoing · 8

Self-contained; withdrawn · 9

Well balanced and friendly · 10

Unstable · 11

Fairly well balanced · 12

Withdrawn; pessimistic · 13

Expansive and outgoing · 14

"Neurotic" · 15

Well balanced · 16

Practical child care

Once confidence grows and certain tasks become routine, a pattern can usually be established in which parents have time to enjoy their children as well as care for them.

Left: A vacation at the coast (The Mansell Collection)

THE NEW BABY

E01 COPING WITH THE BABY

A new baby brings many changes to the parents' lives.

Feelings of anxiety in the early days are quite normal. Many mothers suffer from a short period of depression after giving birth to a child - "postpartum blues" - probably caused by hormonal changes in the body. If depression lasts more than a few days, the mother should consult her doctor. Anxiety about coping with the baby's needs is very common - particularly for new mothers or mothers whose lives were busy even before the new arrival. It is in such cases that understanding relatives and friends, baby-sitters, play groups for older children, and groups where mothers can discuss their problems can be so useful.

A major problem at first is that the parents do not know the baby's typical behavior patterns. In time they will learn what to expect, but meanwhile the baby will make his needs known by crying.

Specific aspects of care such as feeding, changing, and bathing may seem problematic to new parents - but will soon become second nature.

Some fathers feel neglected after the arrival of a new and demanding baby. Understanding is needed on both sides in the partnership of parenthood, and a mother should encourage her partner to take an active interest in the care of their child.

Parents should avoid neglecting their own interests; self-imposed imprisonment can lead to harmful resentment. Babies do not ask for total sacrifice - only for love, food, and warmth.

E03 EQUIPMENT FOR A BABY

Preparations for the arrival of a new baby include the assembly of a wide range of equipment. This should be done well in advance, as shopping trips become more difficult in late pregnancy and after the baby's birth.

Many items need not be bought new; buying used furniture and nursery equipment can save a considerable amount of money. (It is important to remember that any repainting must be done with leadless paint.)

Large items, such as the crib and baby carriage, can sometimes be borrowed from friends.

There is no need for the layette to include large numbers of first-size garments - babies grow extremely quickly in the early months. (Also see E34).

E02 EARLY ROUTINE

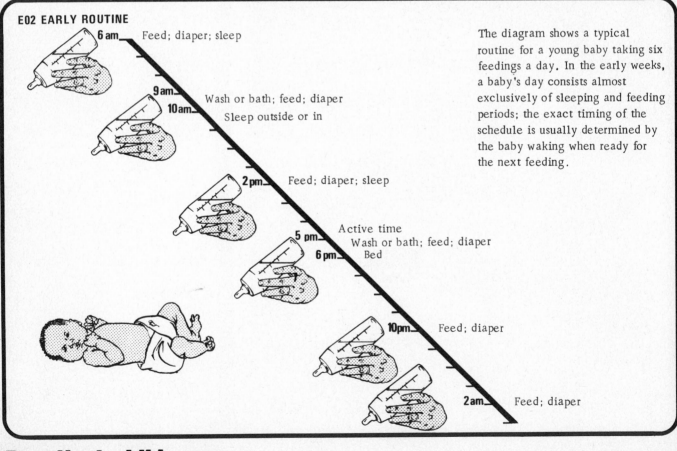

6 am — Feed; diaper; sleep

9 am —
10 am — Wash or bath; feed; diaper
Sleep outside or in

2 pm — Feed; diaper; sleep

Active time
5 pm — Wash or bath; feed; diaper
6 pm — Bed

10 pm — Feed; diaper

2 am — Feed; diaper

The diagram shows a typical routine for a young baby taking six feedings a day. In the early weeks, a baby's day consists almost exclusively of sleeping and feeding periods; the exact timing of the schedule is usually determined by the baby waking when ready for the next feeding.

Practical child care

E04 EQUIPMENT CHECKLIST

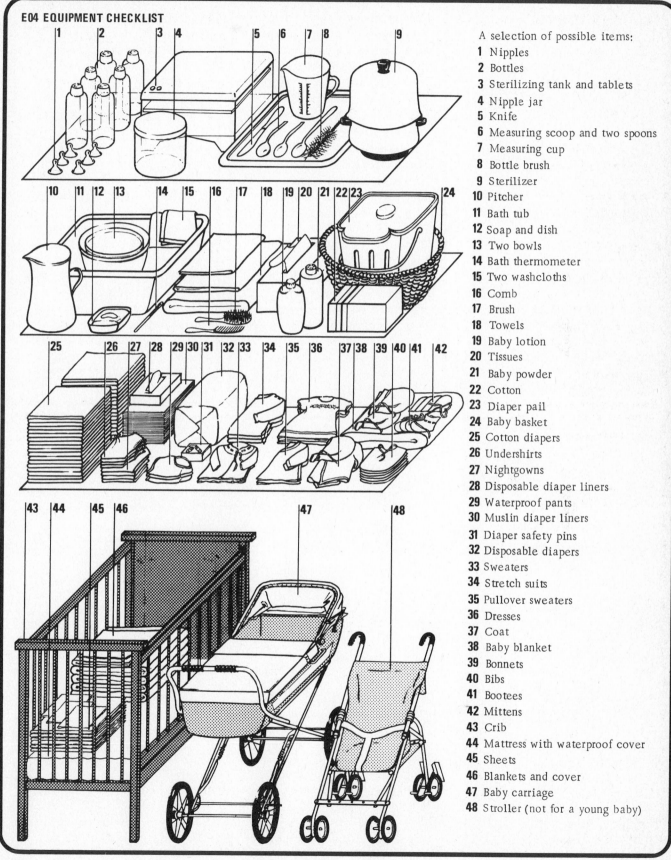

A selection of possible items:

1 Nipples
2 Bottles
3 Sterilizing tank and tablets
4 Nipple jar
5 Knife
6 Measuring scoop and two spoons
7 Measuring cup
8 Bottle brush
9 Sterilizer
10 Pitcher
11 Bath tub
12 Soap and dish
13 Two bowls
14 Bath thermometer
15 Two washcloths
16 Comb
17 Brush
18 Towels
19 Baby lotion
20 Tissues
21 Baby powder
22 Cotton
23 Diaper pail
24 Baby basket
25 Cotton diapers
26 Undershirts
27 Nightgowns
28 Disposable diaper liners
29 Waterproof pants
30 Muslin diaper liners
31 Diaper safety pins
32 Disposable diapers
33 Sweaters
34 Stretch suits
35 Pullover sweaters
36 Dresses
37 Coat
38 Baby blanket
39 Bonnets
40 Bibs
41 Bootees
42 Mittens
43 Crib
44 Mattress with waterproof cover
45 Sheets
46 Blankets and cover
47 Baby carriage
48 Stroller (not for a young baby)

E

©DIAGRAM

CONTACT AND COMFORT

E05 PHYSICAL CONTACT

A reliable and continuous loving relationship experienced from birth on provides a baby with a firm basis for future development. Research suggests that close physical contact, and not food, is the most important factor in the formation of a baby's first emotional attachments - with parents or parent substitutes.
Babies like to be held in close body contact - being particularly happy in positions that simulate clinging - and a reassuring cuddle will often work wonders when a child is upset.
Aids such as baby carriers and baby carriages may be a blessing to mothers, but if used to excess can deprive a baby of valuable physical contact. Baby slings or backpacks worn by the parent can be useful alternatives.

E06 THUMB OR PACIFIER

Young babies have an instinctive need to suck, and many like to suck their thumbs in addition to sucking during feedings. Thumb sucking may continue later, by which time it is essentially a comforting device.
Only if thumb sucking continues after a child has his adult teeth is there a risk of permanent damage - and by this time even the most enthusiastic thumb sucker is likely to have given up the habit.
Some parents prefer their baby to suck a pacifier or dummy, and it does seem to be easier for a child to abandon his pacifier than to give up sucking his thumb.
If a pacifier is used it must be kept scrupulously clean - and never dipped in tooth-decaying sweet substances.

E07 HANDLING A BABY

Handling a baby may seem a daunting prospect to the new parent. In practice, however, most people soon master all the procedures they will need.
When lifting or carrying a young baby it is important to support his neck to prevent it from jerking back; supporting the neck with your hand or arm is all that is needed to prevent an alarming shock reaction.
A baby is likely to be startled if he is picked up suddenly, especially if he is unaware of the handler's approach. Talking to him as you approach him will remove the element of surprise. Illustrated here are two basic handling techniques - a method for turning and lifting the baby, and for raising him to a sitting position.

E08 CARRYING A BABY

Illustrated here are four ways of holding and carrying a baby.

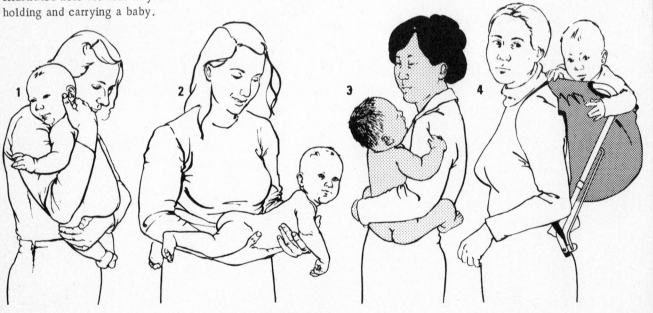

1 A traditional "comforting" position with the baby's head against the parent's shoulder.
2 A forward-carrying position that allows the older baby free movement of his arms and legs.
3 Hip-carrying position - a good way of carrying an older baby who can control his head movements.
4 Baby backpack - also for an older baby who can hold his head up - gives everyone mobility.

Practical child care

TURNING AND LIFTING

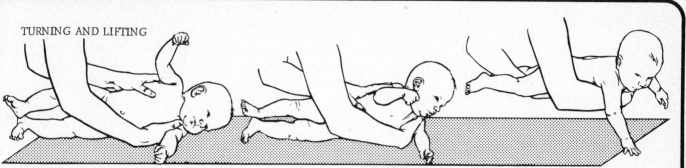

Grip upper part of baby's body.

Turn baby to rest against your arm.

Using your free arm, reach through baby's legs and lift.

RAISING TO A SITTING POSITION

Grip baby by his upper arms and shoulders.

Turn baby slightly to one side.

Supporting head, raise baby to sitting position.

E

E09 COLD AND HEAT

It is possible for a baby, from birth, to regulate his body temperature in response to changes in temperature around him. But the body mechanisms that allow him to do this are still inefficient.

COLD

Cold is generally more of a problem for babies than heat. A baby who is inadequately dressed in a cold environment needs a lot of energy to keep himself warm. A baby who has become chilled normally responds to the cold by using energy to create additional body heat - but he is unable to store this heat, and so is forced to continue his efforts until relieved by outside warmth.

Serious problems can occur if the air temperature drops suddenly and markedly when the baby is asleep. It seems that a baby's temperature control mechanisms start to function only when he is almost awake. A controlled bedroom temperature, and swaddling or a sleeping bag are therefore strongly recommended. If a baby has become chilled it is important to get him warm before adding clothing - otherwise the extra clothing will merely keep in the cold. If the chilled baby is lethargic, with reduced respiration and pulse rates, medical attention should be sought at once.

HEAT

High environmental temperatures are less likely to cause serious problems than low ones. A baby will soon cry if he is too hot - and the problem is easily identifiable. Removing a layer of clothing, wiping away the perspiration, and perhaps a drink of water are usually all that are needed to restore his comfort.

E10 FRESH AIR AND SUN

Babies and children generally benefit from spending part of the day outdoors.

Fresh air improves the appetite, brings color to the cheeks, and probably reduces the risk of infection by preventing the air passages from becoming too dry. It is normally quite safe for even a young baby to be taken outside in his baby carriage - provided that he is suitably dressed, well sheltered from the wind, shaded from the sun, and that there is no fog. Most older children enjoy a daily walk or a period of outdoor play.

Babies and children have sensitive skin that burns easily, and care must be taken to avoid sunburn (see N41). A short sunbath - two minutes maximum on the first day - can be beneficial. A light sunhat is a must even for older children when the sun is hot.

©DIAGRAM

CRYING

E11 COPING WITH CRYING

Crying is the only way a young baby can communicate with his parents; if he cries it may be an indication that something is wrong. Babies have characteristic ways of crying depending on what is troubling them, and most parents soon learn to distinguish between cries for different reasons.

Normally the causes of crying are straightforward, and once they have been dealt with the crying soon stops. Frequent causes include hunger, gas (wind), teething, general discomfort, and loneliness. Crying may also be caused by disturbing a child to undress or change him. A baby crying for no apparent reason is probably only asking to be cuddled.

Some reasons for crying are, however, more difficult to remedy. Notable among these is colic, which is painful for the baby and can cause great distress to the helpless parents.

Another difficult problem is that of dealing with what are sometimes called "hypertonic" babies. These babies are particularly tense, and start at even the slightest noise or handling. Many suffer from colic, or are prone to long periods of irritable crying. In time a hypertonic baby will calm down, but for the first few months it is best to disturb him as little as possible.

If crying is in any way unusual, particularly persistent, or if the child appears in any way unwell, medical advice should be sought without delay.

In general, most parents find that coping with crying becomes much easier once they have become accustomed to their own baby's individual behavior patterns.

DISCOMFORT causes babies to cry. The baby should be dressed in light clothes, and kept in a warm draft-free room away from noises and bright lights.

GAS is often relieved by cuddling the baby over the shoulder. Vigorous back-slapping is usually a waste of time. (See F25.)

HUNGER will make a baby cry. A baby who has taken insufficient milk at a feeding typically wakes after about an hour and cries for another feeding.

LONELINESS Babies cry for attention and love. They need to be cuddled and cannot be "spoiled" in the first months of life. (See E05.)

Practical child care

WET DIAPERS do not seem to worry most babies, unless they have diaper rash. (See E15.) When a baby is wet, he should be changed, but it is probably handling that stops the crying.

HYPERTONIC babies are unusually irritable and difficult to manage. A doctor will sometimes prescribe a mild sedative.

COLIC is a severe abdominal pain that recurs daily in some babies between the ages of two weeks and three months. It is notoriously difficult to treat. (See F30.)

TEETHING begins at different times in different babies, but most have a miserable time. A doctor may give special pain-killers in severe cases. (See J10.)

ILLNESS may make a baby cry. A doctor should be called if the baby looks or behaves unusually, vomits (see F29), has a raised temperature (K31), or is drowsy.

DIAPER CHANGING

E12 DIAPERING EQUIPMENT

Various styles of diaper are currently available.

Traditional cotton diapers are usually square, but other shapes can also be bought.

To make laundering easier many people favor using muslin or disposable diaper liners along with cotton outer diapers.

Plastic pants are usually used over the diaper, but should be avoided if the baby is suffering from diaper rash.

Disposable diapers either have a plastic outer lining, or are worn under specially designed plastic pants. Although comparatively expensive, disposable diapers are often preferred by people who are short of time or away from home. Constant use of disposables, however, can cause chafing or diaper rash in some babies.

1 Cotton diapers and pins
2 Muslin liners
3 Pants for disposable diapers
4 Cotton for cleansing
5 Tissues
6 Baby lotion or cream
7 Baby powder
8 Disposable liners
9 Disposable diapers
10 Waterproof pants for fabric diapers
11 Diaper pail

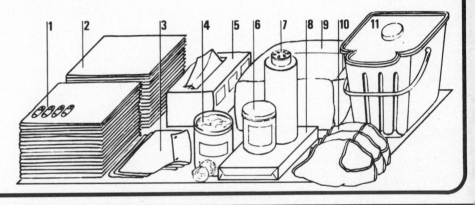

E14 CHANGING A DIAPER

It is useful to have a flat surface on which to change a baby's diaper. All the equipment needed should be directly at hand as a baby must never be left alone where he may fall.

The method illustrated here is for a triangular-fold diaper but stages 1 and 2 apply whichever folding method is used. (Also see E13 for diaper folding methods.)

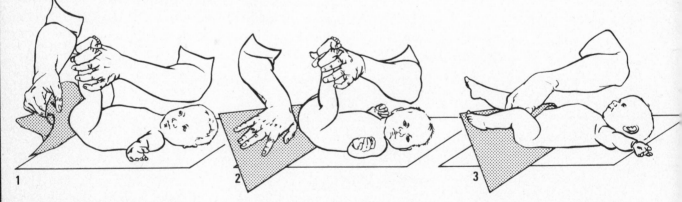

1 Raise the baby's body by grasping his legs with one hand, the index finger between his ankles. Remove the soiled or wet diaper and place in pail.

2 After a bowel movement, wipe the diaper area with tissues. Wash with cotton moistened with warm water, working from front to back. Apply lotion or powder, if used. Slide folded diaper under baby.

3 Fold one corner of the diaper across the baby's stomach and tuck it between his legs.

Practical child care

E13 FOLDING A DIAPER

Illustrated here are three popular ways of folding a regular square diaper.

TRIANGULAR FOLD
Fold the diaper into a triangle and fasten the three corners with a single pin. (For detailed instructions see E14.)

KITE FOLD
Fold in two sides to give a long, pointed shape. Fold over top and bottom flaps; secure with two pins. This method gives a thick center panel.

TRIPLE FOLD
Fold over one-third of the diaper and then fold the rectangle into three. Fasten the diaper with two pins. The extra thickness should go at the back for girls and in front for boys.

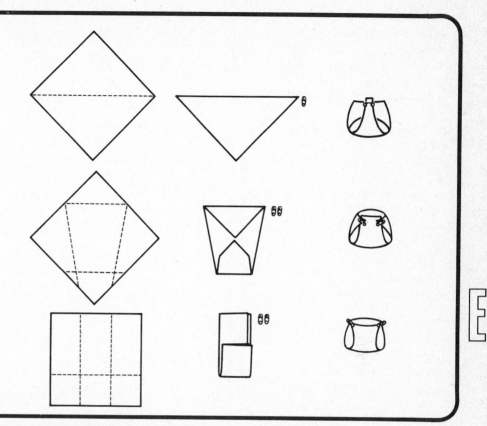

E

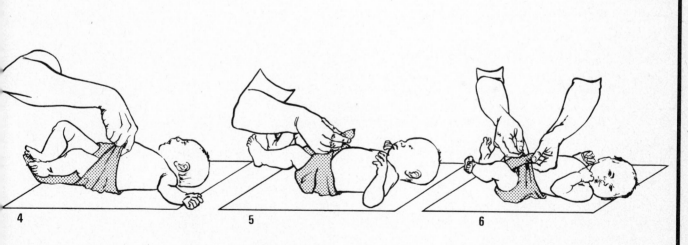

4 Lay the second corner of the diaper across the baby's stomach.

5 Bring up the third corner of the diaper between the baby's legs.

6 With the fingers beneath the diaper to protect the baby's stomach, pin all three thicknesses together, placing the pin horizontally.

©DIAGRAM

DIAPERS AND HEALTH

E15 DIAPER RASH

Diaper rash - patches of redness and spots in the diaper area - is a cause of great discomfort.
It can result from sensitivity to soap, bleaches, or fabric rinses used on the diapers; from powders or lotions used directly on the skin; or from irritation caused by wet or dirty diapers. In older babies, it is usually caused by the reaction of the skin to ammonia formed by bacteria in the urine.
To treat the condition: boil diapers for 10 minutes and rinse with an antiseptic rinse; try using one-way liners or disposable diapers; change the diaper as frequently as possible; do not use waterproof pants; use a cream on the diaper area; and expose the area to the air as much as possible.

E16 CLEANING DIAPERS

The traditional method of cleaning diapers is by washing. The stools are first scraped from the diaper into the toilet and then the diaper is rinsed and washed in very hot, soapy water. Diapers should also be boiled for a few minutes to sanitize them.
The task of cleaning diapers has recently been made easier with the development of special sanitizing products. In this method the diaper is scraped clean, immersed in a sanitizing solution in a plastic pail for two or more hours, and then rinsed several times in clean water.
Diapers are ideally dried in the sun or in an automatic drier; both methods destroy many bacteria. Many people now decide to use labor-saving disposable diapers or liners, or to make use of a local diaper-cleaning service.

E17 NORMAL STOOLS

The stools (bowel movements) of babies vary in appearance and frequency according to age and method of feeding.
During the first two or three days of life a baby normally passes "meconium stools" which are sticky and green-black in color. These stools consist of the waste products that accumulated in the intestines during the last weeks before delivery. For many babies, the first of these stools is gray in color and is called the "meconium plug."
As the baby adapts to milk feeding the stools become green-brown and are known as "changing stools." When milk feeding is established the stools become mustard yellow. The transition from "changing stools" can take just a few days or as long as four weeks.
The frequency of passing stools can vary enormously. Some breast-fed babies produce stools after every feeding during the first few months; others produce as many as 15 daily. Bottle-fed babies tend to produce fewer stools at this time - usually between one and four a day.
In general the stools of a breast-fed baby are softer and less well formed than those of a bottle-fed baby.
As they grow older, both breast-fed and bottle-fed babies tend to produce stools less frequently. Breast-fed babies in particular are likely to have very irregular bowel movements at times; an interval of seven days between stools is not rare, but the doctor should be called if the baby appears unwell.

E18 PROBLEMS WITH STOOLS

DIARRHEA in infants is a serious complaint that needs medical attention.

Sudden onset is usually a result of infection. Gradual onset can be a result of careless formula mixing - too much sugar is often responsible - or the introduction of a new substance to the diet.

CONSTIPATION is most common in bottle-fed babies. Stools are hard and difficult to pass.

Adding brown sugar or maltose to formula can help. Laxatives should only be given on medical advice.

BLOOD IN STOOLS

Blood in stools of newborn babies results from swallowing maternal blood at delivery. Streaks can result from fissure in anus caused by constipation. Large quantities indicate a serious disorder needing urgent medical attention.

STOOLS OF UNUSUAL COLOR

Introduction of any new substance to diet can cause change of color. Bulky gray stools result from over-concentrated formula mix. Black stools can be caused be medicinal iron prescribed for anemia.

Practical child care

E19 TOILET TRAINING

The paragraphs below describe a typical pattern of toilet training, but obviously there will be considerable individual variations. Some babies are put on a pot from a very early age in the hope of "catching" urine or stools. It is now generally agreed, however, that true toilet training cannot begin until the child is getting near the age at which he is physically able to control his bladder and bowels.

Between 15 and 18 months, some children give a signal that the diaper has been wetted or soiled. This should be encouraged and most children then progress quickly to indicate that a bowel movement or urine is imminent. At this stage, the notification and the action of the bowels or bladder may be simultaneous so that on many occasions it is too late to get the child to the pot in time. Nevertheless, praise should still be given. Later, the child will be sufficiently familiar with the sensations of emptying his bladder or bowels to give plenty of warning on most occasions.

Some young children are frightened of falling from the toilet seat, or by the sound of the flush, and should always be accompanied by an adult or older child. Graduating to the toilet from a pot can be made easier if a special infant seat is used.

Accidents will occur, especially with urine, when the child is tired, ill, or excited. But no reprimand should be given.

Night dryness is hardest to achieve, although taking a child to the toilet or pot at around 10pm can often prevent wet bedclothes. (For bedwetting in older children, see G42.)

E20 TRAINING EQUIPMENT

The most basic item of equipment used during toilet training is a pot. Most pots are made of plastic and some have a shield that makes them suitable for boys and girls. It is important to wash and sanitize the pot thoroughly after use. Training pants - made of terry cloth with a waterproof backing - are useful in the early stages of training. Later, a special seat and step for the adult toilet may be used. Some infants prefer a commode chair.

1 Commode chair   **4** Toilet seat
2 Training pants   **5** Toilet step
3 Pot

E21 STAGES IN TRAINING

Children go through the same stages in toilet training but timing varies from child to child.

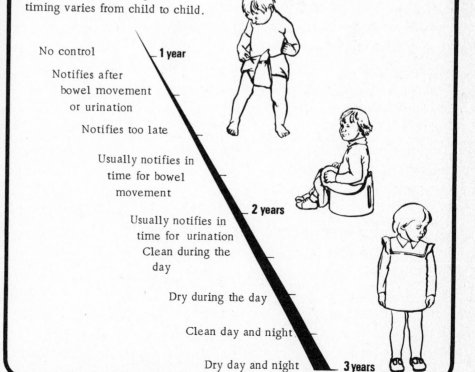

No control   **1 year**

Notifies after bowel movement or urination

Notifies too late

Usually notifies in time for bowel movement

Usually notifies in time for urination
Clean during the day   **2 years**

Dry during the day

Clean day and night

Dry day and night   **3 years**

©DIAGRAM

BATHING 1

E22 BATHING A BABY

A bath is part of most babies' daily routine, and is usually given just before either the mid-morning or early-evening feeding.

It is usually possible to give a new baby a tub bath, but an all-over wash or "sponge bath" may be recommended for the first few weeks. (Procedures for sponge and tub baths are described in E27.) Whatever bathing method is used, it is important to have all the necessary equipment at hand.

This includes all items used during the bath itself, and also towels, a clean diaper, and fresh clothing. For tub baths a plastic tub on a stand or table is useful, but the sink is a good substitute.

A bath thermometer is useful if it provides reassurance, but is not really necessary.

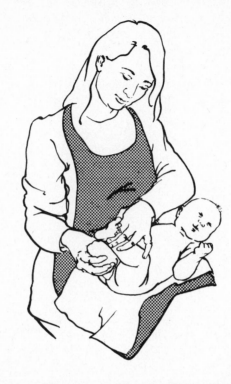

1 Basin
2 Pitchers of hot water
3 Baby shampoo
4 Soap in dish
5 Bath towel
6 Cotton
7 Washcloth

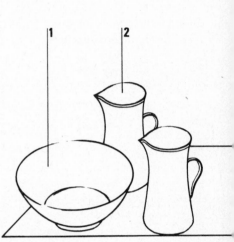

E23 BATHING CHILDREN

Many older babies and children like being bathed together, and simple bath toys can add to their enjoyment. It is important never to leave young children unattended in the bath tub.

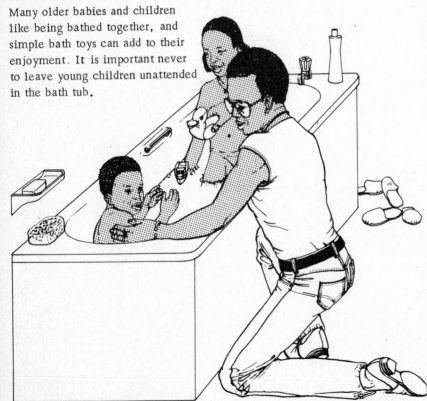

E24 NAIL CARE

A baby's nails may be cleaned very gently with the blunt end of a toothpick.

Nails may be trimmed with blunt-ended scissors, but nail clippers should not be used as their action may cause damage to a baby's nails.

It is a good idea to trim nails when the baby is asleep.

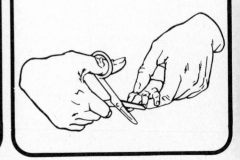

Practical child care

8 Bath thermometer
9 Toothpicks; cotton-tipped sticks
10 Baby powder or cornstarch
11 Baby lotion
12 Diaper

13 Clean clothes
14 Safety pins
15 Bottle for after the bath
16 Tub
17 Waterproof bath apron

E

E25 EAR AND NOSE CARE

A baby's ears and nose are very delicate and should be cleaned only when they become clogged. For this, moistened cotton swabs or cotton-tipped sticks are usually used. It is important to clean only the outer areas, as deeper penetration may cause damage.

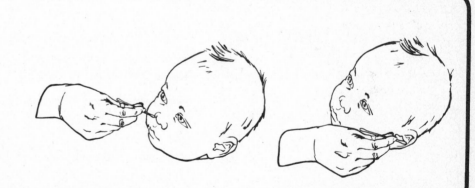

E26 HAIR CARE

A young baby's hair and scalp should be washed with gentle soap or shampoo up to three times a week, and with warm water at other bathtimes. The baby's head should be supported over the tub or basin, as shown. Care must be taken to rinse the head carefully if soap or shampoo is used.
Cradle cap - a yellowish, waxy crust that commonly forms on the scalp at about six weeks - should be treated by massaging with baby oil before washing. An older baby need not have his scalp rinsed so often, but should have his hair washed regularly. Clean, good-quality soft brushes and combs should always be used, and care taken not to tug the hair when removing tangles.

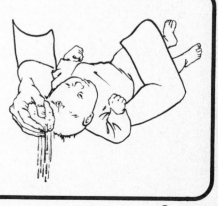

BATHING 2

E27 BATHING PROCEDURES

Bathe the baby in a warm room, using water comfortable to your elbow (95-100°F, 35-38°C). Use mild soap or baby cleansing lotion. The baby may be given a sponge bath or a tub bath (see E22). If a tub is used, the baby may be soaped before or after placing in the tub.

SPONGE BATH

Take off clothes above waist. Apply soap to neck, chest, arms, and hands. Pay special attention to folds and creases. Carefully rinse with clean, warm water. Pat dry with soft towel. Unpin diaper but do not remove.

Turn the baby over, supporting neck with one hand. Apply soap to back and, lowering diaper, also to buttocks. As before, pay attention to all folds and creases. Rinse carefully with clean, warm water. Pat dry. Return baby onto back.

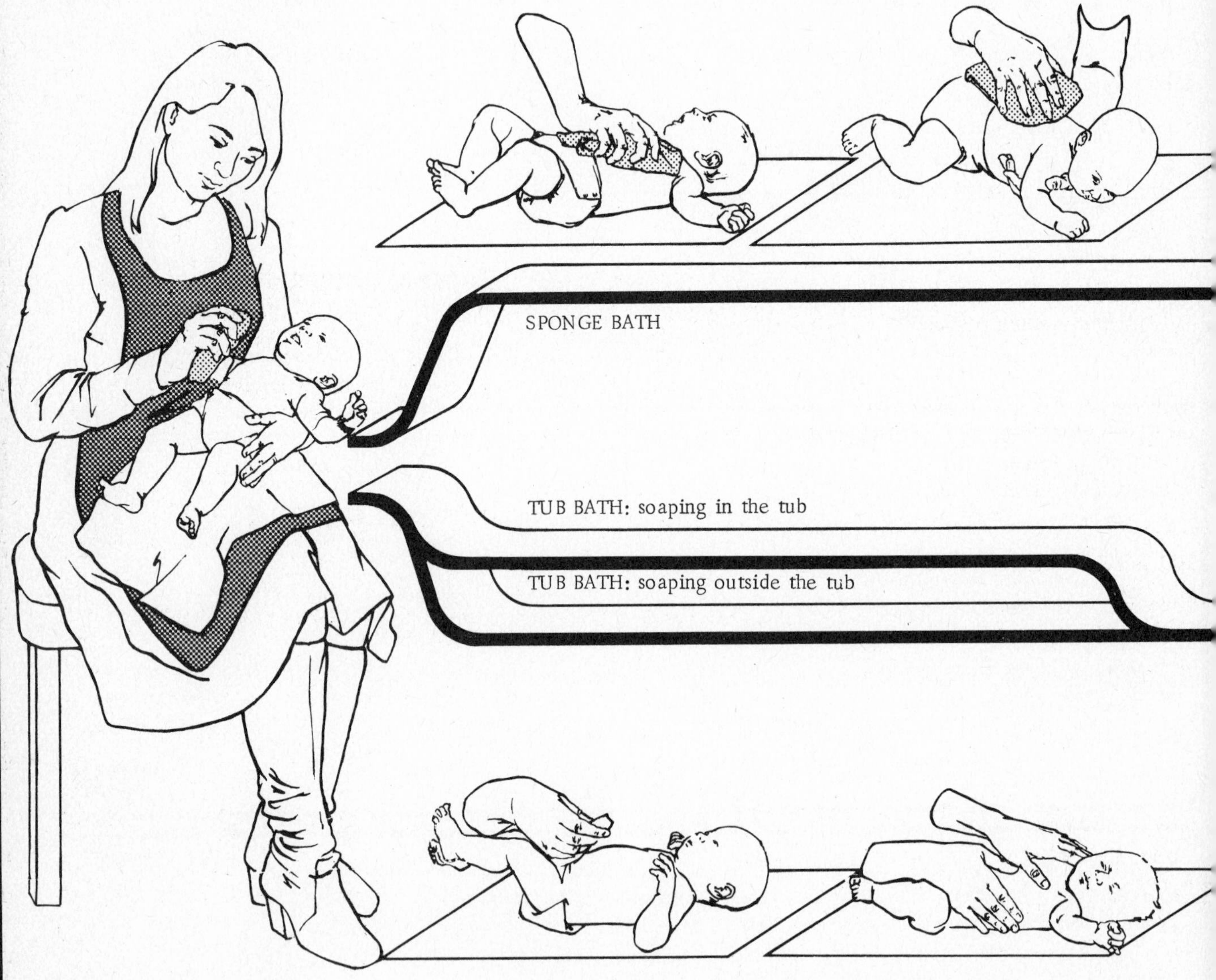

SPONGE BATH

TUB BATH: soaping in the tub

TUB BATH: soaping outside the tub

Collect everything you will need and wash your hands. Sit down with the baby on a big towel on your lap. Clean ears and nose (see E25). Gently clean face with washcloth or cotton dipped in warm water. Wash hair (see E26).

TUB BATH

Remove the baby's clothes - leaving his diaper until last. The baby is now ready to be soaped. This may be done either before or after the baby is placed in the tub.

If the baby is to be soaped outside the tub, this should be done quickly to prevent lather drying on the skin. Using hands or a cloth, apply soap to baby's body and limbs. Use front to back movements in the genital area.

Practical child care

Remove diaper. Wash, rinse, and dry the baby's abdomen, being very gentle with the navel. Wash, rinse, and dry the legs, feet, and genitals, being careful always to use a front to back movement in the genital area.

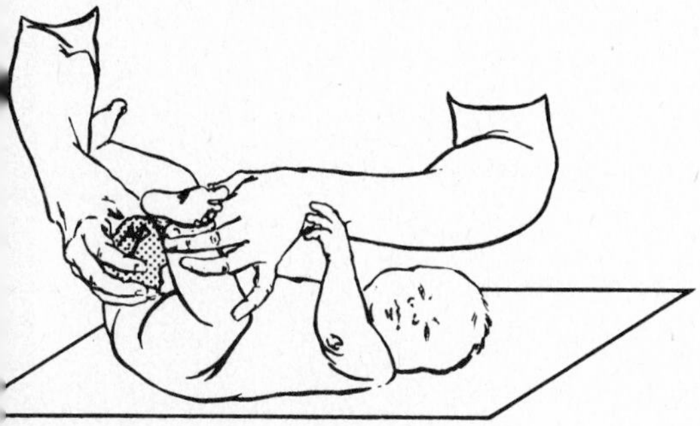

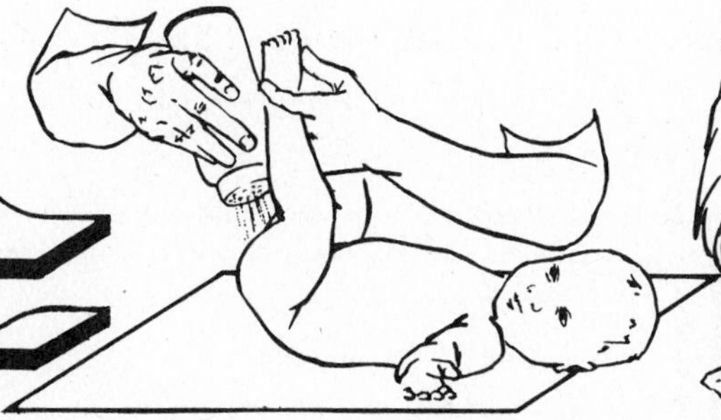

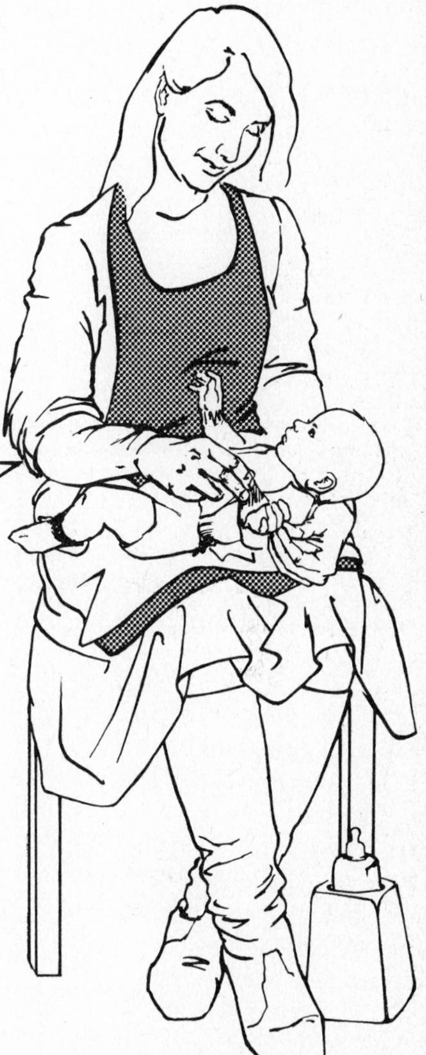

Lower baby into tub - supporting his head and back, and grasping his ankles as illustrated (forefinger between them). Continue to support the baby's head and back with one hand, while soaping or rinsing with the other. Lift out.

To prevent any chafing always make sure that the baby is patted completely dry, particularly around the navel and wherever the skin is folded. Baby powder, lotion, or cream may then be applied as required.

The baby is now ready for a fresh diaper and clean clothes. Babies should never be fed just before a bath, but a bottle or breast feeding should be very welcome once the bath is finished.

EVERYDAY ROUTINE

E28 ROUTINE AT ONE YEAR

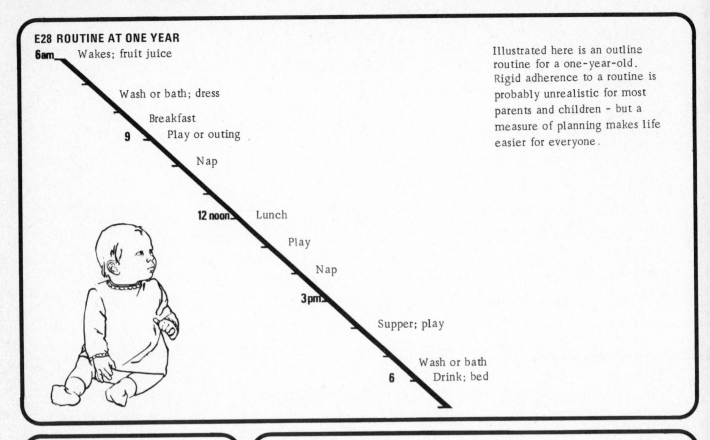

6am Wakes; fruit juice

Wash or bath; dress

Breakfast

9 Play or outing

Nap

12 noon Lunch

Play

Nap

3pm

Supper; play

Wash or bath
6 Drink; bed

Illustrated here is an outline routine for a one-year-old. Rigid adherence to a routine is probably unrealistic for most parents and children - but a measure of planning makes life easier for everyone.

E29 ROUTINE FOR A BABY

A regular daily routine can make life easier for new parents and help give a young baby a valuable sense of security. In addition, performing the same set of actions every day can give confidence to an anxious mother in the few weeks following her baby's birth. In the early months, the routine will be largely dictated by the baby's physical demands. These demands, and their timing, may vary slightly from day to day and it is important that the routine should be flexible enough to accommodate them. It is not, for instance, essential to bathe a baby at the same time each day, nor is it necessary to diaper him before each feeding if his hunger seems to outweigh his discomfort. (A typical daily routine for a young baby is given in E04.)

E30 PRE-SCHOOL ROUTINE

After the first few months the daily routine for a baby becomes more varied. The number of fixed points in the day decreases, as less of the infant's time is spent asleep or feeding. By 12 months a baby is typically taking three meals a day and having a nap in the morning and afternoon. (An outline routine for a one-year-old is given in E28.)

During the next few years much of the parents' time and energy will be spent in guiding the child's early exploration of the world about him. It is an exhausting and demanding time for parents - particularly if it is accompanied by the addition of a new baby to the family (see G06).

A day with some degree of structure is recommended throughout the pre-school years. (An outline routine for a three-year-old is given in E31.) Careful planning will make life easier for all the family; children will know what to expect, and parents should gain time to pursue interests of their own. Realistically, however, a considerable element of flexibility is going to be required.

Except when the weather is bad, children generally benefit from spending some part of the day outdoors (see E10). Also recommended in the daily routine is a period of play with other children. The very young child plays alongside rather than with his contemporaries, but from about two-and-a-half he will enjoy joining others in their games. Organized groups for pre-school children have become increasingly popular in recent years, and a well-run group has advantages for both child and parent.

Practical child care

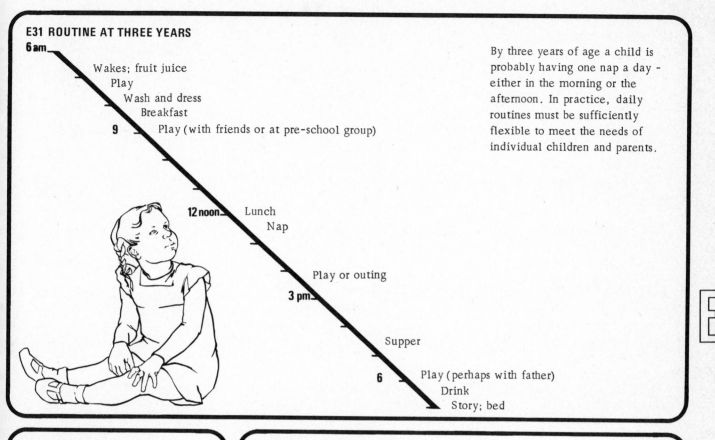

E31 ROUTINE AT THREE YEARS

6 am
Wakes; fruit juice
Play
Wash and dress
Breakfast
9   Play (with friends or at pre-school group)

12 noon   Lunch
Nap

Play or outing
3 pm

Supper

6   Play (perhaps with father)
Drink
Story; bed

By three years of age a child is probably having one nap a day - either in the morning or the afternoon. In practice, daily routines must be sufficiently flexible to meet the needs of individual children and parents.

E32 DISTURBED ROUTINE

Children vary in their ability to cope with a disturbed routine, but parents should be reassured that an unfavorable reaction is not unusual at some stage. In general, understanding handling can usually minimize the trauma.

A visit to the home of relatives or friends can impose extra strain on even the most placid and easy-going child. Good behavior is expected from him in unfamiliar surroundings and he may become exhausted and react with tears or bad temper. A similar reaction can occur after or during the visit of an indulgent relative - perhaps a grandparent.

A family outing, planned as a special treat, can end disappointingly. The excitement of the occasion can quickly tire a child and make him balky and irritable.

E33 SCHOOL-AGE ROUTINE

A child's daily routine changes radically when he first starts attending school, and most children need a good deal of parental support to help them in this new situation (see G12-13). A school-age child spends much of his day away from home, but a fair amount of routine planning is still required.

In the morning, different members of the family must try to coordinate their times of waking, using the bathroom, eating breakfast, and leaving home. Schoolchildren should always be given a nourishing breakfast, with ample time allowed to eat it. Preparing for school should also be as unhurried as possible, and parents should ensure that their children remember any special equipment that may be needed. Whether or not a parent actually accompanies a child to school,

it is ultimately the parents' responsibility to ensure that children arrive at school on time. At the end of the school day, a parent picking up a child should make every effort to arrive on time. If the child is old enough to come home alone, ensuring that someone is there to greet him will increase his sense of security.

If a child has schoolwork to do at home parents should try and see that it is done, providing a quiet work place if possible.

Evening activities and eating times vary a great deal from home to home. Each family must work out a pattern that suits it, and children should learn from an early age the need to fit in with other people's plans.

Views on bedtimes also vary. In general, children should go to bed early enough to ensure that they will not be tired at school.

CLOTHING AND SHOES

E34 DRESSING A BABY

Babies grow quickly, so careful planning is needed when organizing baby clothes. Seasonal requirements vary and should be remembered when selecting baby clothes of different sizes. Garments should be easy to launder and dry, and preferably need no ironing. Deeper colors look fresh longer than the traditional pastel shades.

Dressing a baby is simplified if clothes have few buttons or frills. Lacy-knit or fluffy garments are best avoided, as the baby may catch his fingers or inhale some of the wool.

In the early days, many people favor simple gowns that tie at the neck. Also very popular are one-piece stretch suits. (Clothes for a new baby are shown in E04.)

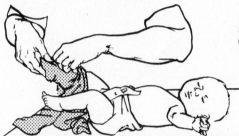

SWEATER: gather sleeve into loop with one hand; with the same hand grasp baby's hand and draw arm down through sleeve;

rock or lift baby onto other side; ease the sweater around baby's neck; draw other arm down through sleeve as described.

STRETCH SUIT: gather one leg of suit into a loop and ease baby's foot and leg into it;

gather second leg of suit into a loop and ease baby's other leg into it; grasp baby's ankles;

E35 CLOTHES FOR CHILDREN

Many factors affect the choice of clothes for children. In general, clothes should be selected that are appropriate to a child's varying activities.

Clothes for play should be in a hard-wearing, easy to launder fabric, and preferably dark in color. Constant nagging about getting dirty is bad for both parent and child - much better to dress the child in play clothes that need little attention.

School clothes should be easy for the child to manage by himself; all unnecessarily difficult fastenings should be avoided. This is particularly important on days when the timetable includes a sporting activity for which the child may have to change. "Best" clothes are worn comparatively little and since

they are soon outgrown it is unnecessary to pay large sums for them. (Shoes must always fit well, and the speed at which children's feet grow makes it particularly uneconomical to keep any for special occasions. Also see E38.) At certain ages children have very definite ideas about clothes and fashion. When this is the case the parents must decide the extent to which they are prepared, or financially able, to let their children have their own way. Hand-me-downs are extremely useful, but to avoid jealousy parents should ensure that younger members of the family receive at least some new garments. Clothes will last longer if they are well taken care of - with regular laundering, prompt mending, and appropriate storage (see E39).

E36 DRESSING THEMSELVES

From about age two, most children show an interest in dressing themselves. By school age, most can manage all but the most

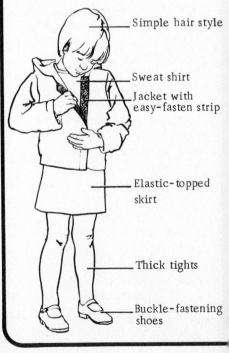

- Simple hair style
- Sweat shirt
- Jacket with easy-fasten strip
- Elastic-topped skirt
- Thick tights
- Buckle-fastening shoes

Practical child care

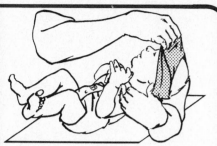

PULLOVER: gather pullover into loop; slip opening over back of head and then forward over front, stretching over forehead and nose.

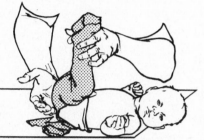

raise baby's legs and ease suit up to waist; put on top of suit in same way as sweater.

E37 CARE OF A BABY'S FEET

A baby's feet are soft and pliable and easily distorted.
In the early months, damage can be caused by bedclothes tucked too tightly around the feet when the baby is lying on his back.
It is important to check that socks and the feet of stretch suits are big enough to allow free movement. Soft shoes for non-walking babies are best avoided as they may hinder the normal development of the feet.
A baby learning to walk should go barefoot as much as possible; shoes worn for outings must fit correctly (see E38).

E38 CHILDREN'S SHOES

The fit of children's shoes matters much more than their appearance. Children's feet grow fast and should be measured regularly for width and length with the special gauges used in shoe stores.
The structure of the shoes is also important. The soles should be flexible to allow a springy step. The uppers should be supple where the toe joints bend but firmer in the arch for support. Shoes that fasten with adjustable straps or laces are recommended as they hold the foot at the back of the shoe and prevent it from sliding forward and cramping the toes. Though it is important to keep the feet dry in wet weather, it is unwise to wear rubber boots for long periods, as they restrict the evaporation of perspiration.

difficult fastenings. It is sensible to encourage independence by providing simple clothes such as those illustrated here.

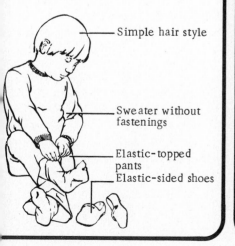

- Simple hair style
- Sweater without fastenings
- Elastic-topped pants
- Elastic-sided shoes

E39 KEEPING TIDY

Accessible storage areas will help children to keep clothes tidy. Ideally there should be enough closet space for hanging up clothes and keeping shoes - with lowered rails for easy reach. Dressers can be used to store underwear and sweaters, and the flat surface on top is a good place to keep combs and brushes.

TRAVEL HINTS

E40 TRAVEL WITH CHILDREN

Trouble-free travel with children relies to a great extent on careful planning by the parents. An important aspect of this is the provision of all the equipment needed for a particular trip.

For babies it is important that the normal routine remains unchanged as far as possible, and it is sensible to carry in a large bag all the equipment needed for feeding and diapering.

A damp washcloth, a towel, and tissues are useful for children of all ages.

Extra garments and a blanket should be carried for changes in temperature, and some form of entertainment - toys, books, or games - should also be included.

For car travel, safety equipment such as a junior car seat or seat belt is essential.

EQUIPMENT FOR BABY

1 Baby carrier and restraining straps
2 Diapers, possibly disposable
3 Prepared bottles
4 Pacifier
5 Baby food
6 Tissues
7 Extra garments
8 Pot
9 Toys
10 Damp washcloth and towel in plastic bags

E42 CAR TRAVEL

Car trips are a regular feature of modern family life, and, with planning, parents can ensure that as little upset as possible is caused to younger members of the family. Two factors need consideration when a trip is planned - safety and comfort.

SAFETY

It is unwise to allow a child to travel in the front seat of a car.

A baby can travel in his carrier, which should be held on the back seat with restraining straps. Children need special safety seats or junior seat belts (see E40). "Childproof" locks should be fitted to doors.

COMFORT

The car should be warm and adequately ventilated; a small child should not be in a draft from an open window. Clothing should be easy to adjust or remove if the child becomes too warm, and an extra garment or blanket should be available if the child becomes cold.

Trip times should be planned to allow for frequent stops - for toilet visits and exercise.

On longer trips, provision must be made for feeding the family. A picnic meal is usually ideal, and a bottle of plain water should always be carried. For a bottle-fed baby, bottles of formula should be made up in advance and either given cold or heated in a pitcher of hot water from a thermos.

It is essential to provide some form of amusement or diversion for children on a trip - even a baby enjoys having a familiar toy close by. (Some suggestions for amusing older children are given in E46.)

E43 BUS AND TRAIN TRIPS

Long-distance travel with young children on buses or trains is never easy, especially when they are crowded. For this reason, it is preferable to travel midweek and, if possible, to reserve seats in advance. Sleeping cars are recommended for overnight travel on trains.

The breast-fed baby presents few problems on a coach or train journey unless the mother is unhappy about feeding the child in anything but strict privacy. Ladies' rooms in stations and hotels often have special facilities. Bottles of formula should be made up in advance for the bottle-fed baby (see F21).

Older children should be given plain food to minimize the chance of sickness.

Practical child care

EQUIPMENT FOR OLDER CHILD

1 Car seat
2 Seat belt
3 Tissues
4 Pillow
5 Blanket
6 Thermos
7 Food
8 Pot
9 Extra garments
10 Diapers, possibly disposable
11 Toys and games
12 Damp washcloth and towel
in plastic bags

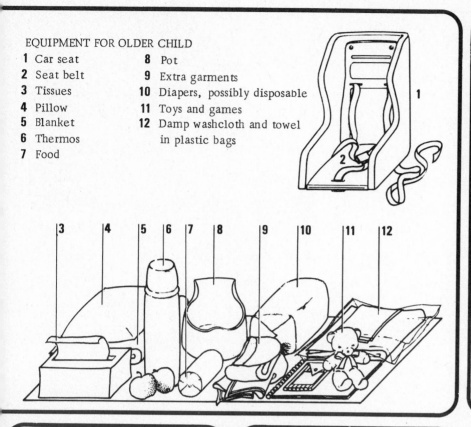

E41 MOTION SICKNESS

If a young child is susceptible to motion sickness, the parents should never fuss or show concern before the trip.

Rich food should not be given before or during a trip. An apple or dry cracker may help relieve feelings of sickness. Adequate ventilation and frequent stops can make car travel more pleasant, and amusements for the child (see E46) may also help. An anti-sickness medication taken in advance can also help ensure a comfortable trip.

During the trip it is useful to have close at hand plastic or paper bags, a damp washcloth, a towel, and a change of clothes; these can give a sense of security to an anxious child.

E44 AIR TRAVEL

Most airlines are extremely helpful to parents traveling with children, especially if they are warned in advance. Some aircraft have cribs, facilities for heating bottles or canned baby food, and a supply of disposable diapers; this should be checked before the trip.

Takeoff and landing can sometimes be alarming for a child. A baby may be given a bottle of boiled water or a zwieback (rusk), and an older baby a candy; these will help equalize pressure in the ears. Children need some form of amusement during the flight and waiting periods (see E46 for ideas). Delays are sometimes unavoidable so provision should be made for extra time spent traveling. This means keeping extra clothing and food at hand and not packed away in baggage in the aircraft hold.

E45 BOAT TRIPS

A short boat trip with children is often more difficult to manage than a long sea voyage.

If cabin accommodation is available, most of the problems associated with feeding and caring for a baby will be solved. Toddlers and older children should be carefully controlled at all times for their own safety. Rich meals should naturally be avoided.

For long trips, most large ships offer special facilities for babies and children, including supplies of formula milk, disposable diapers, and baby foods; special mealtimes; and a supervised nursery.

Before a long trip it is important to find out about the places visited en route so that the child may be dressed comfortably whatever the temperature.

E46 TRAVEL ENTERTAINMENT

Travel can be easier and more pleasant for everyone if some effort is made to entertain the children during a trip.

For a special trip, reading in advance a book about boats, trains, or aircraft can greatly increase a child's enjoyment and interest.

On trains, aircraft, and boats reading or drawing books and play materials such as modeling clay can be useful, though this kind of activity can cause a headache or sickness in a car.

Spotting games like "I spy" are entertaining and can be instructive. Also popular are counting and guessing games. Singing or reciting for short periods can amuse children of all ages, and stories, told by parents or children, can provide an enjoyable diversion.

E

E47 TYPES OF CRIB

A baby spends much of his time asleep, so all the equipment must be both safe and comfortable. In the early months, many babies sleep in a bassinette, or baby carrier on a stand. These have enclosed sides that reduce the risk of chilling from drafts. When buying a full-size crib there are several points to consider. It should be sturdily built with vertical bars no more than $2\frac{1}{2}$in (6.4cm) apart, and a safe latch on the side that can be raised and lowered. The mattress, either foam or horsehair, should have a waterproof cover. A pillow is not recommended for the first year. Fitted sheets are timesaving and easy to use. Blankets should be light, warm, and easy to launder; acrylic fiber is a good choice.

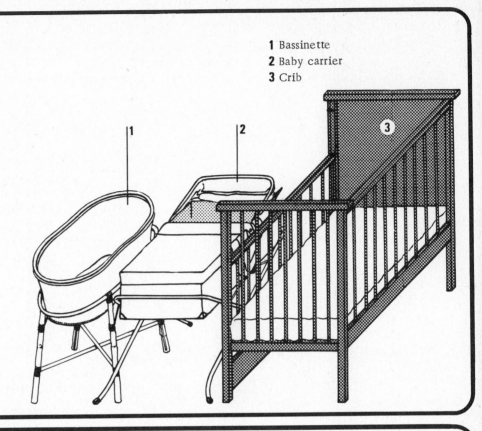

1 Bassinette
2 Baby carrier
3 Crib

E48 EQUIPPING A NURSERY

A room of his own is ideal, but a baby can successfully share his parents' room if necessary. The crib is the only essential item of equipment in a nursery. A flat surface for diaper changing and a storage unit for baby clothes and equipment are, however, strongly recommended. Also useful is a comfortable nursing chair for feeding.

A number of safety and health factors need careful consideration. Walls and furniture should be painted with leadless paint. Drapes and blinds should be made of flameproof fabric. Flooring should be easy to clean and non-slip. Scatter rugs may cause a serious fall.

The room should be kept warm - not lower than 65°F (18°C) - and the crib should be placed in a draft-free position.

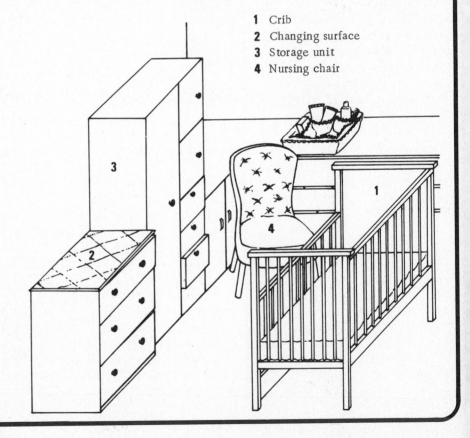

1 Crib
2 Changing surface
3 Storage unit
4 Nursing chair

Practical child care

E49 BABIES' SLEEPWEAR

A simple cotton gown (1) is the traditional sleepwear for young babies. Many people, however, now favor dressing their babies for sleep in an easy-to-wash terry cloth stretch suit (2). As babies become more active and are likely to kick off their cot covers it is a good idea to use a sleeping bag (3).

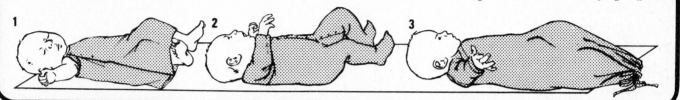

E50 SLEEPING POSITIONS

For the first three months a baby sleeps in the position in which he is placed. The front position (1) is sometimes recommended, as any regurgitated feeding can easily trickle out of his mouth. The back position (2) allows the baby to look around when he wakes. Only from about six months old are babies able to sleep unsupported on their sides (3); a younger baby can be kept in a side sleeping position by supporting his back with a rolled towel or sheet.

E51 HOW MUCH SLEEP?

Individual sleep needs vary enormously. Some young babies sleep as much as 80% of the time, while others seem to be wakeful from birth. Children and adults, too, appear to have very different personal sleep requirements.
In general, however, sleep needs decrease with age. An indication of sleep needs at different ages is given here in the diagram (based on on the findings of H. P. Roffwarg, J. N. Muzio, W. C. Dement).
Researchers have discovered that there are two basic types of sleep: light, or REM, sleep (when rapid eye movements can be observed), and deep, or NREM, sleep (without rapid eye movements). In older children and adults, dreams are most likely to occur during REM sleep. In infants, REM sleep is thought to be not necessarily related to dreaming.

Typical sleep needs and types of sleep at different ages

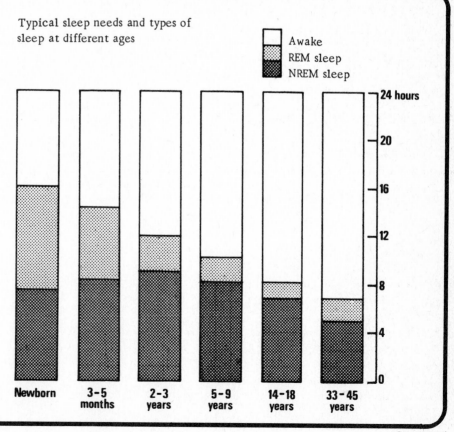

©DIAGRAM

SLEEP 2

E52 SLEEPING PATTERNS

The distribution of sleep during a 24-hour period changes with age. A young baby typically has five or six sleep periods a day, waking when hungry and sleeping when fed. As the baby gets older he spends more of the time awake, with sleep concentrated into a long night sleep and a number of daytime naps (see also E54). A two-nap-a-day pattern is usually established in the second half of the first year. This is followed, usually early in the second year, by a one-nap-a-day pattern that persists through early childhood. From about age four children usually sleep only at night, with total sleep needs decreasing as they get older (also see E51).

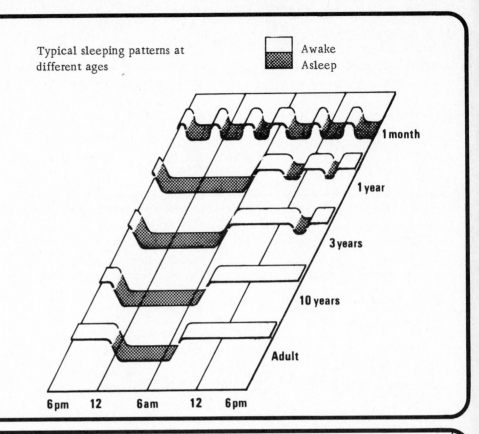

Typical sleeping patterns at different ages

▢ Awake
▨ Asleep

1 month
1 year
3 years
10 years
Adult

6 pm   12   6 am   12   6 pm

E55 BEDTIME ROUTINE

The establishment of a regular bedtime routine can be comforting and reassuring for a young child, and may in some cases prevent the formation of severe sleep problems. Though exact procedures vary with the age and temperament of the child and with the particular family situation, the observation of a few general points can help make bedtime easier for both child and parent.

The period before bed should be as calm as possible and a story can be an ideal way of rounding off a child's day. Most children thoroughly enjoy a story and derive considerable satisfaction and a valuable sense of security from receiving the undivided attention of a parent - even for just a few minutes.

It can also be helpful to encourage a child to take an active part in bedtime preparations. He can be allowed to turn on the bath tap (under supervision), undress himself, help dry himself, and put on his nightclothes.

Ideally, the child should go to bed at approximately the same time each evening. The parents' attitude to bedtime should be pleasant but firm; if the pre-bed routine is tackled with an air of certainty the child will quickly learn that he cannot successfully delay going to bed by discussion, argument, or pleading.

A certain amount of bedtime ritual is comforting - indeed necessary - for children. Many insist on having particular toys or playthings in bed with them; such objects can help give a child a feeling of security when he is left alone and may help him not to disturb his parents if he wakes in the night or early in the morning. Others may ask for a drink or an extra kiss, or that the bedroom door be left open a certain distance. As long as bedtime requests remain reasonable it is probably sensible to grant them. Some children, however, may use them as a deliberate delaying tactic, and parents should guard against the establishment of long and involved bedtime rituals.

In general, the parent should settle the child and leave him with a firm but cheerful farewell. Some children will fall asleep almost immediately, or at least lie quietly until they are ready to sleep. Others are more troublesome, beginning to cry as soon as the parent has left the room. Refusal to settle down is discussed in E56.

Practical child care

E53 CHILDREN'S NIGHTWEAR

Nightwear should be carefully chosen to meet a child's needs. A sleeping suit is a good idea for young children. Simple, short nightdresses may be worn by young girls, but long ones should be reserved for older girls for safety reasons. All children's nightwear should be made from flameproof fabric.

E54 NAPS

Babies and young children need to supplement their night sleep with daytime naps (E52). The timing of a child's naps is influenced by sleep needs at different ages and by general family routine. Problems sometimes occur when the child is making the change from two naps a day to one. If he does not sleep in the morning, he is too tired to eat lunch. If he naps in the morning, he becomes overtired in the late afternoon. A very early lunch followed by one long nap is probably the best solution at this stage.

Similar flexibility is often needed when the child is almost ready to give up naps altogether. A quiet period in the afternoon or a short sleep somewhere other than in his bed may help a child over this period.

E

E56 REFUSING TO SETTLE DOWN

Almost every child goes through phases of refusing to settle down when put to bed. There are a number of common reasons. Childhood is interspersed with countless new experiences, and at bedtime the child may be left too excited to sleep. Children, like adults, need time to unwind before sleep is possible.

A young child's growing enjoyment of the company of others can make him reluctant to leave the family, and his unwillingness to sleep can be reinforced by interesting sounds from elsewhere in the home. Alternatively, he may simply not be tired. Afternoon naps continued too long or taken too late in the day may lead to problems at bedtime. Ajdusting the daily routine as the child gets older should put matters right.

Sometimes a child's refusal to settle down is due to anxiety or a genuine fear of being left alone in the dark. Parental reassurance, together with a comforting toy, a nightlight, or leaving the bedroom door open and another light on should help the phase to pass more quickly.

Some toddlers refuse to lie down in their cribs at bedtime. They should be left sitting or standing; the parent can return later to cover the child.

Many young children habitually cry when left for the night. In most cases this is merely a "testing cry;" it rarely warrants the parents' return as the child usually drifts to sleep quite quickly. More persistent bedtime crying is more of a problem, and in severe cases a a doctor may prescribe a very mild sedative to help reestablish the habit of falling asleep.

E57 EARLY WAKING

Many children regularly wake very early in the morning. This is perfectly normal but can cause an unwelcome disturbance of the parents' sleep, especially in the case of a young child who is at his brightest and most sociable after a night's rest.

It is often possible to encourage a young child to play quietly in his bed in the early morning; a mobile to watch or toys to play with may delay any disturbance.

In some cases a "bribe" of a drink or cookie set out the night before may also be useful.

Older children can sometimes be taught not to make too much noise until they hear a certain sign - for instance, the ringing of their parents' alarm clock.

Sharing a room may also help solve the problem as the children may amuse each other and play quietly until a reasonable hour.

E58 DISTURBED NIGHTS

Young babies, provided that they are tired, comfortable, and not hungry, sleep very soundly. From the age of about six months, however, children wake more easily, and may do so frequently for a variety of reasons. Disturbance by other people is a common cause of waking at night. Too many visits by over-anxious parents can cause the child to wake up and demand attention. Sharing a room - either with the parents or another child - can also cause problems. Bedtime preparations must be made with the minimum of noise and fuss if a child is already asleep in the room. If two children are sharing a room and one of them wakes in the night it is extremely likely that he will disturb the other - either deliberately or not.

Accustoming a child to complete silence when he is in bed is not necessarily a good idea - making it difficult for him to sleep away from home or if there is any unusual noise in the night. It is not, of course, reasonable to expect children to sleep through high levels of noise, for example, from a loud television or party. Some children wake at night simply because they are no longer tired - a later bedtime, or cutting out a nap, may be the solution. Many children need to visit the toilet during the night - leaving a convenient light on can persuade an older child to manage alone. Nightmares are another common cause of disturbed nights. Gentle reassurance from the parent will usually get the child to go quickly back to sleep.

E59 MOVING TO A BED

The age at which a child is moved into a bed can vary considerably - some children are ready at two while others are happy in a crib until they are four. When a toddler begins to climb out of his crib regularly, he is probably safer in a bed. Although it represents "growing up" some children may be anxious about moving from a crib to a bed. The transition need not be made suddenly; a child can become accustomed to a new bed by taking naps there, and only moving on to sleeping in it at night when he feels ready.
If the crib is needed for another child, it is wise to establish the toddler in his bed well before the new baby's arrival in order to avoid giving him the impression that he is being "pushed out."

E60 CHOOSING A BED

The first essential for any bed is a firm mattress to support growing bones and encourage good posture. In the early months it is wise to place the bed against a wall, and to have a special guard rail or a chair against the other side of the bed for extra reassurance.
Junior beds, smaller than the regular single version, are widely available, but have the disadvantages of needing special bedding and being soon outgrown. Bunk beds save floor space, and their play potential makes them popular with many children.
It is a good idea to store a camp bed under the child's bed, for use by visiting friends.

1 Secure ladder
2 Guard rail
3 Firm mattress

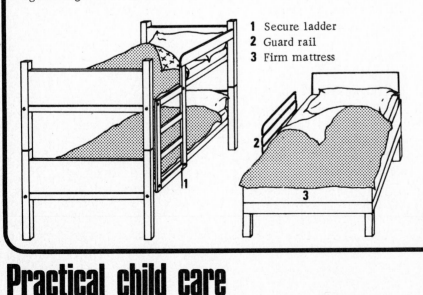

E61 SHARING A ROOM

In many families it is necessary at some stage for two or more children to share a bedroom - a situation that has both advantages and disadvantages.
Young children often enjoy sharing a room and perhaps will amuse each other in the early morning, so allowing the parents a little extra sleep. At the other end of the day, however, it can sometimes be a problem to persuade children sharing a room to go to sleep. Also, a disturbed night for one child can often mean a disturbed night for both.
As they get older, children may resent the lack of privacy in a shared room. It is a good idea at this stage to allocate specific areas of the room to each child, either by using some form of room divider or by giving each child his own storage and display areas.

Practical child care

E62 BABY-SITTERS

GENERAL PROCEDURE
1 Agree in advance the hours, pay, and duties expected of the sitter.
2 Indicate whether you allow the use of the TV, radio, and telephone; whether you allow the sitter to bring a friend; and whether you will provide food.
3 Show the sitter around the house.
4 Pick up the sitter and take home if necessary.

CARING FOR THE CHILD
1 Choose a person who can cope with the needs of a particular child, and preferably someone the child knows.
2 Check that the sitter can, if necessary, change a diaper and give a bottle. Indicate where the equipment is kept.
3 Warn the sitter of any point of routine such as leaving a door ajar, or any favorite toy, that the child finds comforting.
4 Establish, in the presence of an older child, details about snacks, drinks, play, bedtime, etc.

EMERGENCIES
Leave a list of telephone numbers, including the number at which you can be contacted, and the numbers of a reliable neighbor, the doctor, and the police.

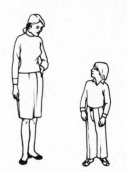

BRIEFING THE CHILD
If the child is old enough, brief him as follows:
1 Warn him in advance that you are going out and that the sitter will be taking care of him.
2 Remind him to behave well.
3 Introduce him to the sitter.
4 Establish, in the presence of the sitter, details concerning snacks, play, bedtime, etc.

E

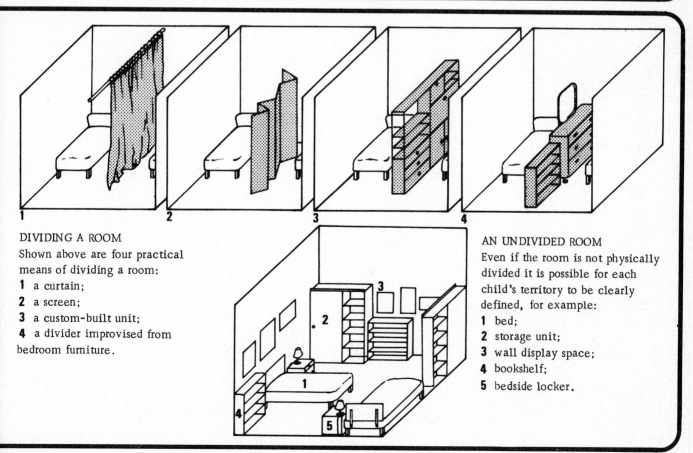

DIVIDING A ROOM
Shown above are four practical means of dividing a room:
1 a curtain;
2 a screen;
3 a custom-built unit;
4 a divider improvised from bedroom furniture.

AN UNDIVIDED ROOM
Even if the room is not physically divided it is possible for each child's territory to be clearly defined, for example:
1 bed;
2 storage unit;
3 wall display space;
4 bookshelf;
5 bedside locker.

©DIAGRAM

Feeding

Few aspects of child care cause more anxiety than feeding. From the birth of the baby onward there are numerous questions to be answered.

F

Left: A park bench feeding (Photo Richard and Sally Greenhill)

MILKS

F01 BREAST MILK CONSTITUENTS

For the first week of a baby's life all his nutritional needs are supplied by milk - either his mother's breast milk or a specially developed formula milk.
The exact composition of breast milk varies slightly from mother to mother - and there is a similar variation in the precise requirements of different babies. The diagram shows a detailed analysis of 100gm of breast milk. Water constitutes a very large proportion of the total, and carbohydrate, protein, and fat account for most of the remainder. Minerals and vitamins have an importance out of all proportion to their weight.

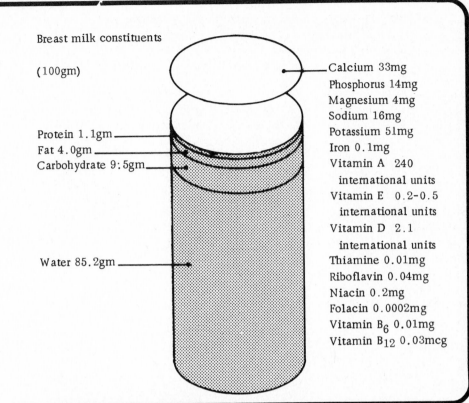

Breast milk constituents

(100gm)

Protein 1.1gm
Fat 4.0gm
Carbohydrate 9:5gm

Water 85.2gm

Calcium 33mg
Phosphorus 14mg
Magnesium 4mg
Sodium 16mg
Potassium 51mg
Iron 0.1mg
Vitamin A 240
  international units
Vitamin E 0.2-0.5
  international units
Vitamin D 2.1
  international units
Thiamine 0.01mg
Riboflavin 0.04mg
Niacin 0.2mg
Folacin 0.0002mg
Vitamin B_6 0.01mg
Vitamin B_{12} 0.03mcg

F03 COMPARISON OF MILKS

Human milk is ideally suited to the developmental needs of a human baby. The needs of the offspring of different types of animal are similarly met by their own mothers milk.
Obviously the needs of human babies and the needs of different young animals vary - and so do different types of milk.
The diagram illustrates the most obvious difference between human milk and various types of animal milk - all milks contain carbohydrate, protein, and fat, but the relative proportions of these different nutrients vary considerably from milk to milk. Human milk is seen to be comparatively rich in carbohydrate and low in protein.

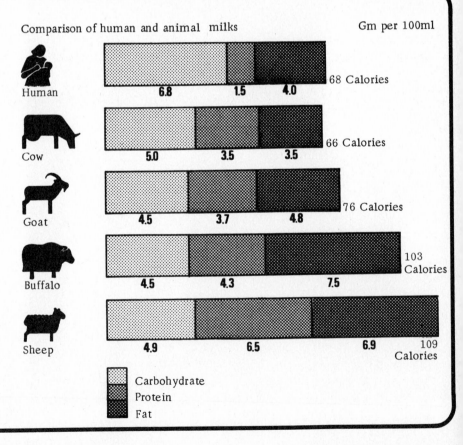

Comparison of human and animal milks   Gm per 100ml

Human   6.8   1.5   4.0   68 Calories
Cow   5.0   3.5   3.5   66 Calories
Goat   4.5   3.7   4.8   76 Calories
Buffalo   4.5   4.3   7.5   103 Calories
Sheep   4.9   6.5   6.9   109 Calories

Carbohydrate
Protein
Fat

F02 HOW MUCH MILK?

The quantity of milk required by a baby varies according to age and weight. In the first few days after birth babies take tiny feedings at irregular intervals. By the end of the first week a more regular feeding pattern is usually established. From this point food requirements increase fairly steadily and are reflected in a correspondingly steady gain in weight.

It is possible to calculate a baby's approximate daily food needs in ounces by multiplying his weight to the nearest pound by $2\frac{1}{2}$. Each baby's requirements are slightly different, and a particular baby's intake may vary from day to day. The diagram is a guide to the amount of milk required by typical babies at different ages.

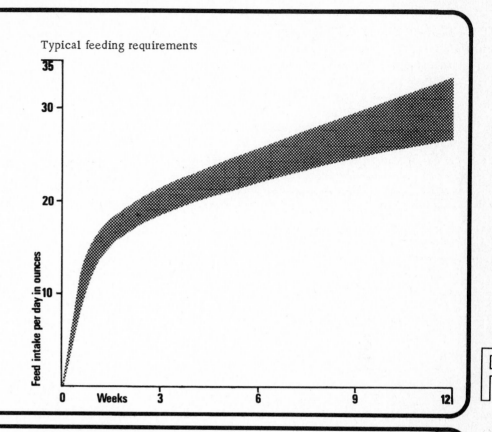

Typical feeding requirements

F04 FORMULA MILKS

A wide range of commercially produced milk formulas is now available for bottle-fed babies. Scientific research into the constituents of human and animal milks has enabled manufacturers to produce milk formulas that are well suited to babies' needs. Baby milk formulas are generally made by modifying cow's milk to make it more like human milk.

One important change is illustrated in the diagram - an adjustment in the relative proportions of carbohydrate, protein, and fat. The actual nature of these nutrients is also modified - as are the proportions of different minerals and vitamins.

A very few babies are unable to take milk of any kind - and special non-milk formulas have been developed to meet their needs (see F27).

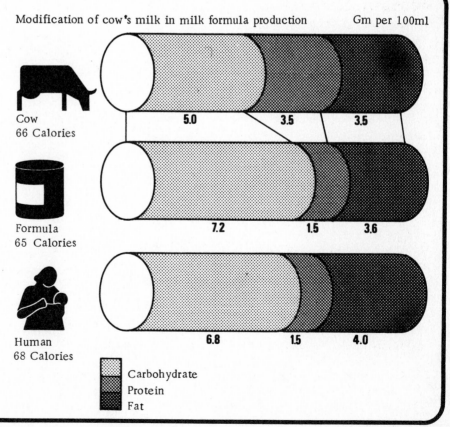

Modification of cow's milk in milk formula production   Gm per 100ml

Cow
66 Calories   5.0   3.5   3.5

Formula
65 Calories   7.2   1.5   3.6

Human
68 Calories   6.8   1.5   4.0

Carbohydrate
Protein
Fat

FEEDING CHOICES

F05 SCHEDULE OR DEMAND

Experts used to recommend a strict four-hour feeding schedule.
At present, however, a more flexible approach is generally in favor - with many babies now being fed on a "self-demand" basis. Most babies, whether fed on schedule or demand, have dropped the late-night sixth feeding by eight weeks.

SCHEDULE
The most common timetable for a schedule-fed baby receiving five feedings a day.

SELF-DEMAND
A typical self-demand pattern for an eight-week-old baby on five feedings a day.

12 Midnight

F06 BREAST OR BOTTLE?

It has been estimated that in recent years up to 75% of babies in the United States have never been breast-fed at all.
There is now evidence that this pattern is changing. More and more women are choosing to breast-feed their babies, and most doctors welcome this as they regard breast-feeding as the safest and most natural method of infant feeding. Mothers who have successfully breast-fed reinforce this view, claiming that breast-feeding is also a unique and rewarding experience.
Some women, however, are uncertain about breast-feeding. Perhaps they have commitments that would make it impossible, or they may find the whole idea unpleasant. And for some women who had planned to breast-feed, illness or problems arising after the birth force them to turn to bottle-feeding.
Current promotion of breast-feeding may make bottle-feeding mothers fear that they are somehow inadequate or uncaring. Such worries are unnecessary - although breast-feeding is usually desirable, the vital physical contact between mother and baby can be as intimate, warm, and loving whether the baby is fed by breast or bottle.
Some of the main advantages and disadvantages of each feeding method are presented here.

QUALITY
The constituents of breast milk are present in near perfect proportions for the baby's optimal growth and development throughout the breast-feeding period.
Colostrum, secreted by the mother in the first few days after the birth, is rich in antibodies and gives invaluable protection against some gastric infections.
Breast-fed babies are less likely to suffer from diaper rash, and less likely to be overweight.

QUALITY
Formula milks have been developed that are very similar in composition to breast milk.
But finding the formula that is most suitable for a particular infant can be a matter of trial and error.
There is no formula equivalent to colostrum.
Bottle-fed babies are more likely to suffer from diaper rash and more likely to be overweight.

Feeding

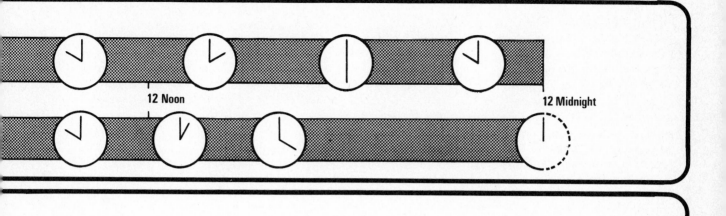

12 Noon   12 Midnight

QUANTITY

Only by test weighing the baby is
it possible to tell how much milk
has been taken at a feeding.
Milk supply generally adjusts itself
to cope with the baby's demands.
But sometimes the amount of milk
produced at a particular feeding
does not coincide with the baby's
needs at the time.

EXPENSE

Breast milk is virtually free. But
the breast-feeding mother may
need to spend rather more money
than usual on her own diet, which
must be rich in protein, calcium,
and vitamins.

CONVENIENCE

Breast milk is instantly available -
at the correct temperature and
usually sterile.
But only the mother can feed the
baby, and her health and
well-being affect the milk supply.
Any medication or alcohol taken
by the mother may also affect the
breast-fed infant.

QUANTITY

It is possible to see at a glance
how much milk the baby has taken.
The quantity of milk offered can
be easily adjusted to meet the
baby's needs at any time.

EXPENSE

Initial expense is involved in
purchasing the various types of
equipment needed for bottle-
feeding.
Milk-formula must be purchased
over a period of several months.

CONVENIENCE

Formulas need mixing, and
strict sterilization procedures must
be followed.
The mother can delegate feedings
- which allows her more freedom
and gives others, particularly
the father, an opportunity to
help in the care of the baby.

F

BREAST-FEEDING 1

F07 SUCCESSFUL FEEDING

For successful breast-feeding, a nursing mother needs a well balanced diet and adequate rest. She must also ensure that she is relaxed and comfortable during the feeding itself, as tension and anxiety affect the supply of milk from the breasts.

DIET
Although most nursing mothers can continue to eat all the foods that they normally enjoy, it is advisable to try and include the following in the daily diet:
a) 1 US quart milk (just over 1.6 Imperial pints: 0.9 liters);
b) meat, poultry, or fish;
c) 1 egg;
d) whole grain bread or cereal;
e) butter or margarine;
f) fruit and vegetables.

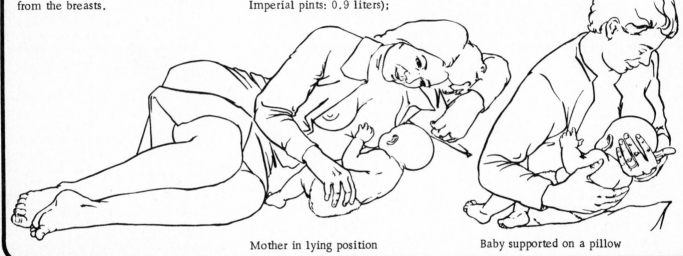

Mother in lying position   Baby supported on a pillow

F09 HOW MILK IS PRODUCED

The breasts prepare for milk production just before childbirth as the estrogen and progesterone output from the ovaries decreases. The reduction of the level of these hormones in the bloodstream affects the hypothalamus which then causes the pituitary to produce prolactin. It is this hormone that sparks off the secretion of colostrum, and later milk, from the breasts. (Milk yield does not start until several days after childbirth.) The flow is stimulated by the baby sucking the nipple. This sends nerve impulses to the hypothalamus which releases oxytocin that travels via nerve fibers to the pituitary. From there, oxytocin flows through the bloodstream causing the alveoli to contract, thus forcing liquid through the ducts to the nipples.
Milk flow usually starts about 30 seconds after nursing begins.

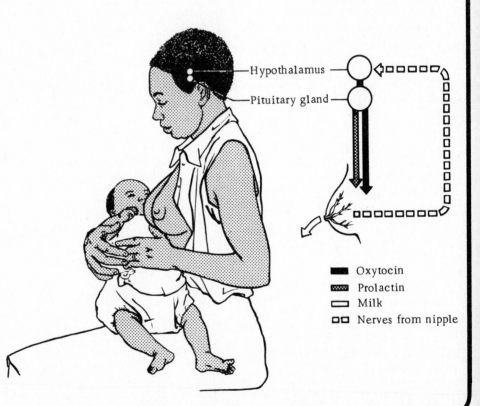

Hypothalamus

Pituitary gland

■■ Oxytocin
▨▨ Prolactin
▢ Milk
▢▢ Nerves from nipple

Feeding

NURSING POSITION

The mother should adopt any comfortable nursing position. Three examples are shown below.

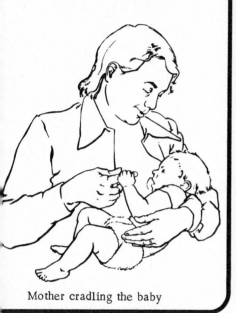

Mother cradling the baby

F08 STARTING FEEDING

As soon as the baby is put to the breast, his rooting reflex (see B21) will help him find the nipple. The mother should ensure that the baby takes into his mouth the entire areola (the dark area around the nipple), and she may also need to hold the breast away from his nose to help him breathe.

At the end of the feeding, the mother can release the nipple by gently inserting her finger into the corner of the baby's mouth. The first few feedings will be very short - perhaps only two to five minutes - but after the first few days the baby will demand longer feedings at less frequent intervals. The changing composition of breast milk during the first ten days is shown in the diagram. The milk itself is preceded by colostrum - a yellow liquid rich in antibodies.

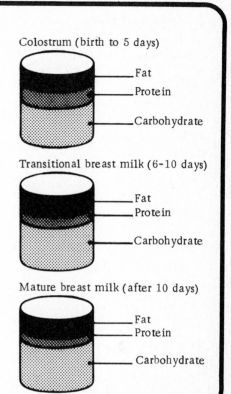

Colostrum (birth to 5 days)
— Fat
— Protein
— Carbohydrate

Transitional breast milk (6-10 days)
— Fat
— Protein
— Carbohydrate

Mature breast milk (after 10 days)
— Fat
— Protein
— Carbohydrate

F10 CARE OF THE BREASTS

Care of the breasts and nipples is extremely important for the nursing mother.

Some doctors advise regular massage of the nipples during the last weeks of pregnancy to prepare for breast-feeding.

The enlarged breasts should be well supported in the later stages of pregnancy and in lactation. Many women find that a special nursing bra is also ideal for the last weeks of pregnancy.

Nursing bras are designed to allow the mother to expose her nipples for nursing without removing the whole garment. Most styles also have an adjustable back fastening. Because the nipples may leak a little milk, some nursing bras have special waterproof cups (alternatively, absorbent cotton pads may be placed in the cups).

Front-fastening nursing bra: this style provides the breasts with good support and unfastens at the front to allow easy access to the breasts for feeding.

Nursing bra with flaps: this style fastens at the back, but the flaps on the cups allow the nipples to be exposed without unfastening the whole of the bra.

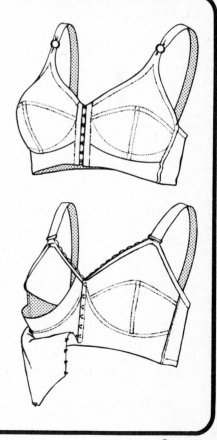

F11 TEST WEIGHING

It is possible to calculate the exact quantity of milk taken by a breast-fed baby by a series of test weighings carried out over a period of 24 hours. It is important to calculate a whole day's intake as the intake at individual feedings varies considerably.

Before receiving the first feeding of the day the baby is weighed in his clothes. Immediately after the feeding he is weighed again in the same clothes without having his diaper changed. The difference between the two weights gives the total milk intake at one feeding. By repeating the procedure at each feeding and totaling the separate milk intakes, the day's total intake can be calculated.

The printed table (right) gives typical results obtained from weighing an infant before and after each feeding. Illustrated below is the calculation of the infant's daily intake based on these results.

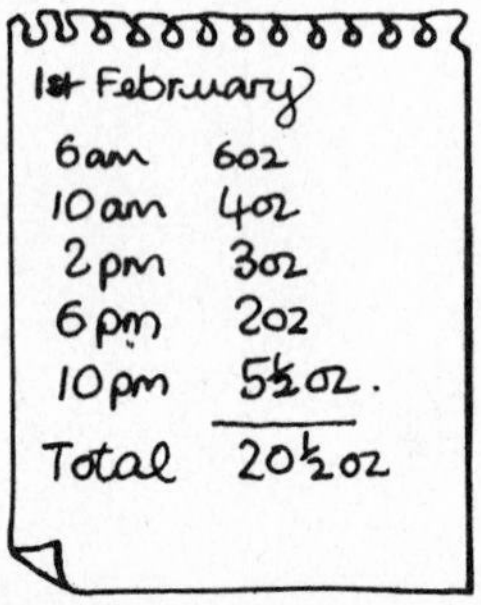

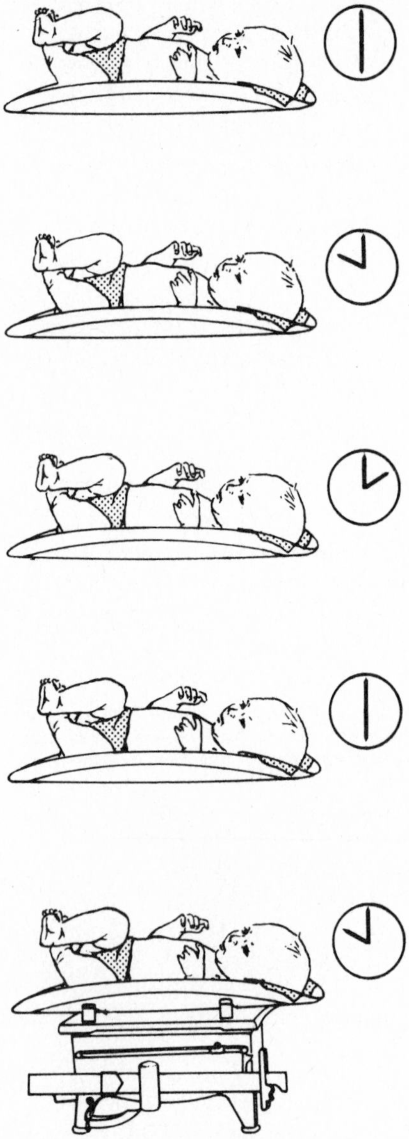

TEST WEIGHINGS		
WEIGHT BEFORE FEEDING	WEIGHT AFTER FEEDING	DIFFERENCE
8lb 1oz	8lb 7oz	6 oz
8lb 1½oz	8lb 5½oz	4oz
8lb 1¾oz	8lb 4¾oz	3oz
8lb 1¾oz	8lb 3¾oz	2oz
8lb 1¾oz	8lb 7¼oz	5½oz

1st February

6am	6oz
10am	4oz
2pm	3oz
6pm	2oz
10pm	5½oz
Total	20½oz

F12 PROVIDING EXTRA MILK

If the supply of breast milk is insufficient, the mother can try to increase it by giving feedings more often, being more relaxed, and increasing her own fluid intake. If these measures are unsuccessful and the mother is determined to continue breast-feeding she will have to increase the baby's milk intake by adding bottle feedings. These may be given in two forms.

COMPLEMENTARY BOTTLES
Feedings given after breast-feeding to "top up" the milk intake are known as complementary feedings. Some mothers find that they need to give their baby a 2-3oz bottle after each breast-feeding. Others find that a complementary bottle is necessary only after the day's scantiest feeding - usually in the afternoon or early evening.

SUPPLEMENTARY BOTTLES
Feedings given instead of a breast-teeding are called supplementary feedings. A supplementary bottle is most commonly given instead of the afternoon feeding. The breasts should then be full enough by early evening to provide the baby with a substantial feeding.

Feeding

F13 MOTHERS' PROBLEMS

Breast-feeding mothers may have to face one or more of the following problems.

SORE OR CRACKED NIPPLES

These conditions may be caused by not allowing the nipples to dry properly before covering them after a feeding, or by the baby "chewing" on the nipple rather than suckling the entire areola area. The mother is often advised to stop or restrict nursing until the nipples heal, during which time she must express her milk for feeding in a bottle. The doctor may prescribe an ointment to speed recovery. In some cases the use of a nipple shield may prove helpful.

RETRACTED NIPPLES

If the nipples are retracted or inverted the baby is unable to take them into his mouth for satisfactory suckling. Gentle massage of the nipples before a feeding may make them stand out a little more; or a nipple shield may be used during feeding.

ABSCESSES

The presence of an abscess is indicated by an extremely painful red patch on the surface of the breast. The condition is often accompanied by a high temperature. It is sometimes possible to continue breast-feeding but it is essential to seek medical advice.

ENGORGEMENT

This is the medical term used to describe the overfilling of the breasts with milk. It is most likely to occur toward the end of the first week, as the mother's milk supply gets under way.

In areolar engorgement only the sinuses behind the nipple are affected, making the areola too firm for the baby to take into his mouth. Expressing a little milk (see below) before the feeding usually solves this problem.

Total engorgement, affecting the whole breast, is also treated by expressing milk and sometimes by massage and hot and cold compresses.

NIPPLE SHIELDS of different styles are sometimes recommended if the nipples are sore or retracted. The baby sucks on the rubber nipple, which creates a vacuum and draws milk from the breast.

EXPRESSING MILK It may be necessary for a mother to express milk from her breasts - to maintain her milk supply if the baby cannot suckle, or if her breasts become engorged. In manual expression (**a**)

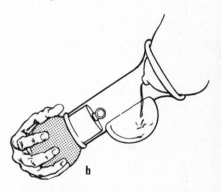

the mother squeezes the areola between her finger and thumb. Milk may also be expressed with a hand pump (**b**) or with a more sophisticated electrically operated breast pump.

F14 GIVING EXTRA NUTRIENTS

Breast or formula milk supplies almost all the nutrients a baby needs during the first few months of life.

Medical opinion, however, now favors the giving of some form of vitamin supplement. The most common of these is a commercial preparation in drop form containing vitamins A, C, and D. The quantity needed by each baby varies according to his age and how he is fed, and because excessive doses of vitamin D can be harmful, it is essential always to follow medical instructions. For bottle-fed babies, the drops are mixed with the formula; for breast-fed babies, they are placed inside the baby's cheek or on his tongue, or mixed with a bottle of cooled, boiled water.

From about four weeks babies can be given diluted, or enriched fruit juices either on a spoon or in a bottle. These are valuable sources of vitamin C and are also thirst-quenching. Fruit juices should not be given just before a feeding, and because of the risk of tooth decay must never be given undiluted on a pacifier.

BOTTLE-FEEDING 1

F15 FEEDING EQUIPMENT

The mother who intends to bottle-feed her baby will need to have all the feeding equipment ready before the birth. Most mothers who breast-feed their babies also keep a small supply of bottles and nipples for the occasional supplementary feeding or fruit drink.

F16 WORKING AREA

It is a good idea to keep close together the different items needed for preparing feedings. Most people find it convenient to store equipment and formula in an area of the kitchen where they are near both a sink and a stove, and where there is a flat working surface. Spare formula and items not in regular use are best stored in in a cupboard or on a nearby shelf.

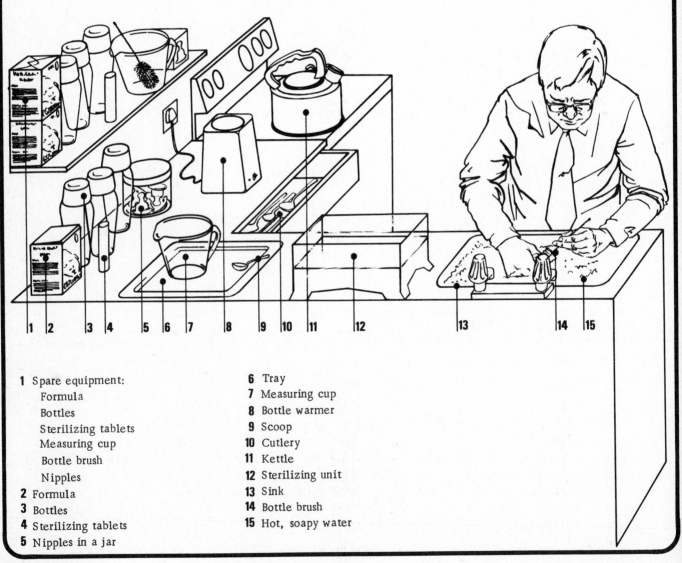

1 Spare equipment:
   Formula
   Bottles
   Sterilizing tablets
   Measuring cup
   Bottle brush
   Nipples
2 Formula
3 Bottles
4 Sterilizing tablets
5 Nipples in a jar

6 Tray
7 Measuring cup
8 Bottle warmer
9 Scoop
10 Cutlery
11 Kettle
12 Sterilizing unit
13 Sink
14 Bottle brush
15 Hot, soapy water

Feeding

1 6 bottles and caps
2 Jar and 6 nipples
3 Knife
4 Spoon for adding sugar (if used)
5 Long-handled spoon for mixing
6 Measuring scoop for formula
7 Bottle brush
8 Measuring cup
9 Tray for storage

F17 FEEDING BOTTLES

Feeding bottles are available in a variety of styles. They are usually made from heat-resistant glass or plastic. A wide-necked bottle (1) has the advantage of being easy to clean with a bottle brush. But a narrow-necked bottle (2) helps prevent the baby from taking in air with the milk. Small bottles like (3 and 4) are useful for using in addition to a breast-feeding or for giving water or fruit drinks. The straight-sided bottle (5) is fitted for convenience with disposable, ready-sterilized, plastic lining sacs.

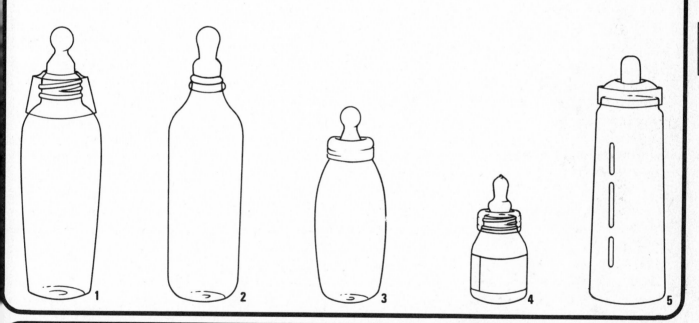

F18 NIPPLES (TEATS)

The size of hole in the nipple is extremely important. Nipples with large holes should not be used because they allow too fast a flow, causing indigestion or even choking. Small holes restrict the milk flow but can be enlarged - either with a hot needle held in a cork (1), or by using a razor blade to make a cross-cut in the end of the nipple (2).

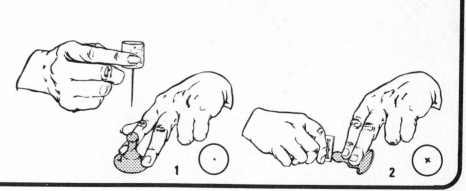

BOTTLE-FEEDING 2

F19 MIXING A FEEDING

There are two basic types of formula milk - powder and liquid. Both are made from modified cow's milk and are reconstituted with water for feeding. Some brands are unsuitable for young babies so it is important to follow the instructions of the nurse or doctor. It is also wise to seek medical advice before changing from one formula to another.

Pour water into sterilized bottle to half the final feeding quantity required.

Scoop powder from package into bottle, leveling each scoop with the back of a knife. Count the scoops carefully. (Sweetening is now added only if specified in manufacturer's instructions.)

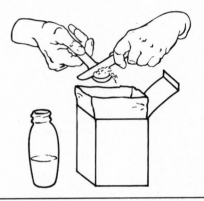

METHOD OF PREPARING POWDER FORMULA

Check that the baby has a dry diaper; change if necessary. Wash hands. Boil water in kettle; leave to cool slightly.

METHOD OF PREPARING LIQUID FORMULA

Scrub and scald top of can. Open can and pour prescribed quantity of formula into sterilized bottle.

Add required amount of cooled, boiled water from kettle.

Feeding

Fix sterilized cap to top of bottle
and shake. Remove cap and top up
to desired level with cooled,
boiled water.

F

Attach sterile nipple. Check
temperature and rate of flow by
shaking a few drops onto the
inside of the wrist. The milk must
not feel hot and should run in a
rapid stream of drops.

Feed, and discard any formula left
in the bottle.

WARNING
1) Never make a bottle too strong
by overloading the scoop or adding
extra formula. Over-concentrated
mixture can cause stomach upsets
or even kidney problems and can
result in overweight.
2) Never add extra sweetening.

Fix on sterilized cap and shake
bottle.

F20 MIXING IN A MEASURING CUP

Some people prefer to mix the formula in a measuring cup before transferring it to the bottle. This method is particularly useful for formulas to which sweetening must be added, or for formulas that need stirring with a spoon or fork. It is also recommended when preparing several feedings at the same time (F21).

With this method, formula for one or more feedings is measured into a large cup where it is mixed to a paste with a little cooled, boiled water. More cooled, boiled water is then added to bring the feeding up to the right amount. The formula is then poured into one or more bottles for use immediately or after storage in a refrigerator.

1 Formula is mixed in a large measuring cup

2 Bottles are filled with formula for immediate or future use.

F21 FEEDINGS FOR THE DAY

If a refrigerator is available it may be preferred to make up enough feedings for the whole day. The bottles can be made up one by one (see F19) or the entire quantity can first be mixed in a large measuring cup (see F20). After making up, the bottles not needed for an immediate feeding should be placed in the refrigerator. Made-up bottles must never be stored for more than 24 hours. When a bottle is required, it is not necessary to reheat it: most babies find cold milk quite acceptable. Many people, however, prefer to warm the milk. This can be done by: standing the bottle in in a pitcher of hot water; putting the bottle in a saucepan of water while the water is brought to the boil; or by means of an electric bottle warmer.

F23 ASEPTIC PREPARATION

When using the aseptic method of food preparation, all equipment is sterilized beforehand and the milk formula is mixed with cooled, boiled water.

1 All equipment - bottles, nipples, spoons, etc - must be sterilized before mixing begins. Many people now do this with a commercially obtainable sterilizing product. Sterilizing liquid or quick-dissolving tablets are added to water in a special container designed to keep the equipment completely immersed. (Note the importance of following the manufacturers' instructions when using these products.) Alternatively, equipment may be sterilized by boiling for 25 minutes in a sterilizer unit (see F24 for illustration) or in a covered saucepan.

2 The formula is mixed in the bottles, using cooled, boiled water, and handling the sterilized equipment as little as possible. Alternatively, the formula may first be mixed in a sterilized measuring cup (see F20).

3 Any bottle not intended for immediate use should have its nipple inverted in the neck.

4 Caps are tightly screwed on to all bottles prepared for future use.

F22 GIVING A BOTTLE FEEDING

It is important that a bottle-fed baby should enjoy the same sort of warm and intimate relationship that a breast-fed baby enjoys with his mother. To achieve this, the baby must be held close and cuddled throughout the feeding. In this way he will come to associate the pleasure of feeding with the people who love and care for him. On some busy occasions it may be tempting to "prop" the bottle on a folded diaper or by means of a bottle-holder. But this is much less satisfactory from the baby's point of view. Very young babies, in particular, must never be left alone with a bottle because of the risk of choking. From the age of about six months a baby may be allowed to hold his own bottle under supervision.

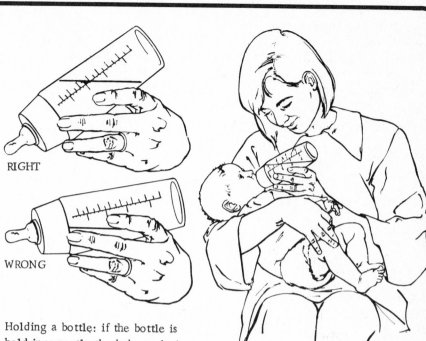

RIGHT

WRONG

Holding a bottle: if the bottle is held incorrectly the baby sucks in a lot of air with his milk, causing discomfort from gas.

A good holding position

F24 TERMINAL STERILIZATION

In the terminal method of sterilization the prepared milk is sterilized along with the bottles and nipples.

1 Milk formula is measured into the bottles, which have previously been washed but not sterilized. (Hot, soapy water is used for washing the bottles and a bottle brush is recommended to get them really clean. Care should always be taken to rinse the bottles thoroughly with clean water.)

2 Cold water from the tap is used for mixing the formula.
3 A clean nipple is inverted in the neck of the bottle. (Rubbing nipples with a little salt before washing will remove the film of milk that collects inside them.)
4 The bottle caps are put on - loosely so that steam can pass under them - and the bottles placed upright in 3in of water in a sterilizer unit or saucepan.

5 The sterilizer or saucepan is covered, and the water brought to the boil. After 25 minutes' boiling the sterilizer should be left to cool with the lid on for about 2 hours. (Gradual cooling prevents skin from forming on the milk.) The bottles are then taken out of the sterilizer, and those not intended for immediate use should have their caps screwed on tightly before storage.

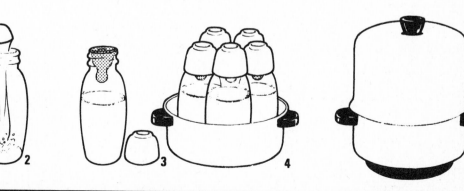

1   2   3   4   5

PROBLEMS WITH FEEDING

F25 BURPING (WINDING)

During a feeding a baby swallows air which forms a bubble in his stomach. If discomfort is to be prevented it is important to get up this air bubble at least once during a feeding and again at the end. Three ways of burping a baby are illustrated here.

1 The baby is held against his mother's shoulder while she gently rubs his back.

2 The baby is held upright in his mother's lap while she gently rubs his back.

3 The baby lies across his mother's lap while she rubs his back.

1

2

3

F26 PREMATURE BABIES

Feeding a premature baby during the first few days, or even weeks, of life, demands the expert attention of hospital staff (B20).

In a premature infant the control of vital functions such as breathing, sucking, and swallowing is restricted and, in many cases, the digestive system is still immature and unable to cope easily with the normal processes of digestion.

One of the major hazards of feeding premature infants is that improperly digested food may be regurgitated and breathed into the lungs, causing choking.

Most premature babies are not fed until 48 hours after birth. They are fed very small quantities of milk, usually every three hours, from a dropper, or by means of a tube passed down the throat into the stomach. The feeding consists of formula milk or breast milk expressed by the mother. When the baby's weight has increased and his sucking ability is more fully developed, he can be fed normally from breast or bottle. The baby will still require very small quantities at frequent intervals.

The premature baby has few nutritional reserves and is often so short of iron that slight anemia results. This can be corrected by a prescription of medicinal iron from about the fourth week. Vitamin supplements (see F14) are usually given from the second week.

F27 MILK ALLERGIC BABIES

A very few babies who fail to thrive are found to be allergic to milk. This allergy is identified by a series of hospital tests, after which the doctor will prescribe the use of a special non-milk formula.

These specially developed milk-free formulas typically contain such ingredients as soybeans, corn and coconut oils, sucrose, and corn sugar. Other formulas have been developed using modified meat protein.

A baby fed on a special non-milk formula can be expected to have normal rates of growth.

Feeding

F28 COMMON FEEDING PROBLEMS

Some babies have feeding problems that can cause considerable distress and anxiety to those around them.

Very young babies sometimes feed for a very short time and then fall asleep, only to wake a few minutes later for more milk. This is frustrating and exhausting for everyone but it is almost certainly only a passing phase. The nervous and digestive systems of some babies do not at first work properly together, so that the baby does not make the connection between sucking and the relief of hunger. He will soon stay awake long enough to satisfy his hunger. Meanwhile the mother could try changing the baby's feeding position, or could move him frequently from breast to breast. Feeding problems may also arise because babies are sensitive to the moods of those who feed them. If the person giving the feeding is tired, rushed, or anxious, the baby may sense this and become restless and difficult to feed. A calm and relaxed atmosphere at feeding times should help reduce problems. Older babies may feed badly when they are teething or if they have an ear infection that makes jaw movements painful. If discomfort temporarily prevents a baby from sucking, expressed breast milk (see F13) or formula milk may be taken from a cup or spoon.

BREAST-FED BABIES

In the case of a breast-fed baby, problems affecting the mother, such as retracted nipples or engorgement, can mean that the baby has considerable difficulty in taking the areola into his mouth to begin feeding. (For further details of these and other problems, see F13.)

Occasionally a baby refuses to nurse during the mother's menstrual period. If this happens, the mother should express her milk and substitute a formula bottle-feeding.

BOTTLE-FED BABIES

A bottle-fed baby may lose interest in his feeding if the milk does not flow quickly enough through the nipple. This can be remedied by enlarging the nipple holes as described in F18.

F29 HICCUPS AND SICKNESS

Many young babies suffer from hiccups after feedings, but they are rarely upset by them. Some mothers find that they can stop the hiccups by burping the baby or by giving a drink of cooled, boiled water.

Some gentle regurgitation or "spitting" of milk is quite normal after a feeding, particularly during the early months. As long as the baby's weight gain is satisfactory there is rarely anything to worry about.

True vomiting - the regurgitation and ejection of the stomach's contents with some force - is much less common. It may be a symptom of infection or obstruction, and cases of persistent vomiting always need medical attention.

F30 COLIC

Colic is a severe abdominal pain that affects many babies between the ages of two weeks and three months. Attacks usually occur daily, often in the evening, and can last up to four hours.

A baby with colic typically refuses to settle down after the late afternoon or early evening feeding. He begins to scream - often adopting the position illustrated. During an attack the baby can be comforted temporarily if he is cuddled or wrapped up tightly but his distress returns as soon as he is left again.

The causes of colic are uncertain and medical opinion is still in disagreement. Some doctors, however, suggest some precautions that may possibly prevent an attack. The baby should not be allowed to feed too quickly; he should be thoroughly burped after a feeding; and he should be kept warm.

The illustration shows a baby with characteristic signs of colic:

a) screaming;
b) legs drawn up to the stomach;
c) tightly clenched fists.

F31 EQUIPMENT FOR WEANING

From the time a baby first begins to take solid food a considerable variety of equipment will be needed at mealtimes.

Learning to eat is always a messy process - particularly when a baby starts to feed himself. For this reason, it is advisable to have terry cloth or plastic bibs to protect clothing, and easy-wipe surfaces or mats to protect the furniture. Some feedings may be given on the parent's lap, but the baby will need a rigid seat with a table when he begins to feed himself. Many baby chairs - like the one shown, right - can be used as a low chair or fitted on a stand for conversion to a high chair.

Cups and dishes should be unbreakable and designed for easy use. Cutlery should be small enough for the baby to handle.

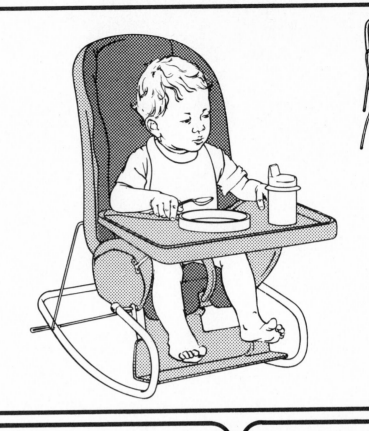

F32 WEANING

Weaning is the term used for the gradual substitution of solid foods for milk in an infant's diet. Exact procedures and schedules for weaning vary considerably - and the advice of a doctor or nurse is the best guide for the optimal growth and development of a particular baby. Typically, weaning begins at three to four months, and by 12 months the infant should be taking a wide variety of solid foods.

PHASING OUT MILK FEEDS
During the first stages of weaning the infant continues to receive five breast or bottle feedings daily, but the amount of milk is reduced at any feeding at which solid food is also given. From about six months an infant may safely be given undiluted cow's milk in place of breast or formula milk, and milk and milk products remain an important aspect of diet throughout childhood.

INTRODUCING SOLIDS
Traditionally the first solid food consists of cereal or a zwieback mixed to a creamy consistency with milk. Some people, however, prefer to start weaning with pureed apple or a small amount of canned baby food.

Whichever solid food is chosen, it is first given at one feeding daily and is given in addition to breast or formula milk. After a week or so solids are given at two of the five milk feedings, and after a few more weeks the infant should be receiving a selection of different solid foods at three of his feedings. Gradually the infant's food pattern becomes more like that of the rest of the family - with three meals a day and drinks on waking and at bedtime.

F33 FEEDING PROCEDURE

In the early stages of weaning, small tastes of solid food should be given on a teaspoon. The spoon is placed in the baby's mouth so that he can eat the food and swallow it. He is likely to fuss at the first few feedings and it is often worth giving at least part of the milk feeding before offering any solids.

A baby should also be encouraged to drink from a cup. An eggcup or a double-handled cup with a spout is suitable for this.

After a few months, many babies begin to pick up food in their fingers and show signs of wanting to feed themselves. This is the start of a messy and lengthy process but it is vital to allow the baby to perservere. The feeding can be speeded up if the parent slips an occasional spoonful of food into the baby's mouth when he becomes tired or fretful.

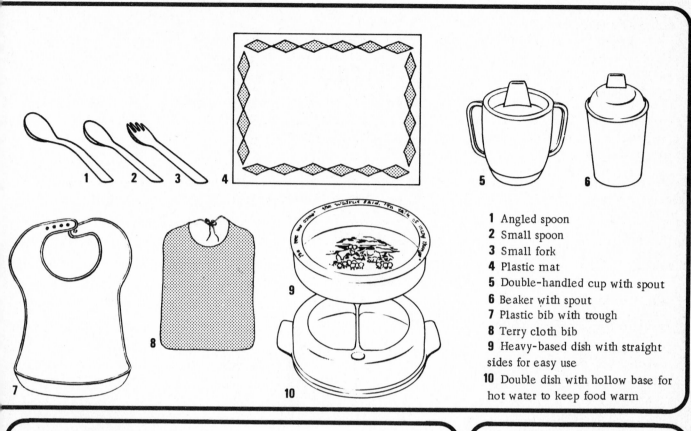

1 Angled spoon
2 Small spoon
3 Small fork
4 Plastic mat
5 Double-handled cup with spout
6 Beaker with spout
7 Plastic bib with trough
8 Terry cloth bib
9 Heavy-based dish with straight sides for easy use
10 Double dish with hollow base for hot water to keep food warm

F

F34 HOME-PREPARED FOODS

Some people like to prepare their own baby foods, and with a little time and trouble many items from the family diet can be adapted to a baby's needs.
Food for the young baby must be in puree form, so a sieve and food mill or blender are essential. As the baby becomes accustomed to solids, mashing, mincing, or chopping is usually sufficient.
Too much salt and sugar is harmful to babies, and seasoning and sweetening of baby foods should be kept to a minimum.
Vegetables - particularly carrots, tomatoes, peas, string beans, and potatoes - are good weaning foods. If they are offered one at a time the baby's likes and dislikes can be easily identified.
Egg yolk is a valuable source of iron, and can first be introduced with a little cereal. (Whole egg may cause an allergic reaction

and should be avoided during the early stages of weaning.)
Meat broth can be used as an early weaning food and the tasty juices from roast meat can be mixed with vegetables. Beef, lamb, chicken, and liver - pureed or minced - are all suitable for the slightly older baby.
Non-oily fish can be served if all the bones are removed.
Cheese is another nourishing weaning food. Grated cheese can be mixed with cereal as an alternative to sweetening. Later, many babies like to hold and eat a piece of cheese.
Firm foods should be given to babies to encourage chewing and teething. Suitable foods include small pieces of toast, crusts of bread, raw carrot, and apple.
Fruit is popular with many babies - particularly apples, bananas, and apricot puree.

F35 COMMERCIAL BABY FOODS

It is often convenient to use commercial baby foods, and manufacturers have undertaken a great deal of research to produce foods to meet the nutritional needs of infants.
There are two basic types - ready to serve in cans or jars, and powdered foods for mixing with milk. Ranges include foods suitable for the early stages of weaning - broths, and purees of fruits, vegetables, and meats - and a great variety of foods suitable for the slightly older child.
Particularly in the early stages of weaning, powdered foods may prove most economical as tiny quantities can be prepared without affecting the quality of the remainder of the package.
Food from a can or jar, once opened, can be stored for re-use provided that certain precautions are taken (see F36).

WEANING AND AFTER

F36 USING COMMERCIAL FOODS

Small quantities of baby food can be heated in a cup over hot water. The food can then be fed directly from the cup or may be transferred to a dish. If the baby has not been fed from the jar or can, and if it has not been heated up, any remaining food can be stored in a refrigerator for up to two days.

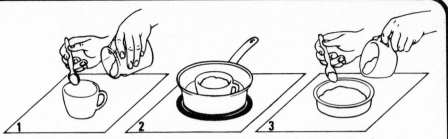

Sufficient food for one meal is transferred to a cup **1**, heated by placing the cup in hot water **2**, and then transferred to a dish for serving **3**.

F37 BABY FOODS COMPARED

Details of the contents of three popular varieties of canned baby food are given here as an indication of the wide range of commercially produced baby foods.

☐ Protein
▨ Carbohydrate
■ Fat

Analysis per 100gm

BEEF AND CARROT CASSEROLE

Contents: beef, carrots, potatoes, tomatoes, flour, soya flour, cornflour, herbs, hydrolyzed vegetable protein, iron sulfate.

Calories: 80

4.2   8.3   3.3

Sodium 40mg
Iron 2.4mg
Phosphorus 45mg
Calcium 20mg
Potassium 155mg

EGG AND CHEESE

Contents: eggs, milk, cheese, semolina, modified cornstarch, vegetable oil, spice.

Calories: 88

4.2   6.9   5.0

Sodium 90mg
Iron 0.5mg
Phosphorus 75mg
Calcium 30mg
Potassium 55mg

BANANA DESSERT

Contents: banana, sugar, modified cornflour, orange juice, lemon juice, vitamin C.

Calories: 77

0.2   18.1   0.2

Sodium 10mg
Iron 0.2mg
Phosphorus 5mg
Calcium 10mg
Potassium 60mg

F38 NUTRIENTS

There are five basic types of nutrient found in foods - proteins, carbohydrates, fats, minerals, and vitamins. All play a part in a healthy diet and are especially important for a growing child.

PROTEINS are complex substances vital for the growth and repair of the body.
The richest sources of protein are animal products such as meat, fish, eggs, milk, and cheese. Protein is also found in some vegetables such as peas and beans, and in grain and grain products like wholemeal bread.

CARBOHYDRATES are the main source of energy for immediate use, and play an important part in the functioning of vital organs. Bread, rice, potatoes, and almost all sweet foods are rich in carbohydrates. An excess of these foods in the diet - particularly of sweet foods that contain few other nutrients - can lead to an undesirable weight gain.

Feeding

F39 EATING SENSIBLY

Most parents appreciate the importance of establishing sensible eating habits in their children. This is not always easy, however, as a variety of feeding difficulties can cause parents considerable anxiety.

Among the most common problems are: refusal to eat particular foods; refusal to eat properly at family mealtimes; and a preference for sweet foods and snacks (see F43). Refusing to eat is rarely serious, and parental anxiety will only communicate itself to the child and make the problem worse. Food should be presented as attractively as possible, and after a certain time removed without fuss if the child is not eating.

Cookies, cake, and candies are best avoided except at the end of a meal. Recommended snacks include fresh fruit, fruit juices, and cheese.

F40 DAILY FOOD GUIDE

A properly balanced diet is essential for the health and well-being of even the youngest child. Assessing whether a child's nutritional needs are being met, however, can be confusing and difficult. A simple means of checking is to use the daily food guide described here.

Devised by a dietitian, the guide divides foods into four groups:
a) milk, cheese, and yogurt;
b) fruit and vegetables;
c) meat, fish, and eggs;
d) cereals and bread.

It is recommended that two helpings from each group should be served each day if possible, though an overweight child may need only one serving from the last group.

Children suffering from certain illnesses, such as diabetes (J67), need diets planned under medical supervision.

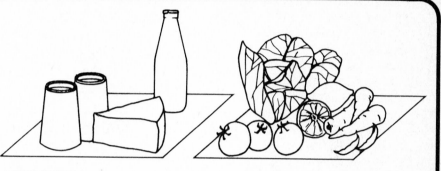

MILK GROUP
Contains protein, carbohydrate, fat, calcium, vitamin A

VEGETABLE AND FRUIT GROUP
Contains carbohydrate, minerals, vitamins C and A

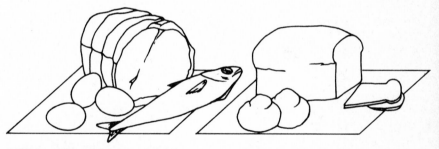

MEAT, FISH, AND EGG GROUP
Contains protein, fat, iron, vitamin A, vitamin B, vitamin C

CEREALS AND BREAD GROUP
Contains protein, carbohydrate, calcium, iron, vitamin B

FATS are a concentrated source of energy. They are found in two main forms.

Saturated fats are normally hard at room temperature. They occur in meat, and in dairy products such as butter and cheese. Polyunsaturated fats are usually consumed in the form of liquid vegetable oils, such as soybean or corn oil, or some margarines.

MINERALS play a vital role in the diet. Calcium, found in milk and cheese, is important for healthy bones and teeth; iron for making red blood cells is present in wheat germ and liver. Other valuable minerals - potassium, phosphorus, sodium, and iodine - are found in a variety of natural foods such as meat, milk, fish, eggs, fruits, vegetables, and whole grains.

VITAMINS are substances that the body cannot manufacture for itself but which are vital to health. Vitamin A is found in carrots, egg yolk, and butter, and vitamin C in fruit and vegetables. Vitamins of the B complex are present in wheat germ and yeast, while the major source of natural vitamin D is sunshine.

F

CALORIES AND WEIGHT

F41 CALORIES

The energy value of food and drink is measured in units called Calories.

People use up Calories every minute of the day - to maintain body functions and as fuel for physical exercise. Children have comparatively high Calorie requirements because energy is also needed for growth.

An individual's Calorie needs vary according to age, sex, size, physical activity, and climate.

If a person takes in as food more Calories than are needed, the surplus is converted into fat to be stored for future use.

If Calorie intake is below requirements, fat stores in the body are converted into energy and body weight decreases.

F42 DAILY CALORIE NEEDS

Daily Calorie needs change with age. Exact estimates of needs vary, but different sets of statistics show the same general pattern. (Our diagram is based on the 1974 statistics of the US Food and Nutrition Board.) For the first 10 years or so, boys and girls of the same age have similar needs. Later, differences reflect changes at puberty, comparative growth rates and body size, and typical exercise levels.

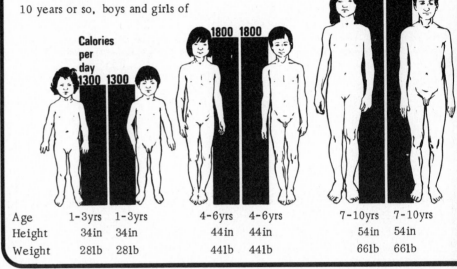

Age	1-3yrs	1-3yrs	4-6yrs	4-6yrs	7-10yrs	7-10yrs
Height	34in	34in	44in	44in	54in	54in
Weight	28lb	28lb	44lb	44lb	66lb	66lb

Calories per day: 1300 1300 1800 1800 2400 2400

F43 SNACKS AND MEALS

Eating too many snacks is a common bad habit among children and adults alike. As this diagram shows, the Calorie content of many popular snacks is comparatively high - making it all too easy to add a few hundred surplus Calories to the daily intake. In addition, snacks may also be responsible for spoiling the appetite for other foods needed to give a balanced diet (see F40).

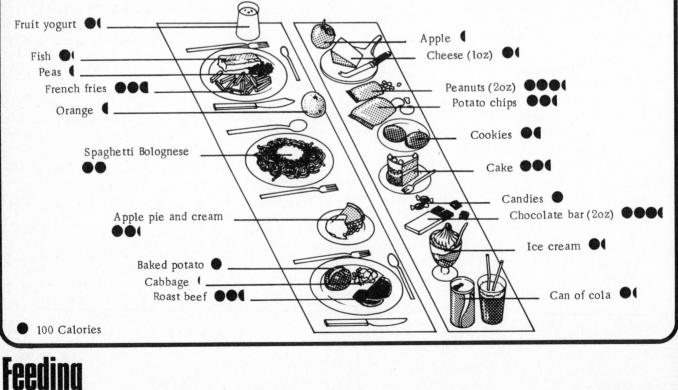

Fruit yogurt ●◖

Fish ●◖
Peas ◖
French fries ●●●
Orange ◖

Spaghetti Bolognese ●●

Apple pie and cream ●●◖

Baked potato ●
Cabbage ◖
Roast beef ●●●

Apple ◖
Cheese (1oz) ●◖

Peanuts (2oz) ●●●●
Potato chips ●●◖

Cookies ●◖

Cake ●●◖

Candies ●
Chocolate bar (2oz) ●●●●

Ice cream ●◖

Can of cola ●◖

● 100 Calories

Feeding

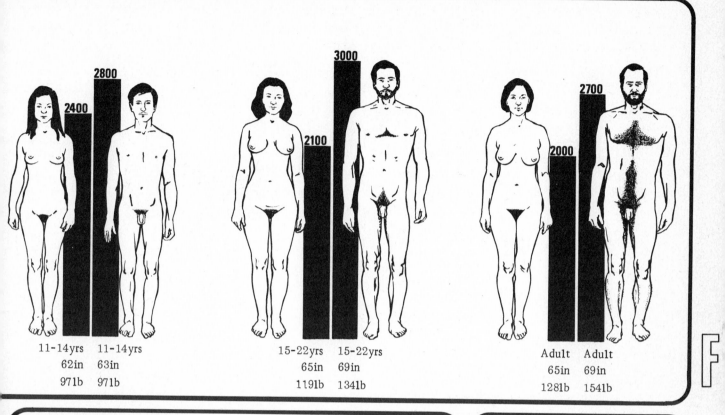

11–14yrs 11–14yrs
62in 63in
97lb 97lb

15–22yrs 15–22yrs
65in 69in
119lb 134lb

Adult Adult
65in 69in
128lb 154lb

F

F44 THE OVERWEIGHT CHILD

In all but a very few cases, overweight in infants and children is caused by overeating. All too often this is the parents' responsibility – bad eating habits are established at an early age, and continue through childhood and adolescence into adult life. Too many parents, either consciously or unconsciously, regard feeding their offspring as a means of expressing affection.

OVERWEIGHT INFANTS
Researchers have found that there is a marked tendency for overweight infants to become overweight children and adults. For this reason it is especially important to pay attention to an infant's diet and to stop him from becoming overweight.
Common errors in feeding include: making formula feeds too concentrated or too sweet;
introducing cereal into an infant's diet unnecessarily early; offering too many sweet foods so that the infant fails to acquire a taste for less fattening savories.

OVERWEIGHT CHILDREN
Excessive weight gain is commonly caused by too many between-meal snacks (see F43). Once a child has acquired the habit of eating fattening snacks it is hard to break him of it – much fairer to limit his intake from the start and try to be firm about when such "treats" are or are not allowed.
Overweight in children is often made worse by lack of exercise. In many cases the child falls into a vicious circle in which he is too embarrassed to take part in sport or active play – and then makes matters worse by overeating for consolation.

F45 HELPING A CHILD REDUCE

A plump child will very often slim down after puberty without special effort. An obviously overweight child is, however, likely to be healthier and happier if he is helped to lose weight. If the child is very overweight, it is recommended that medical advice be sought before embarking on any drastic reducing program. The parents of an overweight child will probably find it useful:
a) to plan menus so that all the family can eat the same thing – for a time excluding fattening foods from everybody's diet;
b) to avoid having fattening snacks in the house – using fresh fruit as a healthy alternative;
c) to check that the child is not overeating because he is unhappy;
d) to gain the child's cooperation so that he does not eat fattening foods away from home.

Child, home, and community

Early experiences with parents and siblings help a child's emotional development and prepare him for life within a larger community.

Left: Fun and games in a popular cartoon strip (Archive K)

CHILD IN THE FAMILY

G01 MEETING A CHILD'S NEEDS

From the moment of his birth a child has many needs that must be met by adults. Some of these needs, such as the provision of food and shelter, are obvious to everyone. Others, notably those involving a child's emotional development, are perhaps harder to recognize and therefore easier to neglect.

Recognizing and meeting their children's various physical and emotional needs is a major responsibility of parenthood. In doing so, the parent helps to prepare his child for physical and psychological independence in later years.

A secure and loving relationship is a basic requirement for the well-being of any child. A child who is deprived of loving contact in the early years is more likely to experience difficulties in forming close personal relationships in maturity.

Parents can show love for their children in many ways - by close physical contact in the form of a hug or a cuddle, or by giving them plenty of attention and showing real interest in their activities and childish chatter. Stimulation is a further need in childhood that may sometimes be ignored. A parent can do a great deal, quite simply, to encourage a young child's developmental progress. Providing interesting toys, reading to him, encouraging him to play with friends, taking him on outings, and, simplest of all, talking to him, all help to enrich a child's pre-school years and prepare him for the future (also see G04).

G02 THE FAMILY CONTEXT

Many of today's children grow up within a small two-generation family unit consisting of father, mother, and children. This "nuclear" family structure - generally resulting from increased population mobility in search of work or a new life - has in many instances replaced the "extended" family structure more typical of earlier generations.

In an extended family, a child is surrounded not only by his immediate family but also by aunts, uncles, cousins, and grandparents, most of whom live nearby. This has obvious advantages for a child. Against a general background of care and affection, he has a first-hand opportunity to become acquainted with members of different generations. From the parents'

G04 PARENTS AND CHILDREN

1 A close and loving relationship with his parents is important for the healthy emotional development of a child, and gives him a firm basis on which to build personal relationships in the future.

2 Parents can help the development of a pre-school child by providing stimulation in the form of toys and playthings that are appropriate to the child's particular age and ability (see H05-H10).

3 Reading stories to a child and sharing a picture book with him can usefully begin before he is 12 months old. Language development is encouraged, and stimulus given to his imagination.

Child, home, and community

viewpoint, an extended family can mean a great deal of on-the-spot support, both emotional and material, and advice - both welcome and unwelcome.

By contrast, the nuclear family requires a greater degree of self-reliance. In many cases this has been gained by a new sharing of responsibilities - with fathers participating more fully than ever before in all aspects of domestic and family affairs.

Support for the nuclear family can also come from the community as a whole. Friends and neighbors can fulfill many of the roles traditionally played by other family members. In consequence, it is essential that the value of a flourishing community is not lost sight of in these present days of rapid social change.

G03 ROLE REINFORCEMENT

In recent years, there has been a widespread questioning of traditional male and female roles. Women are no longer viewed necessarily as child rearers, nor men as breadwinners, and this has also led to changing attitudes to parental roles in the family.

As a result, a child's imitative play is no longer clearly "masculine" or "feminine" in the traditional sense. Many children still prefer the activities and toys traditionally associated with their sex, but others prefer to spend their time playing in a style once thought more appropriate to members of the opposite sex.

G

4 Drawing is an activity that should, if possible, be encouraged in a pre-schooler. It familiarizes him with basic materials, helps fine muscle control, and is an excellent means of self-expression.

5 A young child needs plenty of opportunity to broaden his horizons. Even the simplest outing - perhaps to a nearby park - provides him with a wealth of new and stimulating experiences.

6 A few minutes set aside each day that the parents regularly devote to a child can be extremely valuable, allowing him to talk through any anxieties and assuring him of his parents' love.

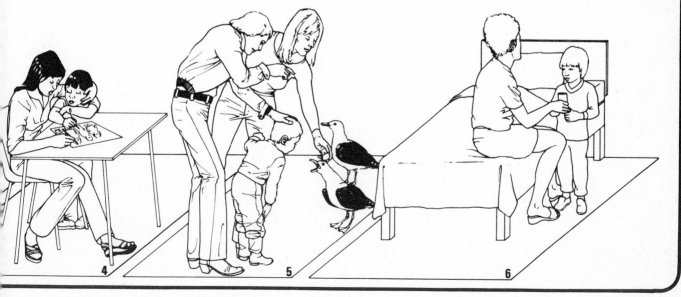

ONE CHILD OR MORE

G05 THE FIRST CHILD

Even if he is later joined by brothers and sisters, every first child begins life as an only child. This means that for some time at least he enjoys a great deal of his parents' undivided attention. His activities and reactions take on a concentrated significance, and he may be the sole object of their anxieties, hopes, and expectations. If the first child remains an only child, wise parents will take care not to develop an overanxious or overprotective attitude toward him. It is important that an only child should not spend all his time with adults. Time spent in the company of other children is his best way of learning about human relationships at his own level.

G06 ADDING TO THE FAMILY

Parents can do a great deal to minimize a child's possible jealousy and displeasure when a new baby joins the family. Even a young child should be told about the new baby in advance - but not so soon that he becomes bored with waiting. Feeling his mother's abdomen may help make the situation more real. Any important event or necessary change in the child's life - like starting nursery school or moving from a crib to a bed - should not be timed to coincide with the baby's birth as this will increase his sense of insecurity.
Before introducing the new baby the mother should make a point of first devoting a little time to the older child - perhaps giving him a reassuring cuddle and a small gift, and listening to his news.

G07 BROTHERS AND SISTERS

It is unrealistic of parents always to expect their children to live side by side in perfect harmony. While still deriving considerable pleasure from being part of a family, each child is an individual - and will sometimes behave like one at his siblings' expense. It is, however, extremely rare for jealousy or resentment between brothers and sisters to grow into the kind of bitterness that damages family relationships.

The age gap between children is a significant factor in their relationship. A gap of just a year or two may mean that they will be good play companions in middle childhood, while a longer gap sometimes means a relationship relatively free of jealousy.

Twins often have an extremely close relationship with each other. They are, however, still individuals, and parents should avoid treating them as a unit.

Aspects of sibling behavior:
a Playing together
b Playing individually
c Interrupting the other's play
d Open confrontation

Child, home, and community

G08 SEXUAL CURIOSITY

A typical child's interest in sexual matters fluctuates according to his age.

Around three, most children begin to show an interest in the genital differences between the sexes.

By four, a child may respond to stress by grasping the genitals and urgently needing to urinate. A year later, at five, he is typically more modest.

Around the age of six, he starts to show a marked awareness of the physical differences between the sexes, and may indulge in mild exhibitionism or sex play.

Sexual curiosity is less obvious in most seven-year-olds, but around the age of eight an interest in "peeping," sharing smutty jokes, and discussing sex information with friends may develop.

By nine, many children seek out pictures on sexual topics in books, and indulge in some childish sex swearing.

Age in years

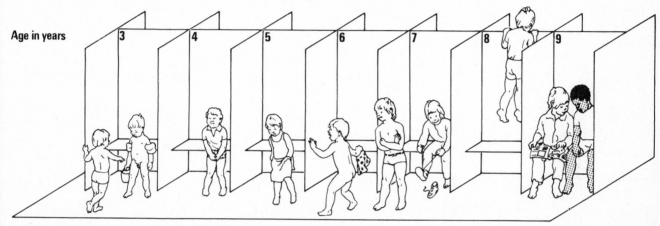

G09 THE FACTS OF LIFE

A child's questions about sex are just one aspect of his need to learn about and come to terms with the world around him.

If possible, parents should answer these questions simply and truthfully as they arise, just as they would answer a question about any other topic.

The temptation to give too much information should be avoided; if a child wants to know more he will generally ask. It is also unwise to postpone answering a question out of embarrassment, as this may make a child think that his natural interest is really an unhealthy curiosity in a taboo subject.

The earliest questions generally begin at the age of about three or four and usually concern babies - where they come from, how they get out, and, later, how they got there. Replies should be simple and direct, and at a level the child can understand.

In later childhood, menstruation and wet dreams should be explained to both boys and girls in the context of growing up and becoming able to produce babies (also see M01-07).

For a parent who is uncertain of how to cope with a child's questions, a great many books are available to help him. In addition, sex education is now included in the curriculum of most schools.

Sex education, however, is not simply a matter of answering a child's questions. The relationship between the parents, and the family approach to topics such as nudity in the home are also influential in the formation of a child's attitudes to sex.

G10 TALKING ABOUT DEATH

A child of any age should be encouraged to ask questions and talk openly about death, even if his attitudes seem immature or illogical. It is generally wise to tell the truth about a death as simply as possible. An explanation that grandfather has "gone to sleep" or "gone away" for ever may make the child fearful of sleeping or of journeys, in case he too may die.

A young child often seems to accept death very calmly, and may be upset more by the grief of those around him.

An older child may ask more thoughtful questions about his own or his parents' deaths - will dying hurt, when will it happen, and why? In these cases, the best reassurance an adult can give is to show that he himself is not overanxious or preoccupied with thoughts of death.

G

OUTSIDE THE HOME

G11 HAZARDS AWAY FROM HOME

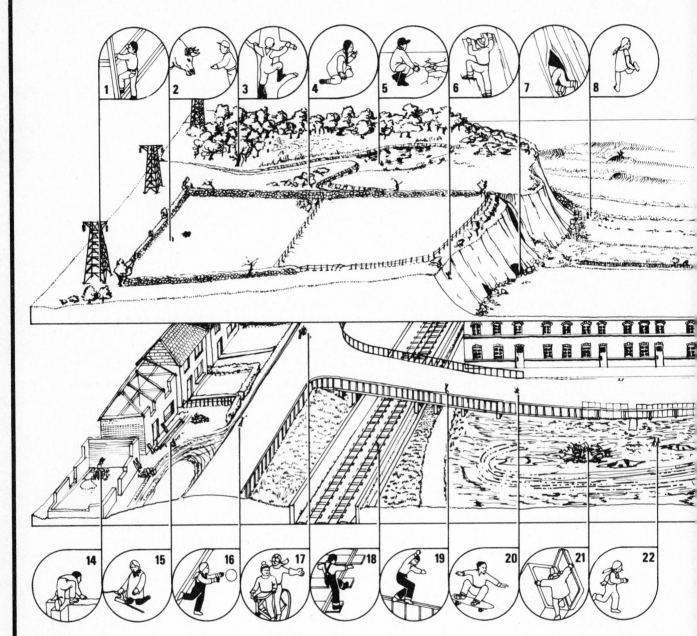

KEEPING SAFE
As soon as children are old enough to go out alone, they are faced with an enormous number of potential hazards. Parents now have the problem of encouraging their children's independence and self-reliance, while at the same time making them aware of how to cope with the many possible dangers they may meet.

WATER SAFETY
Water can be a major hazard. Ideally all children should be taught to swim as soon as possible, and should then be strongly discouraged from swimming where it is dangerous. Life jackets are a wise precaution for young children and nonswimmers playing near water, and are a must for water activities like sailing.

SAFETY WHEN CLIMBING
Most children love climbing and it is sensible that they should be taught to climb as safely as possible - always keeping at least three limbs "mountaineer-style" in contact with whatever is being climbed. At the same time they should be actively discouraged from climbing rotten trees or dangerous cliff faces, and from

Child, home, and community

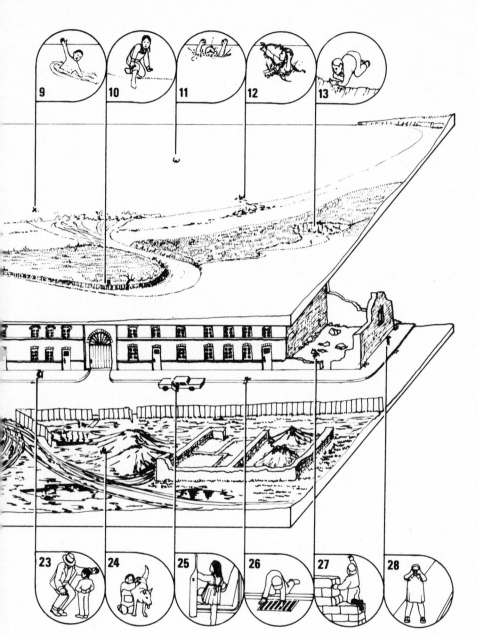

COMMON OUTDOOR HAZARDS

1 Climbing electric pylons
2 Approaching dangerous animals
3 Climbing unsafe trees
4 Eating unidentified berries or fruits
5 Sliding or playing on thin or untested ice
6 Climbing cliffs, rock faces, or quarries
7 Exploring caves or tunnels
8 Stepping barefoot on sharp stones or broken glass
9 Dangerous currents
10 Paddling in a fast-flowing or dirty river
11 Swimming too far from land
12 Becoming entangled in seaweed
13 Leaning out too far over the edge of a pond, lake, or river
14 Climbing high walls
15 Playing with dangerous tools and implements
16 Running out into the road while playing
17 Two riding on one bicycle
18 Walking on railroad tracks
19 Balancing on dangerous railings
20 Playing in the road on a skate board or roller skates
21 Playing with discarded items such as an ice box
22 Running with a lollipop-stick in the mouth
23 Talking to strangers and accepting gifts from them.
24 Stroking unknown animals, especially dogs
25 Accepting rides from strangers
26 Playing in dirty gutters
27 Playing on demolition sites
28 Going too far from home

playing in places such as quarries, building sites, and demolition areas.

ROAD SAFETY

Teaching children the rules of road safety is an obvious and important precautionary measure that parents should take. It is also vital to stress the dangers of accepting car rides or going for walks with strangers.

GOING TO SCHOOL

G12 STARTING SCHOOL

Some children look forward eagerly to starting school and enjoy it from the very first day. Many others, however, find the experience overwhelming, frightening, or simply disappointing, and may take a little longer to settle down.

During their first weeks at school it is quite common for children to show signs of strain. They may be generally irritable and ready to cry, have nightmares, begin nailbiting, or return to thumb sucking or bedwetting (see G42). This is normally a short phase; if it persists beyond the early weeks the parents should see the child's teacher.

In a very few cases the parents' reluctance to let go of a child may make it more difficult for him to adjust to his new life.

G13 PREPARING FOR SCHOOL

Beginning school is one of the most important events in a child's life. Inevitably it entails significant changes in daily routine (see E33), and there are several ways in which parents can help a child with this big step. Preparation begins ideally at birth as a child from a secure and loving family background generally finds it easier to adapt to school life.

The pre-school child should be encouraged to take an interest in a wide variety of topics. Parents can help by talking to him, reading him stories, and by taking time to answer his many questions with care.

In addition, he should be made familiar with the basic "tools" of the educational trade - books, pencils, paints, and paper.

Playing with other children outside his own home helps accustom a child to being separated from his parents, and visiting the school before he becomes a full-time pupil is invaluable if it can be arranged. Otherwise, taking him past the gate or the school yard may help alleviate some anxieties. Simple practical preparation is also extremely helpful. The child should be able to dress and undress himself (also see E36) and take care of and recognize his own possessions - labeling them with his name or a patch of color may help.

He should be able to listen to and carry out simple instructions, and should be familiar with the basics of road safety.

G14 STRUCTURE, SUBJECTS, AIDS

Since most parents were at school, significant changes have taken place in the internal structure of schools, in the subjects taught, and in the methods and aids used.

STRUCTURE

The traditional single-teacher system is still most common for pupils in their first years at school. This system - in which one teacher is responsible for all the subjects taught to a class - gives young children an opportunity to develop a deep relationship with an adult outside the family.

A subject-teaching system - in which each subject is taught by a different teacher - allows older children to benefit from specialist teaching in different fields.

A more recent development is team teaching, in which several teachers share responsibility for a group of children. Within this system a child with a learning difficulty can receive individual attention.

"Streaming," or "tracking," is commonly used as a means of providing a style and level of teaching appropriate to the needs of different pupils. Some schools divide children into general ability groups, in which they are taught for all subjects. Others favor a system in which children are divided into groups, or "sets," for individual subjects according to their ability in each.

CURRICULUM

The subjects in the daily curriculum vary from school to school. Though determined to some extent by the facilities available, the curriculum at any school is generally designed to cater as fully as possible for the needs of its pupils at different ages. In most schools, the traditional academic subjects such as math, sciences, and languages dominate

the curriculum - with arts, technical subjects, and sporting activities also included.

Increasing concern to emphasize the link between one subject and another, together with a growing enthusiasm for sociological and environmental topics, has in recent years led to the development of a combined-subject approach to lesson planning.

TEACHING AIDS

Mechanical teaching aids play an important part in modern education. Movies and programs on television and radio provide material about specialist topics and are used as a basis for further class teaching. Tape recorders are particularly valuable in language teaching; some schools have laboratories in which each child has his own machine and can, under the teacher's supervision, progress at his own pace.

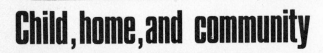

Child,home,and community

G15 PROBLEMS AT SCHOOL

DISLIKE OF SCHOOL

Dislike of school may be shown in various ways. In a mild form, the child may be tearful, or complain of headaches or stomachaches. At its most serious, it may amount to absolute refusal to go to school - school phobia.

Reasons for dislike of school include the following.

a) Parental influences may have convinced the child that school is unpleasant or frightening.

b) When at school, the child may make poor progress in his work and perhaps fail to match up to the expectations of his parents.

c) He may be worried about catching up after an absence, or be afraid of a particular teacher.

d) He may be the object of bullying or teasing, or he may feel that he is unpopular.

In most cases, punishment for school-refusing is useless. The child should be encouraged to go to school every day, and the reasons behind the problem should be investigated.

BAD BEHAVIOR

Persistent bad behavior at school is damaging for a child and may also have a disruptive effect on his fellow pupils.

The following are examples of underlying causes of behavioral difficulties at school.

a) A child may be bored with easy lessons, or struggling to keep up.

b) The problem may result from a desire to attract attention - a common side effect of neglect or even rejection at home.

c) A child may have a problem that needs professional treatment (see G17).

G16 PARENTS AND SCHOOL

Parents can help their school-age child most constructively by taking a real interest in his activities at school. This can mean simply listening to him describe the day's events, or may involve a deeper commitment - in a parent-teacher association, or by helping as a volunteer in the school library or on trips.

"Open" days are a useful guide to the way a school operates and offer a valuable opportunity for discussing with the teacher a child's particular problems or difficulties. It is generally wise to cooperate with the teacher if possible; open disagreement between teacher and parent can severely test a child's loyalties. At home, parents can encourage their child by seeing that he has a quiet place to do his homework.

G17 SPECIAL SERVICES

Many schools now include on the staff some personnel specially trained to deal with pupils' individual problems. At the center of this network is the teacher who is responsible for referring pupils to the appropriate staff member. The health unit may include a nurse who gives day-to-day health care and copes with emergencies, and a doctor who makes regular visits to give checks or advice.

A social worker or guidance counselor may be available to help with problems arising from the pupil's family situation such as unemployment or lack of money, and they may refer pupils with severe emotional problems to a psychologist or psychiatrist.

Specific learning difficulties can be helped by specialist staff such as speech therapists and remedial reading teachers.

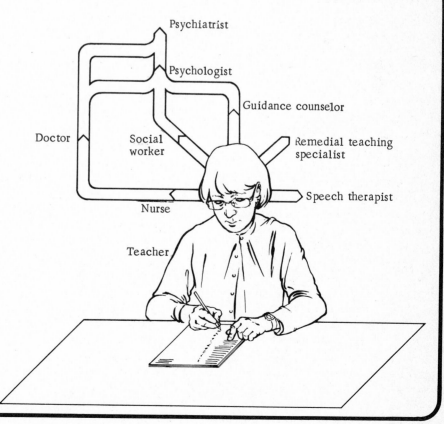

Psychiatrist
Psychologist
Guidance counselor
Doctor
Social worker
Remedial teaching specialist
Speech therapist
Nurse
Teacher

©DIAGRAM

GIVING A PARTY

G18 GIVING A PARTY

The secret of a successful party is good planning: time, place, guest list, food, games or entertainment must all be given thought in advance.

Outdoor parties are in many ways ideal for all ages, but it is essential to make advance plans in case a move indoors becomes necessary.

Parties for younger children need adult supervision and parents of some of the guests may be willing to help.

Older children enjoy helping to arrange their own parties - they should be consulted over the plans and encouraged to take part in the preparations.

Teenagers often enjoy cooking their own food, especially at a cook-out around a barbecue or fire.

G19 PARTY FOOD

Party meals should coincide with a regular mealtime if possible. Disposable plates, cups, and tablecloths can look attractive, and prevent anxiety about breakages and spills.

Young children often squabble about food. A satisfactory solution - and one enjoyed by the children themselves - is to give each child his own "basket" or box of food. The children may like to sit picnic-style on the floor - in which case a sheet can be spread out to protect the carpet.

Party food popular with young children includes hamburgers, hot dogs, potato chips, chocolate cookies, ice cream, and a sponge birthday cake.

Older children may prefer more "grown up" food and it is wise to consult them first.

G20 A YOUNG CHILD'S PARTY

Parties for young children should be reasonably short - probably no more than 90 minutes. The number of guests should also be limited - young children are happier with three or four friends rather than a lot of comparative strangers.

Very young children are happy simply to play with toys - a swing, slide, or rocking horse, perhaps borrowed for the occasion, will prove a certain center of attraction.

Until the age of four or five organized games are rarely successful, but even the youngest child enjoys a party atmosphere and the thrill of dressing up. Outdoor parties, if the weather permits, are ideal; indoors, as large a play area as possible should be cleared and anything of value put out of reach.

G23 PARTY GAMES

Games for a children's party need careful planning in advance. A balanced program can be devised by choosing games from the different categories described here. Before the party it is essential to check that you know the rules for the various games and that you have all the equipment you will require.

BLINDFOLD GAMES
Blindfold games can be a lot of fun. Good games include: blind man's buff (a); pin the tail on the donkey.
SPOKEN WORD GAMES
Good games for less active moments include: I-spy; spelling bee; a quiz; charades.

CONTESTS
Ideas for contests include: tug-of-war (b); seeing who can flick a balloon farthest; arm wrestling.
PENCIL AND PAPER GAMES
Possible games for parties are: categories; consequences.

Child, home, and community

G21 A TRADITIONAL PARTY

From the age of about four, most children take a delight in a party run on traditional lines - with games or entertainment, party food, and a small gift to take home. Since much of the party will be spent playing games, it is wise to have a schedule carefully planned in advance. A varied program should be the aim, with boisterous games alternating with quieter activities. Extra games or activities should also be kept in reserve to fill any spare moments or to replace a game that is not going well. (Some ideas for games are suggested in G23.) Small prizes awarded to the winners of competitive games are always popular. Prizes of candy are generally best avoided, certainly with young children. Another point to remember with young children is that some may not fully understand the concept of winning and losing; it is wise to move quickly to a new activity to console the disappointed. A sitting down game such as pass the parcel or a word game is recommended just before food is served. Confusion over seating arrangements for eating can be avoided if each child's place is labeled with his name or initial. Boisterous games should be avoided directly after eating; if any entertainment is to be provided, now is the ideal time.

Giving each child a small take-home gift helps round off the party successfully; to avoid squabbles it is a good idea to give each child a similar gift.

G22 PARTY ALTERNATIVES

A conventional party is not the only possibility for a children's celebration. Outings to the zoo, movies, theater, circus, skating rink, swimming pool, or bowling alley are all popular, especially if followed by an informal meal in a restaurant.

A cheaper alternative is a picnic - a favorite with children of all ages. The choice of location is obviously important. Parks, rivers, lakes, or a beach are all good picnic spots, but if the group is to include several young children some attention must be paid to safety aspects.

Picnic entertainment usually requires only a small amount of organization - most children will enjoy exploring the area, collecting interesting objects, or joining in a ball game.

RACES
A great variety of amusing races can be devised with a little imagination. Races may be for individual competitors, or relay races for teams. A few examples are: newspaper walk (c); burst the bag; bead threading race; pass the orange (f); matchbox on nose race.

MUSICAL GAMES
Games played to music are always popular. Good examples are musical chairs (d); pass the parcel.
TRICKERY GAMES
Examples include: Simon (or O'Grady) says; do this - do that!

GOAL-SCORING GAMES
Examples include: balloon volleyball (e); hockey played with walking sticks and a rag ball.
HUNTING AND OBSERVATION GAMES
Old favorites include: hunt the thimble; hunt the slipper; hide and seek; matching pairs.

©DIAGRAM

KEEPING PETS

G24 CHOOSING A PET

The first thing to ensure when choosing a pet is that it is suitable for the particular home and family situation. This is essential for the happiness and well-being of both the animal and the child.

A major consideration must be the size and exercise requirements of the animal; a very large dog, for instance, is unsuitable for a small apartment or for a city home with a small garden and no easy access to open spaces. A better choice in this case may be a small pet such as a mouse, hamster, guinea pig, or gerbil, or even "pets" from nature such as caterpillars, stick insects, or tadpoles.

The responsibility for caring for a pet also needs to be given thought in advance. Even quite a young child may enjoy helping with the care of a pet, but someone older will have to do most of the work. Older children often like to feel that they have full responsibility for their pets, and, as far as possible, should be encouraged to look after all their pets' needs. Ultimately, however, it is the parents' responsibility to ensure that every pet is properly cared for.

Vacations may be a problem if the pet cannot accompany the family; before choosing a pet it is advisable to check that it is going to be possible to make arrangements for its care during the family's absence. Cost is a further consideration; a large dog may be quite expensive to feed, while a rabbit may cost very little. Similar variations may be reflected in the fees charged by a veterinarian.

G25 POPULAR PETS

The most popular household pets tend to be those that respond well to humans and those that can be easily tamed. These are most suitable when there is a young child in the family, as a properly trained and healthy animal is unlikely to bite or transfer infection.

1 Dog
2 Cat
3 Horse
4 Pony
5 Canary
6 Parakeets
7 Hamster
8 Mouse
9 Rabbit
10 Guinea pig
11 Fish

Child, home, and community

G26 UNUSUAL PETS

Less common animals are now enjoying increasing popularity as family pets. Many of them need special handling and feeding and it is essential to find out in advance from a pets book the exact requirements of a particular pet. In addition, some unusual pets present a slightly increased health risk to a child and a veterinarian should be consulted.

Many children enjoy collecting their own "pets" from a field, a river, or the sea; many fish, crabs, and insects are quite suitable, but attempting to domesticate some species is obviously both cruel and unwise.

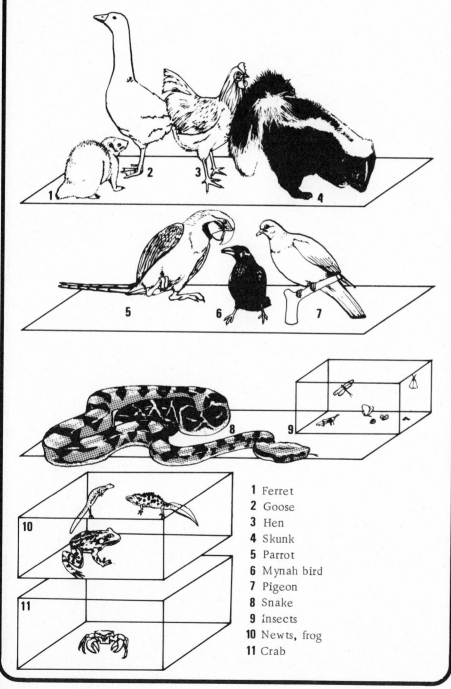

1 Ferret
2 Goose
3 Hen
4 Skunk
5 Parrot
6 Mynah bird
7 Pigeon
8 Snake
9 Insects
10 Newts, frog
11 Crab

G27 OWNING A PET

For a child who longs for one, a well chosen pet can be a source of considerable pleasure. In addition, owning and caring for a pet can provide a child with some useful learning experiences.

The day-to-day care that most pets need can help encourage him to develop a sense of responsibility.

In the case of many popular pets, the child may have the chance to become familiar with the processes of mating and birth in a very natural way. Also, experiencing the loss or death of a pet may help him later in coming to terms with a human bereavement. Perhaps the most valuable aspect of owning a pet, however, is that it gives a child something on which to lavish his affection and innate caring instincts.

G28 PETS AND HEALTH

Only in rare cases does a pet present a serious health hazard to a child. It is advisable to have any new pet looked over by a veterinarian; the examination will include any injections necessary to protect the animal's health and ensure the child's safety.

The most common health problems caused by pets are skin disorders and allergic reactions; these can often be controlled by grooming the pet regularly and keeping it as free as possible of fleas, ticks, and mites.

More serious is the possibility of infection after contact with an animal's bowel movements, so early house-training is vital. With some pets, there is also a risk of bites and a child should be warned against teasing. (For the treatment of animal bites see N31.)

HOBBIES AND INTERESTS

G29 HOBBIES AND INTERESTS

The development of hobbies and special interests usually takes place after the child has begun school. An invaluable form of recreation and self-expression, hobbies can also be an important source of self-education and can in some cases influence career choice.

The range of pursuits that may interest a child is limitless. Some are individual occupations, others group activities; some may seem worthwhile and others pointless; some rely mainly on money and others on the child's own resourcefulness.

For many children, interest in a particular topic is stimulated by their friends' choice of hobby. In other cases, the parents' own leisure activities may be a decisive influence.

G31 COLLECTING

At some time most children enjoy collecting as a hobby. The objects they collect cover a wide range, and favorites include model cars, dolls, coins, stamps, photographs, sport cards, rocks, seashells, and flowers.

Displaying or mounting these objects may be a major part of the child's enjoyment, and special storage - an album, drawer, or shelf - helps encourage tidiness. Though collecting is essentially an individual pursuit, some schools and neighborhoods organize societies for children with specialty interests such as stamps or coins.

Stamp collecting   Shell collecting

G30 CLUBS AND SOCIETIES

Clubs, societies, and other group activities are an important leisure interest for many children, particularly after the age of about seven.

Most organizations for younger children rely on a common interest, and among the activities especially popular with seven- to ten-year-olds are Brownies and Cub Scouts. In addition, many schools arrange extra-curricular clubs and societies for rather more specialized leisure interests.

For older children and teenagers group activities such as youth clubs or camps are especially important as they offer an opportunity to meet and make friends outside the context of the family home, and can in this way play a valuable part in the child's social and emotional development.

G32 MUSICAL ACTIVITIES

A young child's enthusiasm for music can be encouraged from an early age with a recorder, or melodica, or a special junior xylophone or glockenspiel. Later, piano or singing lessons, or instruction in an orchestral instrument or guitar may be appreciated and can lead to participation in enjoyable group activities such as ensembles, orchestras, and choirs.

Listening to music should be an integral part of a child's enjoyment and parents can encourage his interest by providing the opportunity to listen to music of every kind on disk, tape, or radio, and, ideally, at a live performance.

Child, home, and community

G33 ARTS AND CRAFTS

Hobbies connected with arts and crafts have wide appeal to children of many different ages Particularly popular with younger children are activities such as drawing, painting, simple cookery, and model making. As manipulative skills develop and his creativity begins to be reflected in these activities, the child's interest may extend to other hobbies including carpentry, sewing, embroidery, and modeling.

Many art and craft interests can easily be encouraged in the home and need not necessarily be a burden on the family budget. "Starter" craft kits containing all the necessary materials for a particular activity are now widely available, if rather expensive, but many hobbies make use of comparatively cheap materials such as paint and glue, natural objects such as flowers, or household items like paper containers, and scraps of fabric.

Clay modeling   Model-making   Needlework

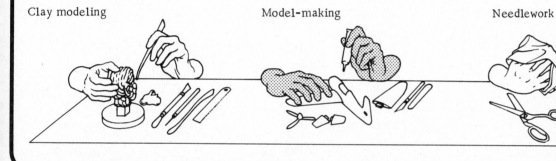

G34 SCIENTIFIC INTERESTS

From the age of about seven, some children develop a deep interest in a variety of scientific subjects including natural history, astronomy, chemistry, and photography. Interest can be encouraged with special equipment - perhaps a good science set, magnifying glass, microscope, or camera - and reference books appropriate to the child's age.

G35 SPORTING ACTIVITIES

Sporting activities are an important leisure pursuit for many children. Great enjoyment may be derived from taking part in individual and team activities, while being a spectator or a follower of a particular team can also be a lot of fun.

Especially popular are team activities which offer the chance of physical exertion combined with the enjoyable social aspects of belonging to a group.

Most schools and many community organizations arrange teams and matches, but for many children an informal ball game organized spontaneously is just as good.

As well as being an excellent form of amusement a childhood interest in sport may continue into adult life, and by encouraging regular exercise can help promote general fitness.

CHILDHOOD ANXIETIES

G36 CHILDHOOD ANXIETIES

Even if they are never involved in a major crisis (see G45), all children experience anxiety at some time or another.

Often the cause of a child's anxiety is easy to recognize. Many "first times," such as a first visit to the dentist, first bus trip alone, or first time away from home, fall into this category. Also very common are age-old childhood fears like fear of the dark, fear of animals, and fear of strangers. Some children regularly become anxious before examinations or tests at school, or worry that their classmates do not like them.

Many childhood anxieties seem unnecessary or illogical to an adult, but the problem is no less real to a child who is upset. In such cases a parent should take care never to ridicule the child, but should gently reassure him and attempt to convince him that his fears are groundless.

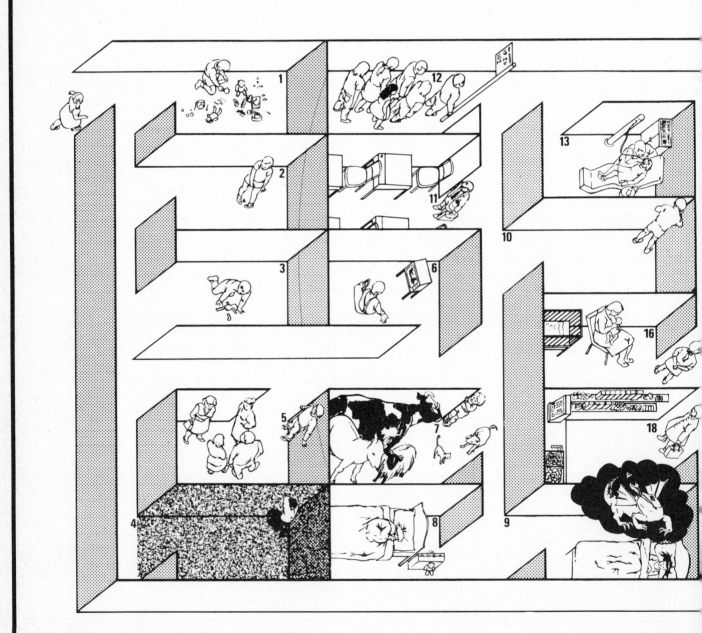

Some children have a naturally anxious and timid temperament, and frequently become upset at apparently trivial occurrences. A parent will need a lot of patience to boost his child's confidence and help him come to terms with his worries.

Other children appear never to be worried by anything, but parents should watch for signs of hidden anxiety (also see G38). Taking time to talk quietly with a child is the best way of ensuring all is well.

Some events in a child's life are almost certain to cause feelings of anxiety and insecurity. Among the most common are the arrival of a new baby (also see G06), and the first few weeks at a new school (G12). In cases such as these an understanding parent will anticipate the child's worries and do all he can to ease the child through each potentially upsetting situation as it arises.

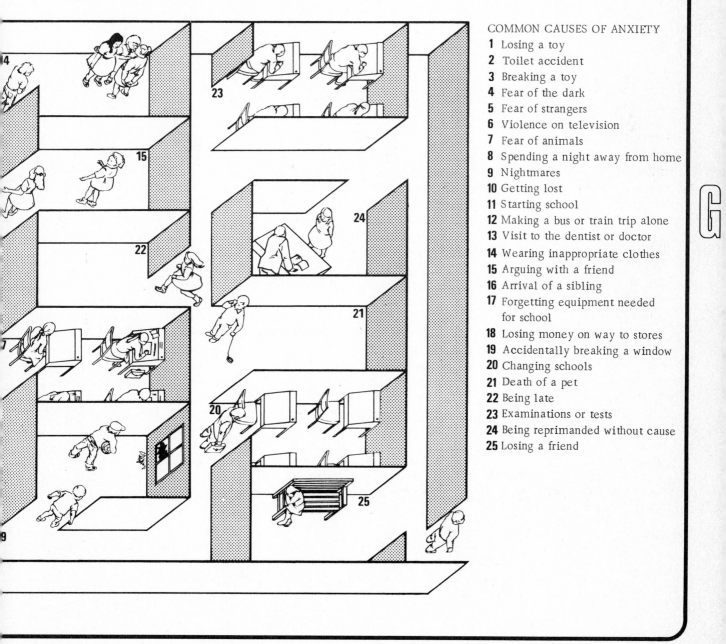

COMMON CAUSES OF ANXIETY

1 Losing a toy
2 Toilet accident
3 Breaking a toy
4 Fear of the dark
5 Fear of strangers
6 Violence on television
7 Fear of animals
8 Spending a night away from home
9 Nightmares
10 Getting lost
11 Starting school
12 Making a bus or train trip alone
13 Visit to the dentist or doctor
14 Wearing inappropriate clothes
15 Arguing with a friend
16 Arrival of a sibling
17 Forgetting equipment needed for school
18 Losing money on way to stores
19 Accidentally breaking a window
20 Changing schools
21 Death of a pet
22 Being late
23 Examinations or tests
24 Being reprimanded without cause
25 Losing a friend

G

BEHAVIOR DIFFICULTIES 1

G37 UNDERLYING CAUSES

Every child displays behavior difficulties at some time or another - expressing anxiety at different situations, or behaving in a manner that is unacceptable to others.

Very often, "bad" behavior has no deep-rooted psychological cause. In some cases the child is simply too young to appreciate that what he is doing is wrong. Sometimes, moreover, his difficult behavior is part of a general developmental pattern - temper tantrums, for example, play a vital part in the emotional development of every toddler. In older children, high spirits and a love of fun and adventure may lead to trouble and clashes with authority that the child never really intended.

In other cases, however, a child's difficult behavior may derive from emotional disturbance - either a temporary upset or a longer-term more serious problem.

A variety of emotional problems may be found to lie behind a child's behavior difficulties. Among the most common are: insecurity resulting from family disharmony or a broken home; jealousy of another member of the family; lack of affection; childhood anxieties (see G36); disfigurement or disability, or sometimes overweight; over-rigid discipline at home or at school; fear of failure; or feelings of guilt, whether real or imaginary. Sometimes an emotional problem resulting in behavior difficulties proves too deep-rooted to be identified and treated by the parents alone. In these cases, professional help from a counselor, social worker, psychologist, or psychiatrist should provide the child with the guidance he needs.

G38 WARNING SIGNS

Children have many different ways of expressing an emotional upset. In general, a parent should take seriously any severe or persistent behavior problem that is uncharacteristic of a particular child or uncommon in other children of the same age.

Persistent crying, obvious anxiety or depression, a return to "babyish" behavior, apparent lack of interest, unusual rudeness, bedwetting, and sleepwalking are examples of behavior that should be investigated as possible indicators of deeper-rooted emotional problems.

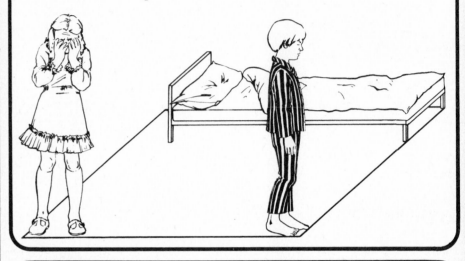

G39 DISCIPLINE

A child's first experience of discipline usually comes from within the family. A parent's aim should be to give the child guidance about expected standards of behavior, encourage him to learn self-control, and help him to acquire a sense of responsibility in maturity.

Lack of parental discipline may cause a child to become insecure and confused as he finds that behavior tolerated at home is unacceptable outside the family. Excessively strict discipline, on the other hand, risks curbing a child's spirit of adventure and may cause him to become fearful of ever trying anything new. In some cases, unnecessarily harsh restrictions on freedom in early childhood lead to open and complete rebellion against authority in later years.

Disciplining a child is not simply a matter of giving out punishments - although sometimes even the most peace-loving parent will feel that some form of punishment is necessary. In fact, one of the most important elements in discipline is parental example: a child learns more from modeling his behavior on that of his parents than he does from raised voices or corporal punishment.

Expectations about a child's behavior must always be in line with his abilities at different ages. It is useless, for example, to expect a one-year-old to feed himself politely.

It is also essential to remember that each child is an individual, and must be treated accordingly. Even within the same family, children have very different temperaments and require varying methods of disciplinary guidance.

Child, home, and community

G40 PASSING PHASES

Certain types of behavior that play a perfectly normal part in a young child's development can sometimes cause parents to become unnecessarily alarmed.

For example, reluctance to participate in cooperative play (**a**) and refusal to share toys (**b**) are passing phases in a typical developmental pattern (see C16, C18). Both will be outgrown without parental interference. Similarly, habits such as nail biting, nose picking, thumb sucking (**c**), genital exploration (**d**), eating strange things (**e**), and temper tantrums (**f**) are common in toddlers and generally require investigation only if they persist well into childhood.

Head banging, cot rocking, breath holding, and air swallowing are rather more alarming aspects of behavior that may be indulged in if jealousy or insecurity are causing a child to feel in particular need of comfort.

G41 SPEECH PROBLEMS

Late talking is a common cause of anxiety to parents. Usually there is no cause for concern, but it is essential that the child has a specialized hearing test to check for any defect (also see L05).

Mild stuttering and frequent stumbling over words are very common in young children, occurring because the child's eagerness to speak exceeds his level of verbal fluency. In almost every case these problems disappear without specialized help.

Persistent stuttering in older children is commoner in boys than girls. Emotional tension makes the problem worse, and parents should avoid drawing attention to the child's difficulty. Speech therapy is always helpful for children who stutter, and in many cases results in a complete cure.

G42 BEDWETTING

Bedwetting is a common problem that may cause considerable anxiety to a child and his parents. In most cases the child would, in time, simply grow out of the problem, but various steps may be taken to help a child remain dry.

CAUSES

Staying dry through the night is a skill that some young children find particularly difficult. In these cases the problem usually results from a small or sensitive bladder in combination with a large urine output.

In other children bedwetting is a temporary lapse, following a prolonged period of night dryness. Often occurring between the ages of four and seven, this type of bedwetting is often the result of a short-term emotional upset such as starting school or the birth of a new baby in the family. Only vary rarely is bedwetting a symptom of severe emotional disturbance.

TREATMENT

In every case it is sensible to restrict fluid intake in the late afternoon and evening.

Because urine production is greatest in the first couple of hours after bedtime, waking the child and taking him to the toilet at this time is often all that is needed to keep his bed dry. A special pad and bell alarm is often helpful in severe cases. A drop of urine on the pad, placed between two undersheets, causes the bell to ring - and wakes the child in time to go to the toilet. An alarm of this kind can greatly boost the confidence of an anxious child.

In rare cases, a doctor may feel that drugs or psychiatric help offer the best chance of solving a child's particular bedwetting problem.

©DIAGRAM

BEHAVIOR DIFFICULTIES 2

G43 BEHAVIOR PROBLEMS

A variety of childhood behavior problems - common and less common - are shown here and in G44. Possible causes are given in G37.

1) LYING

Lying takes two basic forms - stories told for effect, and untruths told to hide a misdeed. The telling of fantastic stories is a normal stage in the development of a young child - a sign of a blossoming imagination. In older children, this type of lying usually involves "improving" a real event. If it occurs very frequently it may be a sign that the child needs to be reassured that great deeds are not necessary to win the esteem of others.
All children tell lies to cover up their misdeeds. In young children it is a sign that they now understand that certain things are not permitted.
An older child who often lies may merely be more adventurous than most - or may be seriously afraid of losing his parents' love if his misdeeds are discovered.

2) SHYNESS

Even outgoing children sometimes feel shy - after moving to a new neighborhood, for example, or starting at a new school. Shyness of this type rarely persists, particularly if the child is gently helped to find his feet. Severe and persistent shyness may be more of a problem, although in these cases, too, the problem often disappears with time and sympathetic handling. A severely shy child should be encouraged to make friends of his own age. Sometimes a child finds it easier to cope in his own territory and inviting another child into the home to play may be helpful. It is particularly important that parents do not allow the very shy child to become too dependent on themselves - he needs to feel loved and secure, but must also learn to stand up for himself.

3) IRRATIONAL FEARS

All children suffer at times from irrational fears. Fear of the dark, fear of strangers, fear of animals, fear of being left alone in quite safe situations, are all examples of common childhood fears. Usually fears such as these are short-lived or, even if persistent, do not in fact cause the child very great disturbance provided that a reassuring parent is comparatively close at hand.
In a few children, however, extreme fearfulness is a sign of some deeper emotional disturbance that may need professional help. Such children may panic at normal, everyday things like a furry toy or pet, be exceptionally afraid of any new experience, be over-anxious about getting hurt in relatively safe activities, or be constantly afraid of failure in very simple tasks.

Child, home, and community

4) COMPULSIVE BEHAVIOR
Children of different ages draw comfort from the performance of ritual actions. Complicated bedtime rituals (see E55) are common in young children and have an importance beyond their value as a delaying tactic. Between the ages of seven and ten a great variety of rituals designed to ward off "bad luck" are extremely common - not stepping on sidewalk cracks, for example, or rapidly touching different parts of the body on seeing an ambulance. Actions such as these are a normal part of any child's development. Sometimes, however, a child's compulsive behavior is a sign of emotional insecurity. Rocking back and forward, head banging, an obsessive interest in neatness or cleanliness, or compulsions about food may mean that a child is subconsciously asking for help.

5) LETHARGY
Although periods of lethargy may become quite common with the approach of adolescence, this type of behavior is less typical of younger children and may be a sign that all is not well.
A child who is sickening for an illness is unlikely to want to join in the boisterous games of his friends. Usually the cause of the problem soon becomes obvious as other sypmtoms appear. If a child is physically quite healthy, frequent lethargy may be a sign that he is in need of help in coming to terms with an emotional problem. This is particularly likely if generally withdrawn behavior is combined with other signs of strain such as absentmindedness, apparent lack of deep feelings, excessive daydreaming, nightmares, or an inability to make decisions.

6) INTEREST IN SEX AND VIOLENCE
Some interest in sexual topics is perfectly natural and normal among young children (see G08). Childish sex games and the use of sex-based swear words may be disturbing to a parent, but are unlikely to represent more than a passing - and important - phase in a child's development.
Violence, too, seems to some parents to play an unnaturally large part in the lives of their children. The acting out of aggressions in games of cowboys, soldiers, gangsters, etc appears to be a fundamental part of growing up and coming to terms with more sophisticated social relations. Only if a child's interest in sex or violence is particularly marked - and part of a wider picture of disturbed behavior - is it at all likely that there is any real cause for parental concern.

G

BEHAVIOR DIFFICULTIES 3

7) TANTRUMS AND TEMPER

Temper tantrums are common in young children, particularly at ages two to four. They result from the child's inevitable lack of self-control, in combination with a developing realization of himself as an individual with wishes of his own. Punishment will certainly have no effect; leaving the child alone to calm down will sometimes do the trick.

Displays of temper usually become less frequent as a child gets older and becomes better able to control himself. But, as with adults, there will always be some things that annoy him: a desire to do something that is forbidden, or frustration at his lack of skill in a particular activity.

In a few cases, excessive and frequent shows of temper may need investigation as indicators of deeper-rooted stress in a child.

8) CHEATING

As with many other childhood behavior problems, cheating can have a variety of causes.

Most worrying is the classic case of a child who, deeply unsure of himself, cheats in an attempt to win the admiration of others. The parents of a child who cheats persistently should ask themselves very seriously whether they are not pushing the child too hard; and must take pains to assure him that their love in no way depends on good results at school.

Occasional cheating may be more simply explained: the child failed to do a piece of work - either deliberately or not - and fell back on cheating to avoid discovery. Another phenomenon quite common among older children is a simple cheating "epidemic" - in which many children cheat for a time just to follow the crowd.

9) STEALING

Most young children "steal" toys or candies from each other - a perfectly normal form of behavior in the early years before a child can properly appreciate the concept of ownership.

Even after they are old enough to know better, many children still steal occasionally. Often the lapse is only temporary - perhaps the child had spent all his pocket money but desperately wanted candy or ice cream.

Another common form of stealing among older children follows a group dare - going into a store and taking something, just to prove it can be done.

Cases of repeated stealing, however, should be carefully investigated as it is possible that the child is using stealing as a means of drawing attention to more serious emotional problems or needs.

Child, home, and community

9   10   11   12

10) SMOKING, ALCOHOL, DRUGS
The widespread availability of
cigarettes, alcohol, and in some
cases drugs, makes it virtually
impossible for a parent to ensure
that his child does not have some
opportunity to try them.
Experiments with these adult
"vices" are common even among
pre-adolescents - perhaps as a
group activity, or perhaps a child
may help himself when his parents
are out. In many cases, these
earliest experiments fortunately
prove unpleasant to the child who
is then quite happy to postpone
his next attempt until he is older
and more mature.
Family attitudes and example vary
a great deal in these matters, and
will obviously affect the child.
It is important in any case that
the child knows his parents' views,
and also that he appreciates when
he is breaking the law.

11) FIGHTING
Many children resort to physical
battle in disagreements with
their friends. To a child with
an immature ability to argue,
actions frequently speak louder
than words. Sometimes the conflict
results more from surplus energy
than from any deep disagreement.
In almost every case there is no
cause for worry - the adversaries
are reconciled within minutes of
the outbreak of hostilities.
Cases of bullying and cruelty
toward younger children are,
however, very much more serious.
A child who consistently fights
with others who are physically
weaker than himself is almost
certainly expressing deep
feelings of hostility that he
cannot understand. Only if he is
helped to come to terms with his
inner conflicts can he learn to
control his aggression.

12) DESTRUCTIVE BEHAVIOR
Feelings of anger often provoke
destructive behavior in young
children; the child throws his toy
on to the floor - and breaks it,
much to his amazement. Even
the deliberate breaking of
another child's toy in a sudden
fit of temper probably signifies
no more than a passing storm.
More worrying is a child who
repeatedly or calculatedly
destroys the belongings of other
children; a child who behaves in
this way almost certainly needs
help with a more serious problem.
Also worrying to parents is a
child who indulges in acts of
vandalism. Activities such as
breaking windows are often
carried out for dares and may not
indicate any emotional problem -
even so, the child risks trouble
with the police and needs to be
kept in check.

G

CRISES IN THE FAMILY

G45 COPING WITH CRISES

When a crisis of any kind hits a family, a child is almost invariably affected, either directly or indirectly.

Occasionally a crisis situation can be anticipated. If a child or parent has to go into the hospital, for example, there may be an opportunity to prepare the child by explaining the event beforehand. (The hospitalized child is discussed more fully in K40-45.) Events such as a serious accident or the death of a member of the family will cause disturbance in even the most stable home. Times such as these are distressing for everyone and, despite his own worries or grief, a parent should try to treat a child with as much understanding as possible.

Other crises in a child's life result from the development of disharmony within the family.

Constant arguing by the parents, physical cruelty, separation, and divorce, are all examples of domestic strife that can have an indirect but profound effect on a child's state of mind.

Not all cases of parental stress are caused by family disharmony. Unemployment, poor housing, and large families can also result in the kind of parental stress that is communicated to a child - at worst, in the form of battering.

Sometimes a child encounters a crisis situation outside the home - for example in cases of social or racial prejudice, civil disturbance, or personal attack.

In some crisis situations the strain on the family as a whole is so great that the needs of a child may be unintentionally neglected. At times like these, support from friends or in the form of professional advisory and counseling services may prove of the greatest value to everyone concerned.

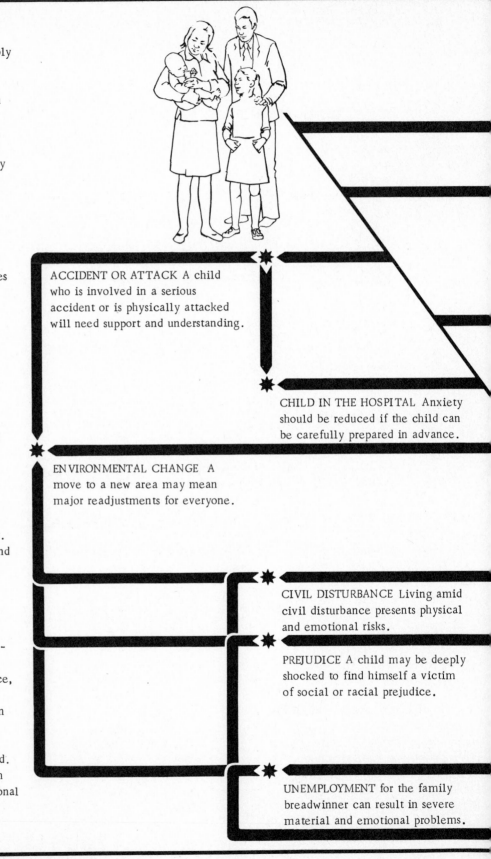

ACCIDENT OR ATTACK A child who is involved in a serious accident or is physically attacked will need support and understanding.

CHILD IN THE HOSPITAL Anxiety should be reduced if the child can be carefully prepared in advance.

ENVIRONMENTAL CHANGE A move to a new area may mean major readjustments for everyone.

CIVIL DISTURBANCE Living amid civil disturbance presents physical and emotional risks.

PREJUDICE A child may be deeply shocked to find himself a victim of social or racial prejudice.

UNEMPLOYMENT for the family breadwinner can result in severe material and emotional problems.

Child, home, and community

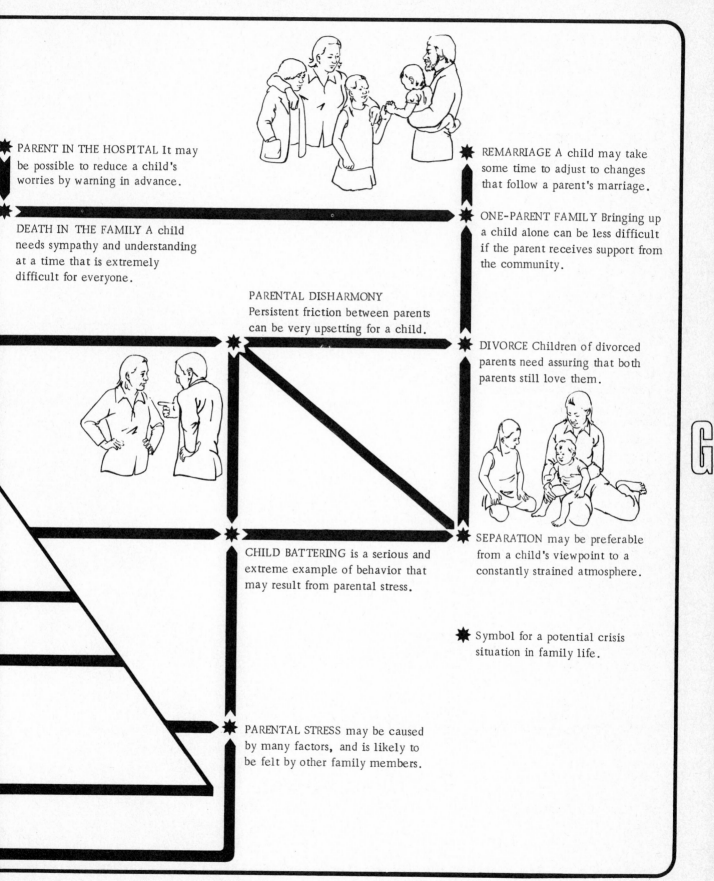

✸ PARENT IN THE HOSPITAL It may be possible to reduce a child's worries by warning in advance.

REMARRIAGE A child may take some time to adjust to changes that follow a parent's marriage.

DEATH IN THE FAMILY A child needs sympathy and understanding at a time that is extremely difficult for everyone.

ONE-PARENT FAMILY Bringing up a child alone can be less difficult if the parent receives support from the community.

PARENTAL DISHARMONY Persistent friction between parents can be very upsetting for a child.

DIVORCE Children of divorced parents need assuring that both parents still love them.

CHILD BATTERING is a serious and extreme example of behavior that may result from parental stress.

SEPARATION may be preferable from a child's viewpoint to a constantly strained atmosphere.

✸ Symbol for a potential crisis situation in family life.

PARENTAL STRESS may be caused by many factors, and is likely to be felt by other family members.

Play

Some adults mistakenly believe that children's play is a pleasant but essentially unproductive means of passing time. This is very far from the truth.

Left: Artists of the future in a 19th-century magazine illustration (The Mansell Collection)

TIME FOR PLAY

H01 THE VALUE OF PLAY

Play is vital to a child's mental and physical development. It is one of his principal means of learning - through which he first masters basic skills, begins to express himself, and learns to get along with others.

Four broad types of play can be distinguished - active physical play, manipulative play, creative and imaginative play, and social play. Obviously some activities can be included in more than one category. The relative importance of different types of play varies with a child's age.

The need for play exists even in a very young baby, and persists in some form throughout childhood. Young children play most happily near the center of family activity. For older children who do not want an adult constantly at hand, it is a good idea, if possible, to have a special play area where boisterous games are permitted and toys do not always have to be tidied away. Materials for play need not be costly toys. Many simple household items make ideal playthings and have the advantage of encouraging creative and imaginative play. The possibilities for improvised playthings are endless, and as a starting point a number of suggestions are included in H03. The importance of commercially produced toys, however, should not be underestimated. Reputable manufacturers have spent a lot of time researching the developmental needs of children of different ages. A well chosen, carefully designed toy will provide a child with much more than entertainment. When buying a toy it is also important to pay careful attention to aspects of safety (see H04).

H02 TYPES OF PLAY

ACTIVE PHYSICAL PLAY

This type of play begins in the womb and continues all through childhood. Involving the larger motor muscles, it teaches control, coordination, and balance, and leads ultimately to all kinds of adventure and·sporting activities.

MANIPULATIVE PLAY

This teaches the control of the finer motor muscles, particularly those in the hands. It begins soon after birth as a baby learns to grasp, lift, and squeeze, and leads eventually to mastery of skills like feeding, dressing, drawing, and writing.

IMAGINATIVE AND CREATIVE PLAY

This type of play is especially significant as it teaches self-awareness, encourages the development of imaginative powers, and allows the safe working out of emotions such as fear and aggression. Imaginative play becomes most important when the child has mastered the basic skills that enable him to express himself.

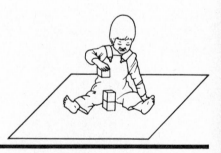

SOCIAL PLAY

This type of play is an essential part of a child's emotional development. By playing first alongside other children and later with them, a child learns about cooperation, communication, and sharing. Social play thus helps him to build satisfactory relationships with others, and eventually to take up his role in the community.

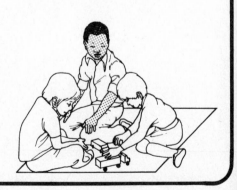

Play

H03 IMPROVISED PLAYTHINGS

Shown here are a few examples of simple household objects that can be used for stimulating play.

1 Plastic bowls and saucepans for filling and emptying.

2 Unbreakable bottles, mugs, and measuring cups for water play.

3 Saucepan lids and wood spoons for banging.

4 Empty boxes for building and model making.

5 Sealed can of stones for rattling.

6 Flour and water dough for modeling.

7 Used bobbins for building or stringing together.

8 Pencil and paper.

9 Old clothes for dressing up.

10 Scissors, glue, and scraps of fabric for collage work.

11 String for cats' cradles.

12 Thread and buttons for threading.

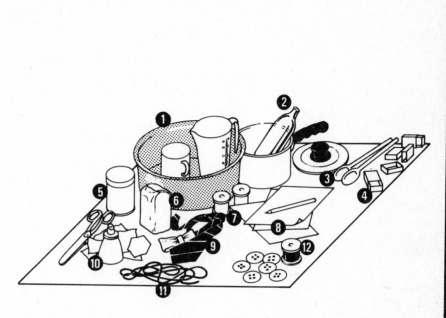

H04 SAFETY OF TOYS

Certain features may make toys unsafe for children who are too young to realize the danger. Toy hazards include the following.

1 Eyes attached with sharp wire.

2 Contents of rattle toxic, or small enough to cause choking.

3 Small wheels to pull off and cause choking or suffocation.

4 Toxic paint.

5 Splinters from rough wood surface.

6 Inflammable doll's clothes.

7 Sharp metal edges.

8 Danger of trapping fingers in clockwork mechanism.

9 Sharp edges on broken plastic toy.

10 Toxic metal parts.

11 Risk of shock from electrically operated toy.

12 Danger of trapping fingers in trigger mechanism.

13 Possibility of an explosion.

H

©DIAGRAM

THE FIRST TWO YEARS

H05 PLAY: BIRTH TO TWO

For the first two years of life, a child spends a large proportion of his waking hours at play. But this play is never aimless, nor just a means of filling in time - it is an essential and integral part of his development, and the basis on which much of his future learning will be built.

A baby's first play activities include kicking, and investigating parts of his body. He also watches, and later copies, the expressions and actions of others.

From about three months, a baby also needs stimulation in the form of simple playthings. At this stage, it is useful to offer objects of different sizes, shapes, colors, and textures, but they must first be checked for suitability and safety (see H04). A mobile suspended above the crib will amuse a young baby and provide excellent visual stimulation. Also valuable are noise-making toys such as bells or rattles, which offer the child a "reward" for his effort.

When a baby can crawl, every item in the home becomes a potential plaything for him to explore and enjoy. As his curiosity should ideally be encouraged and not construed as "naughtiness," it is wise to put away any objects that are valuable or potentially dangerous. A playpen may be useful for short periods, but should only be used if the child is happy to play there.

Even before his first birthday a child starts to benefit from being read to and told simple stories. This is vital for language development. It also gives a toddler a valuable opportunity to enjoy the undivided attention of another member of the family.

H06 TYPES OF PLAY

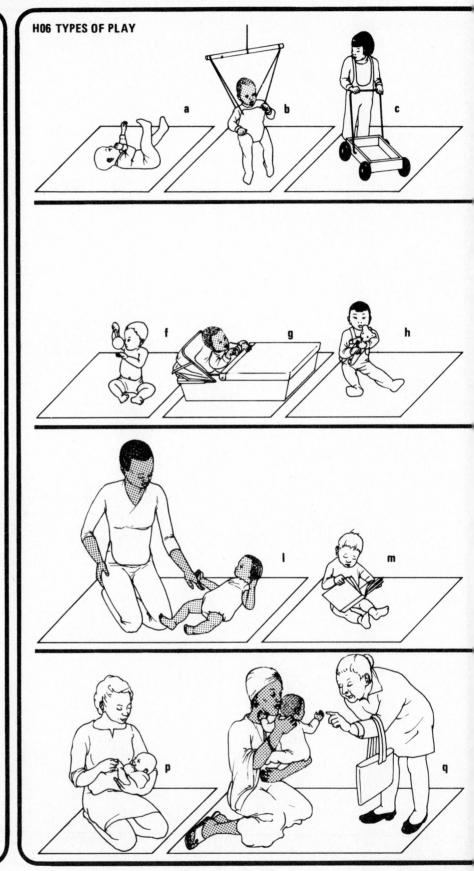

Play

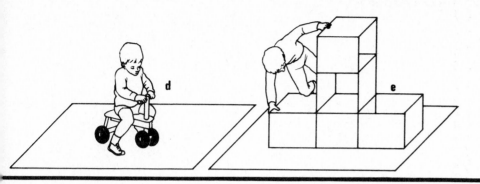

ACTIVE PHYSICAL PLAY
A baby's first form of active physical play involves kicking, reaching, and stretching (**a**). An older baby may enjoy a "bouncer" (**b**). Wheeled toys (**c** and **d**) are popular when the child can walk, and climbing activities (**e**) are useful for strengthening limbs and increasing muscular control.

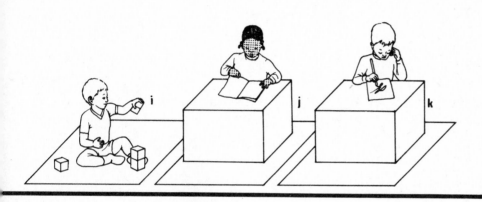

MANIPULATIVE PLAY
For most babies, clutching an adult's finger is the earliest experience of manipulative play. A rattle (**f**), beads (**g**), a squeaky toy (**h**), and blocks (**i**), encourage an older child to grasp, lift, and build, and teach fine muscle control. Turning pages (**j**) and scribbling (**k**) are useful preparation for future imaginative and creative play.

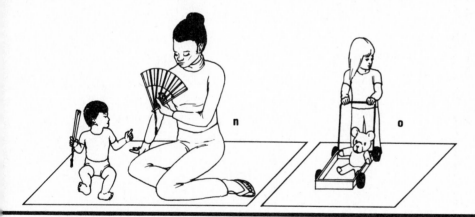

IMAGINATIVE AND CREATIVE PLAY
Among the earliest forms of imaginative play is the imitation of sounds and expressions, often copied from a parent (**l**). Picture books (**m**) and the identification and association of familiar objects (**n**), stimulate the child's imagination. Simple day-to-day events provide a basis for "acting out" situations (**o**).

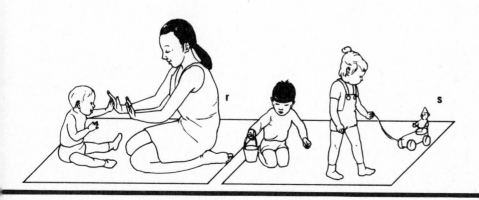

SOCIAL PLAY
A baby's first social play consists of the simple responses such as smiling that result from contact with his mother (**p**); sometimes this sociability extends to strangers (**q**). Older babies enjoy games with person-to-person contact such as pat-a-cake (**r**). By age two, most toddlers start to enjoy playing alongside others (**s**) - though not yet with them.

H07 PLAY: TWO TO FIVE

Between the ages of two and five play continues to be a vital and integral part of learning. Experiences gained at this time provide a basis from which learning in school can develop.

Active physical play increases in importance as the child devotes more of his time to outdoor activities and learns to run, jump, skip, hop, and climb.

By the end of the period, manipulative skills are much better developed and the child starts to use them in an imaginative and creative way. For example, a young child may enjoy handling a modeling material and may appreciate its feel and texture, but an older child will use it to create objects from his imagination. Playing with other children becomes important in these years, and pre-school groups may be useful in this respect.

At first, toddlers will play alongside each other, or play contentedly on the edge of a group of older children. This "parallel" play is gradually superseded by "cooperative" play in which the child actually includes others in his activities.

Toys and books remain extremely important as tools of learning. Natural materials such as sand, water, and even mud, make ideal playthings for a young child. Manufactured toys should be fairly simple; elaborate toys that make little call on the imagination have very little value.

Powers of concentration are limited even in a five-year-old, and regular changes of activity are needed. To help a child over this, a few toys - perhaps birthday or Christmas gifts - can be kept on one side for giving as "surprises" when the child is ill or disappointed.

H08 TYPES OF PLAY

Play

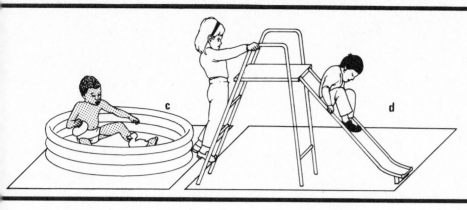

ACTIVE PHYSICAL PLAY
From two to five active play is very important. A tricycle (**a**) or scooter (**b**) are favorite toys, and a wading pool (**c**) may be popular (though supervision is vital). Larger pieces of equipment such as a slide (**d**) are usually found in playgrounds and may be bought or borrowed for garden use.

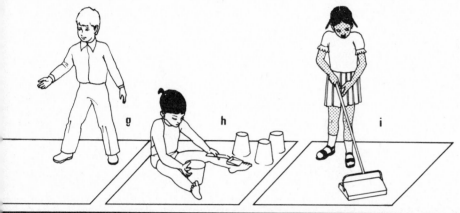

MANIPULATIVE PLAY
At this stage activities that challenge a child's increasing dexterity such as building (**e**), jigsaws (**f**), and throwing and catching (**g**) are very popular. Water and sand play (**h**) are fun and help teach basic scientific principles. Using "household equipment" (**i**) increases a child's manipulative skills and exercises the imagination.

IMAGINATIVE AND CREATIVE PLAY
A child starts to get the most out of this kind of play when he has mastered basic manipulative skills. Modeling (**j**) and drawing (**k**) are two important expressions of creativity, and dressing up (**l**) can add an extra dimension to dramatic play. Some children may now begin to appreciate a musical instrument as a means of self-expression (**m**).

SOCIAL PLAY
The parallel play of infancy is giving way to cooperative play. From the age of about four, simple board and card games (**n** and **o**) are popular, and an older child may be happy to join a younger child in his play (**p**). Elaborate group activities such as "tea parties" (**q**) have a valuable social function as well as being a major form of imaginative play.

H09 PLAY: FIVE TO TWELVE

After the age of five the role of
playthings as instruments of
learning gradually becomes less
important. Play for school-age
children is more significant as a
means of recreation, balancing
the educational and developmental
demands of school. Another change
at this time is the development of
long-term hobbies and interests
(G29) from simpler play activities.
Active physical play continues in
a variety of forms, ranging from
simple outdoor pursuits like tree-
climbing to organized sporting
activities that appeal to a child's
growing competitive spirit.

A vast selection of "playthings" is
available for active play in this
period, but in general a child's
natural inventiveness will allow
him to play contentedly for some
time without special equipment.
Manipulative skills develop
considerably in these years, and
creative pastimes assume greater
importance. Craft sets and
construction kits are popular and
may help establish a lifelong
interest in a subject.

An expensive manufactured set,
however, is not always essential:
paper, card, wood, empty
containers, glue, and paint are
just a few of the items that can be
used for model making, collage,
and similar crafts.

Imaginative and creative play is
at its most significant at this
period and helps the process of
concept learning (D23-25).
Group activities are especially
valuable from the age of about
seven. As well as being a lot of
fun, being a member of a group
or belonging to a club or society
may help a child come to terms
with some of the complexities of
human relationships.

H10 TYPES OF PLAY

Play

ACTIVE PHYSICAL PLAY

Outdoor pursuits such as tree climbing (**a**) or simple games like hopscotch (**b**) are popular throughout this period. A variety of equipment is available for active play, ranging from skipping ropes (**c**) and hoops (**d**) to scooters (**e**), bicycles, roller skates, and skate boards (**f**).

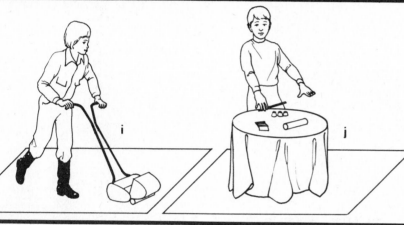

MANIPULATIVE PLAY

A child's rapidly developing manipulative skills may be applied to an almost endless range of activities in this period. Model making (**g**), embroidery (**h**), and gardening (**i**) are examples of popular pastimes. Particular favorites among "playthings" appropriate for this age group are science and magic sets (**j**).

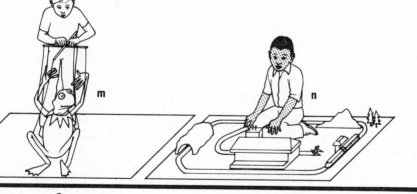

IMAGINATIVE PLAY

Between the ages of five and 12, creative art and craft activities and literary pursuits (**k**) have widespread appeal. In this age group, many children may also enjoy dramatic play through the medium of "acting out" games (**l**) or with puppets (**m**). Elaborate equipment such as a scale version of trains (**n**) can also be a useful basis for imaginative play.

SOCIAL PLAY

After starting school a child becomes increasingly involved with others and starts to enjoy sharing his favorite activities and pastimes. More complex card games (**o**) and board games (**p**) encourage shared play, but most children seem automatically to seek each other out for group activities like a walk, a bike ride, or a ball game (**q**).

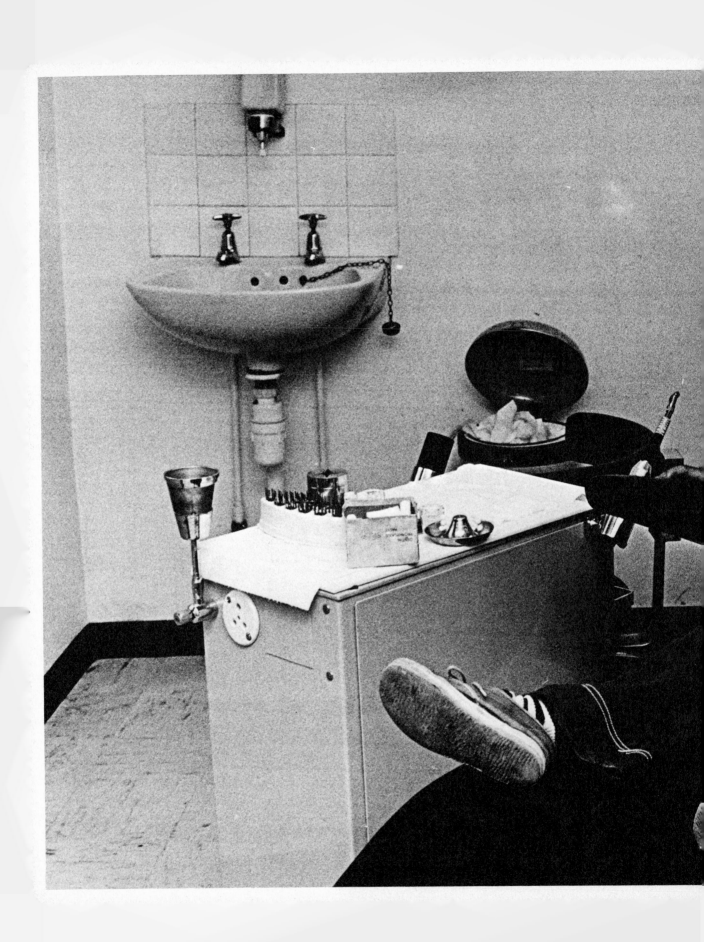

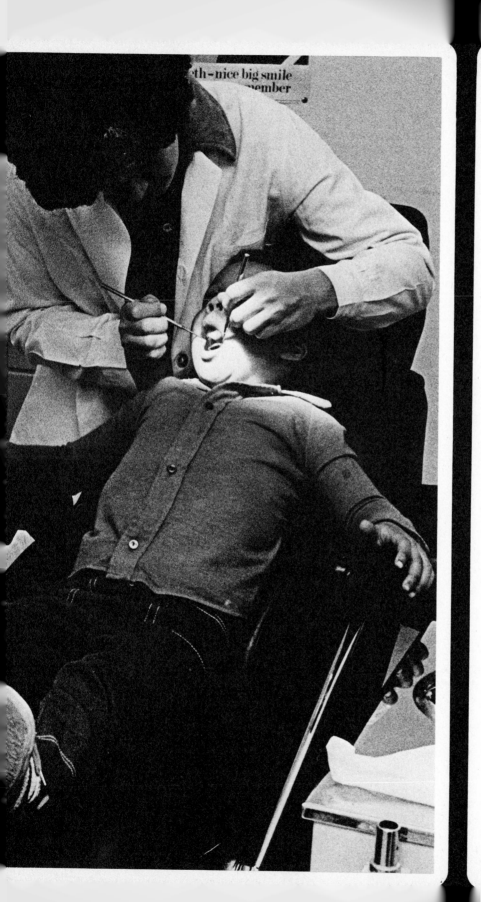

Parts of the body

The body of a child is an extremely complex and fascinating machine.

Left: An appointment with the dentist (Photo Richard and Sally Greenhill)

BONES AND JOINTS

J01 THE SKELETON

The skeleton gives structure to the body and affords protection to delicate internal organs. The human skeleton develops gradually from connective tissues that become first cartilage and then bone. In fact, at birth, some "bones" are still cartilage, and the process does not complete itself until about age 25. At the same time, many bones fuse together, so that the 330 in a baby's skeleton become 206 bones in an adult. Proportions also change. A newborn baby has a short neck, high shoulders, and a round chest. Between ages three and 10 the shoulders lower, the neck lengthens, and the chest broadens and flattens. (Also see DO3.) Posture changes too: bow legs and knock knees, for example, are common to age five.

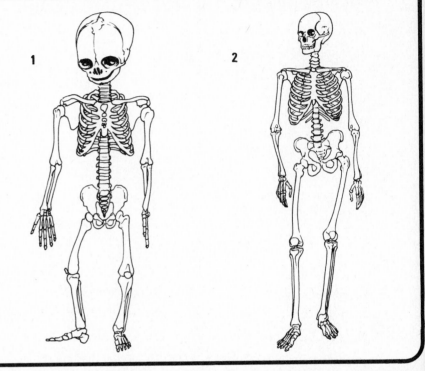

Skeletal differences between a newborn male (**1**) and an adult male (**2**)

J04 FONTANELS

The fontanels are softer areas of cartilage between the bones of a baby's skull. They make birth easier by allowing the head to distort. The largest fontanel - the "soft spot" - is on the top of the head toward the front. The fontanels gradually disappear as the skull bones fuse together. This process is usually completed by the age of 18 to 26 months.

Diagrammatic representation of a baby's fontanels - soft areas of the skull

J05 BONE GROWTH

A bone is first formed by the calcification of cartilage, and grows in the same way. Stages in the development of a bone are:
1 cartilage model;
2 formation of a small area of calcified cartilage (bone);
3 growth of calcified area as blood vessels bring in new bone cells;
4 formation of new bone is concentrated in growth areas at each end of the bone;
5 fusion of growth areas with the bone itself to form the mature bone.

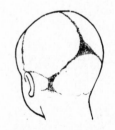

- ▨ Cartilage
- ☐ Bone
- ⤳ Blood vessels

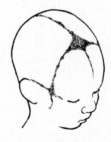

1   2   3   4   5

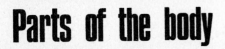

Parts of the body

J02 BONES

Bones may be long, short, flat, or irregular. All bones have a hard outer casing, and a porous honeycomb interior where minerals are stored. Many bones also have a growth area at one or both ends (see JO5), and a hollow center that contains marrow where blood cells are made.

Cross section of a bone

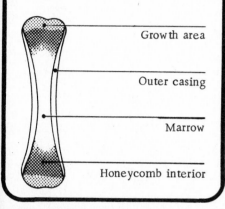

- Growth area
- Outer casing
- Marrow
- Honeycomb interior

J03 JOINTS

Fully movable joints consist of a layer of cartilage around each bone end, and a joint capsule with a lining membrane that secretes lubricating fluid.
Different types include:
a hinge (eg elbow);
b pivot (eg neck);
c ball and socket (eg shoulder).

Cross section of a joint

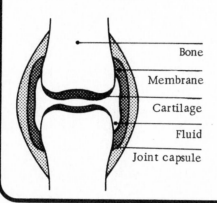

- Bone
- Membrane
- Cartilage
- Fluid
- Joint capsule

Types of joint

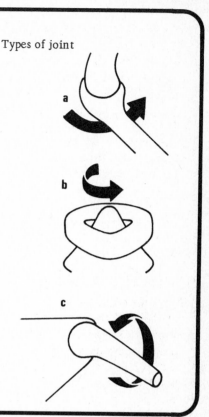

J06 HIP DISLOCATION

Congenital hip dislocation is found in four to five live births per 1000, and is four times more common in girls than boys. In this condition the thigh bone is out of its hip socket (usually only one thigh is dislocated). It is usually checked for soon after birth, and can then be corrected by fitting a special splint. Surgery may be necessary if discovery is delayed.

Normal hip joint   Congenital dislocation

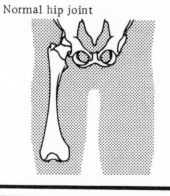

J07 CLUB FOOT

This condition occurs in about one in 1000 live births, and one or both feet may be affected.
The foot is twisted out of position, with malformation of bones and abnormal stretching or shortening of muscles and tendons.
The condition is discovered at a post-birth check, and treatment must be started at once.
Mild cases can be cured by manipulating the foot into its correct position, putting it in plaster for about six months, and then possibly into a splint.
Special shoes may have to be worn for a time, and exercises will be needed to strengthen weak muscles and tendons.
More severe cases require surgery to correct the condition.

Types of club foot

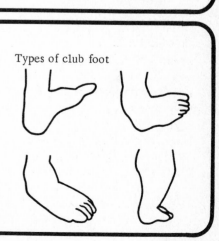

TEETH 1

J08 TEETH

The root of a tooth is embedded in the jaw. The part of the tooth projecting from the jaw is called the crown. Where the root and crown meet is called the neck. Each tooth is made up of enamel, dentine, pulp, and cementum. Enamel is the hardest tissue in the body, and protects the tooth's sensitive crown. Dentine is a hard, slightly elastic, honeycomb material that forms the bulk of the tooth under the enamel. It is sensitive to heat and chemicals. Pulp is the soft tissue inside the dentine, and contains nerves and blood vessels that enter the root of the tooth by a small canal. A thin layer of cementum covers the root, protecting the underlying dentine. It also helps attach fibers from the gum to the tooth.

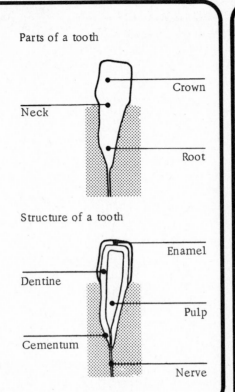

Parts of a tooth

Crown
Neck
Root

Structure of a tooth

Enamel
Dentine
Pulp
Cementum
Nerve

J09 TYPES OF TOOTH

There are three basic types.
a Incisors are sharp, chisel-like teeth at the front of the mouth, used for cutting food.
b Canines are pointed teeth at the corners of the mouth, used for tearing and gripping food.
c Molars and premolars are square back teeth with rounded projections ("cusps") on top, used for grinding and slicing food.

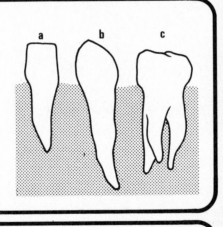

a   b   c

J10 TEETHING

Most babies experience some discomfort when teething. In some, the only evidence of an erupting tooth is an inflamed gum. But in others, the gum may become painfully swollen, causing extreme irritability and crying. Something to bite on - a teething ring, a piece of hard food, or even the fingers - can relieve minor discomfort. In severe cases the doctor may prescribe a painkiller, but these must be used with extreme caution.

Teething has often been linked incorrectly with illness. If any symptoms do occur (such as loss of appetite or diarrhea) they should be investigated for their real cause and not dismissed as an inevitable part of the teething process.

J11 PRIMARY TEETH

When a baby is born, the primary or "milk" teeth are already formed except for their roots. But they are still hidden in the jaw, and the time of their appearance varies from child to child. A few babies have one or more teeth showing at birth, but first teething more commonly begins some time between three and 12 months of age.

The full primary set is made up of 20 teeth: eight incisors, four canines, and eight molars.

The order in which they appear - with typical ages for the appearance of the different teeth - is shown here in a series of diagrams.

6-8 months: lower central incisors

7-9 months: upper central incisors

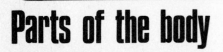
Parts of the body

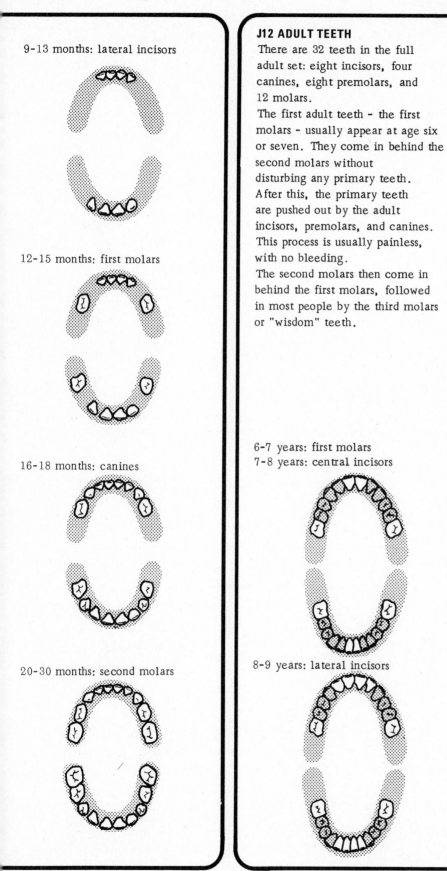

9-13 months: lateral incisors

12-15 months: first molars

16-18 months: canines

20-30 months: second molars

J12 ADULT TEETH

There are 32 teeth in the full adult set: eight incisors, four canines, eight premolars, and 12 molars.

The first adult teeth - the first molars - usually appear at age six or seven. They come in behind the second molars without disturbing any primary teeth. After this, the primary teeth are pushed out by the adult incisors, premolars, and canines. This process is usually painless, with no bleeding.

The second molars then come in behind the first molars, followed in most people by the third molars or "wisdom" teeth.

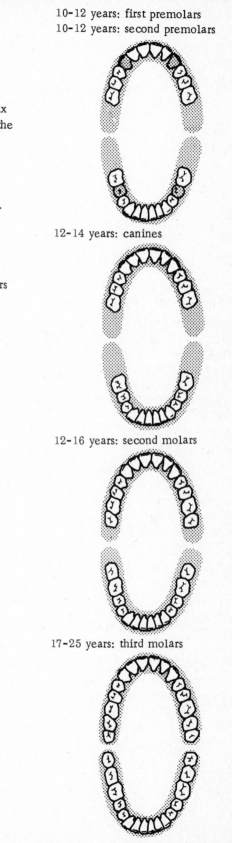

6-7 years: first molars
7-8 years: central incisors

8-9 years: lateral incisors

10-12 years: first premolars
10-12 years: second premolars

12-14 years: canines

12-16 years: second molars

17-25 years: third molars

TEETH 2

J13 CARE OF THE TEETH

BEFORE BIRTH

a) Calcium and fluoride are important for the proper formation of the baby's teeth. The mother should eat plenty of milk and cheese, and fluoride tablets can be used if the local water is not fluoridated.

b) Some drugs should be avoided; tetracycline antibiotics, for example, if taken in pregnancy, may discolor and even weaken the enamel of the unborn baby's teeth.

THE CHILD'S DIET

a) Milk and cheese are still vital, to form strong adult teeth.

b) A good general diet (see F40) will provide trace minerals needed by the teeth. Also, by keeping the body healthy, it will help the mouth to fight bacteria.

c) Food should not be too soft. Food that needs chewing massages the gums, cleans out food particles from between the teeth, and stimulates the flow of saliva.

d) Most important, sugars and carbohydrates should be limited to mealtimes: there is more saliva to wash them out of the mouth, and the teeth can be cleaned immediately after. Sweet snacks are fatal to dental health. A baby should never be given a pacifier (dummy) dipped in honey, fruit syrup, etc.

CLEANING THE TEETH

Teeth should be cleaned after every meal, and also last thing at night. When the first few teeth appear, they can be wiped with a damp cloth. Later, clean the child's teeth for him with a recommended children's toothbrush and plain water. From about two years old, many children enjoy cleaning their own teeth with toothpaste. Encourage the child to do so, but give his teeth a final brushing until he becomes more practiced. (See J14 for brushing techniques.) Dental floss is good for cleaning between the teeth, and is particularly useful for older children with temporarily overcrowded teeth.

GOING TO THE DENTIST

There should be regular dental checks every six months, starting at about two years. Introduce the child to the idea gradually, and explain what the dentist will do. Make the first visit brief, and do not worry if the child will not even open his mouth. Be particularly careful not to give the impression that a visit to the dentist is something to fear.

J14 BRUSHING THE TEETH

A child needs to be shown how to use a toothbrush properly. "Scrubbing" actions should not be used: a side-to-side action will leave food in gaps between the teeth, while scrubbing up and down can damage gums.

Ideas on toothbrushing vary, but four commonly recommended actions are illustrated here: repeated downward strokes for the upper teeth (**a**); upward strokes for the bottom teeth (**b**); a back-and-forth action for the tops of the molars (**c**); and an up-and-down action for the rear surface of the front teeth (**d**).

Electric toothbrushes are a good alternative: they clean the teeth effectively, massage the gums, and are often popular with children.

WRONG: Scrubbing side to side

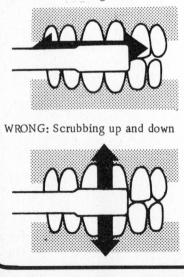

WRONG: Scrubbing up and down

RECOMMENDED TECHNIQUES

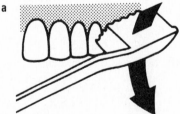

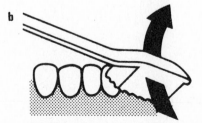

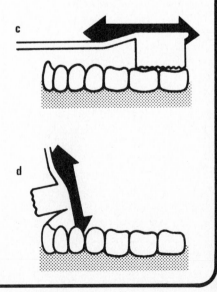

Parts of the body

J15 TOOTH DECAY

This occurs because bacteria in the mouth change carbohydrates in the food into acids that attack the tooth enamel (**a**). Gradually the enamel is broken down and bacteria invade the dentine, forming a cavity. The pulp reacts by forming secondary dentine to wall off the bacteria, but without treatment it becomes inflamed and painful (toothache). Finally the infection may pass down the root (**b**) and cause an "abscess" - a painful collection of pus under pressure.

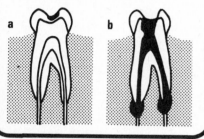

J16 GUM DISORDERS

Gum disorders are often due to overconsumption of soft food, which does not stimulate and harden the gums. The gums recede from the teeth (**a**), tooth sockets enlarge, securing fibers are destroyed, and teeth loosen. There may be pain from the exposed dentine, and, later, from abscesses. But often the process is painless until it is too late. Many teeth are lost in this way. In other cases, food deposits irritate and infect the gums (**b**), causing inflammation and bleeding.

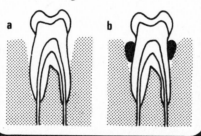

J17 ORTHODONTIC PROBLEMS

These involve bad tooth position or formation, causing problems in eating, swallowing, speaking, breathing, or appearance. The jaws may not meet in a good "bite" (for example, if one jaw projects as shown). Individual teeth may not grind together or overlap as they should. Teeth may protrude or show ugly gaps. Extra, or missing, primary teeth may cause displacement in the adult set (which is why premature loss of a primary tooth requires careful dental attention).

Protruding lower jaw

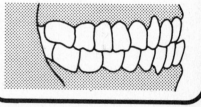

J18 DENTAL TREATMENT

FILLING CAVITIES
All the decay must be drilled out, or it will spread beneath the filling. High speed drills and injected anesthetics are now usual. Treatment of very young children is difficult, however, and may make extraction necessary.

EXTRACTION
This is needed if teeth are badly overcrowded, irretrievably decayed, or broken beyond repair. Forceps are used to work the tooth loose; anesthetic makes this painless (general anesthetic is usual for young children).

TREATMENT OF GUM DISORDERS
Long-term treatment aims to improve oral hygiene, diet, and general health. Acute conditions may need pus drainage, antiseptic mouthwashes, antibiotics, tooth extraction, and even surgery.

ORTHODONTIC TREATMENT
This may include: exercises for the jaw muscles or for mouth movement; extraction of overcrowded teeth; and surgery to recontour the jaws. But most common are "braces," which put constant pressure on certain teeth so that they shift position.

REPAIR AND REPLACEMENT
Childhood accidents often damage teeth. A dentist should be consulted immediately. Mild cracks can be smoothed over; more serious ones covered until the child nears adulthood, when a permanent jacket can be fitted. Broken teeth may need replacing with a solid crown on the existing root, or with an entire false tooth, perhaps on a bridge. Teeth knocked out whole can sometimes be replanted in the jaw. Loosened teeth can be splinted to neighboring ones until they become naturally secure again.

Crown

Bridge

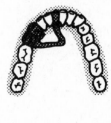

J

SKIN

J19 SKIN STRUCTURE

Skin consists of two distinct layers. The outer layer (epidermis) is made of dead, flattened cells, bound together by proteins to form a tough, flexible, waterproof surface. It is constantly worn away and replaced from below. The lower layer (dermis) contains nerves, blood vessels, and fat deposits; hair roots ("follicles") and their erector muscles; and various glands. The sweat glands release sweat to the surface; the sebaceous glands secrete a grease that helps keep the skin supple.

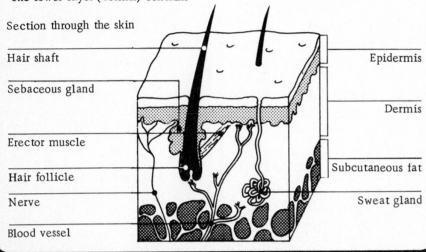

Section through the skin

Hair shaft

Sebaceous gland

Erector muscle

Hair follicle

Nerve

Blood vessel

Epidermis

Dermis

Subcutaneous fat

Sweat gland

J20 SKIN FUNCTIONS

a) The skin protects delicate internal organs from physical damage, harmful sun rays, and bacterial infection.

b) It acts as a sensory organ, being more richly supplied with nerve endings than any other part of the body. Sensations of touch, pain, heat, and cold from the skin give a continuous flow of information about the surroundings.

c) The skin helps regulate body temperature: 85% of body heat loss is through the skin. Blood vessels near the surface dilate or contract, so that more or less blood heat is lost according to need.

d) Perspiration also helps control body heat, as well as getting rid of waste matter.

e) Finally, the skin plays a part in making vitamin D and also certain antibodies.

J21 SKIN COLOR

A person's skin color is due partly to color pigments found in the skin cells, and partly to the presence of tiny blood vessels near the surface of the skin.

Most important of the pigments that color the skin is melanin - a brown pigment present in skin cells known as melanoblasts.

The melanoblasts of dark-skinned people contain more melanin granules than those of people with fairer skins. The concentration of melanin in an individual's skin is largely determined by heredity, but can be considerably modified by exposure to sunlight.

There are a few individuals whose bodies contain no melanin pigment at all. Known as albinos, such people have white hair, light-colored eyes, and a pale skin tinted pink by blood vessels.

J22 BIRTHMARKS

Most marks on the skin at birth are just temporary. But a few can be troublesome.

a) "Strawberry marks": red, slightly raised, spongy areas of skin. Usually tiny at first, they often enlarge for a time, then may disappear without treatment. If one persists, it may be shrunk by injections or removed surgically.

b) "Port wine stains": dark red, flat areas of skin, often on the neck and face. Various treatments can now make these less noticeable, and special cosmetics help to conceal them effectively.

c) Vitiligo: a condition in which an area of skin always stays white. It can be concealed but not treated.

d) "Liver spots": dark patches like large freckles, caused by concentrations of the brown pigment, melanin.

J23 SKIN CARE

Spots, peeling, and blotchiness are common in new babies, and usually soon pass (see B18). But the condition of the skin can be helped in various ways.

a) Always wash and dry well in the creases of skin: under the armpits, behind the ears, in the groin, and in folds of fat at the neck and thighs.

b) Use lotion on any redness that does develop.

c) Avoid tight clothing which can cause soreness at the groin, armpits, and neck.

d) Follow the routines recommended in E14 and E27.

e) If a child has a dry skin, keep his face and hands covered against wind and cold, and use baby lotion or oil to clean the face, rather than soap and water.

Parts of the body

HAIR AND NAILS

J24 HAIR STRUCTURE

Every hair in the body grows from its own individual follicle in the skin, and each follicle has its own sebaceous (oil) gland and a tiny erector muscle. Capillaries supply nutrients from the bloodstream. A cross section through the shaft of a single hair reveals a hollow core (medulla), surrounded by an outer cortex. This in turn is covered by the cuticle - a thin coating of horny cells containing the binding protein "keratin."

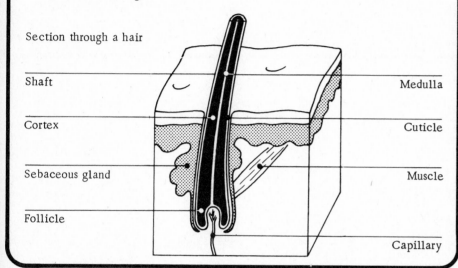

Section through a hair

Shaft

Cortex

Sebaceous gland

Follicle

Medulla

Cuticle

Muscle

Capillary

J25 HAIR TYPE

Hair color and curliness are decided by heredity (see A06). Pigment cells in the follicle give a hair its color, while curliness depends on the cross section shape of the follicle.

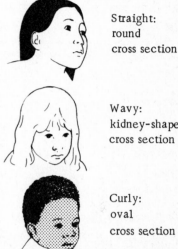

Straight:
round
cross section

Wavy:
kidney-shaped
cross section

Curly:
oval
cross section

J26 HAIR DEVELOPMENT

Hair follicles form gradually between the second and fifth months of fetal development. The first hair to be produced is lanugo: fine, soft hair with no pigment that covers many parts of the body. It usually disappears by the seventh or eighth month of pregnancy, but is sometimes still present in full-term babies. A second type of hair then develops. Known as vellus, this hair includes the baby's first crop of head hair. It is fine and soft, rarely over 1in (2.5cm) long, and may or may not be pigmented. Pigmentation may differ from a child's eventual hair coloring. Vellus is followed on the head and elsewhere by coarser, longer-growing, pigmented hair. Often the change is quite gradual, as the child's hair slowly coarsens and changes color.

J27 HAIR GROWTH

Hair on the scalp grows by about ½in (1.25cm) per month. (So the end of a hair measuring 18in (45cm) is about three years old. The root is the only live part of a hair: it grows and pushes the dead shaft out above the skin. Hair growth is cyclical, with a growth phase followed by a rest phase in which the hair is gradually loosened. The loosened hair is then pushed out by a new hair growing in its place. In this way, up to 100 hairs are lost each day from a normal head of hair. The thickness of growth of a head of hair depends on the number of hair follicles. The follicles are established before birth and no new ones are formed later in life. The thickness of individual hairs is also decided by hereditary factors.

J28 NAILS

Toe and finger nails are present at birth. Each consists of a small plate of dead cells. The horny visible part is made of keratin, a substance found in skin and hair. The nail grows from a bed, or matrix, which is protected by a fold of skin at the base. The white crescent of the nail (or "lunula") is the visible part of the nail bed.

Section through fingertip

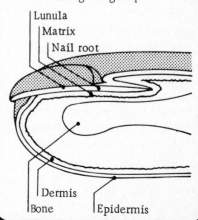

Lunula

Matrix

Nail root

Dermis

Bone

Epidermis

J

J29 EXTERIOR OF THE EYES

The eyebrows (**a**) prevent moisture running down into the eyes. The eyelids (**b**) protect the eyes when closed. Eyelashes (**c**) keep out foreign bodies, and trigger off blinking if touched. The eyeballs show as black in the center (**d**), with a colored ring (**e**) around this, and white (**f**) at the edges.

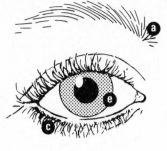
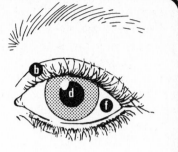

J31 THE EYEBALL

The conjunctiva (**a**) is the membrane covering the front of the eyeball and the inside of the eyelids. The cornea (**b**) is the clear part of the eyeball, which lets in the light. The iris (**c**) controls the amount of light entering the eye: by contracting, it reduces the size of the hole in front of the lens, or "pupil" (**d**). The lens itself (**e**) is contained in a fibrous capsule. The suspensory ligaments (**f**) hold it in place, and the muscles of the ciliary body (**g**) control its shape. Behind the lens is the vitreous body (**h**) - a transparent jelly-like substance that fills out the eyeball, giving it its shape. The retina (**i**) is a thin layer of light-sensitive cells lining much of the eyeball. The optic nerve (**j**) is a direct connection to the brain.

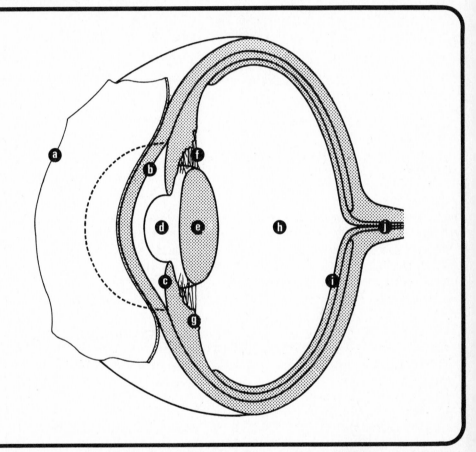

J33 HOW THE EYES COMBINE

The nerves from the left side of the two retinas travel to one side of the brain, those from the right sides to the other side of the brain. So the images received in the two visual centers (at the rear of the cerebral hemispheres) are composite images from both eyes, mixed 50:50.

Nevertheless, each eye sees a slightly different view of the same object. The farther away the object, the less is the discrepancy between the two views. This, plus the amount of tension needed to focus and the amount of blurring, is the basis on which distances are judged.

a Right eye image
b Left eye image
c Composite image

Parts of the body

J30 TEARS

The lacrimal glands (**a**) produce a watery, salty fluid that cleans and lubricates the front of the eye. The lacrimal ducts (**b**) drain it away into the lacrimal sacs (**c**). Tears occur when an irritant or emotion causes fluid to be produced more quickly than it can drain away.

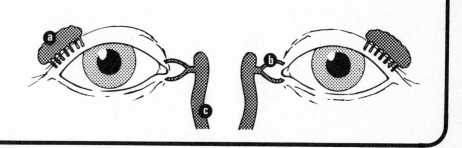

J32 SIGHT

Objects are seen by the light they reflect. When the rays of light from an object enter the eye, they are bent ("refracted") by the cornea and lens. This focuses an upside-down image of the object onto the retina.

The diagrams show how the shape of the lens is changed by muscular action to focus rays from objects at different distances.

The effect of the light on the cells of the retina triggers off impulses that travel down the optic nerve to the visual center in the brain. Here the impulses are interpreted, and "seen" as colors and shapes the right way up. The ability to interpret these impulses has to be learned. It takes time for a baby to learn to use his eyes, and to correlate present with past information to bring about recognition.

Focusing rays from a far object: eye muscles stretch the lens to refract the rays only slightly.

Focusing rays from a near object: the eye muscles relax and the lens bulges to give greater refraction.

J34 COLOR VISION

There are two types of light-sensitive cell in the retina: "rod" shapes and "cone" shapes. Only the cones give color vision, and they need fairly high intensity light to function. (The rods, which can work in low light, only give monochrome vision.)
The actual process of color vision is not known, but it is thought that there are three different classes of cone, each containing a different pigment. Each pigment would be sensitive to a different color: blue, green, or red. Other colors would be combinations of these. Light of the relevant color probably breaks down the pigment for a fraction of a second, bleaching the cone; and this triggers off a nerve impulse to the brain.

a Cross section of the retina
  ⁘ Cones ⁛ Rods
b Cone
c Rod

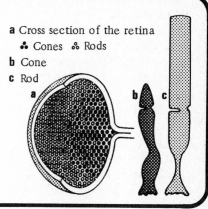

J35 FARSIGHT

This is by far the most common vision deficiency. A person who is "farsighted" can see distant objects clearly, but is unable to bring near objects into focus. Farsightedness is due either to the eyeball being too short, or to the eye's refractive power (ability to bend light rays, J32) being too weak. In each case the effect is the same: rays from near objects would theoretically be in focus behind the retina (**a**) instead of on it. As a result, a blurred image is transmitted from the retina to the brain.

Convex correction lenses are used to bring near objects into focus. They work by bending the light rays in slightly (**b**). Less refraction is then demanded of the eye itself, and the rays can be focused farther forward, on the retina.

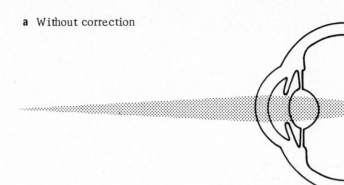

a Without correction

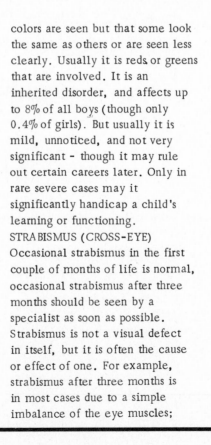

b Correction by convex lens

J37 VISUAL DEFICIENCIES

A child's eyes should be tested for visual ability at about $2\frac{1}{2}$ years - or earlier if any deficiency is suspected. Tests can be repeated at yearly intervals. Apart from farsight and nearsight (see J35 and J36) the most common types of deficiency are astigmatism and color vision deficiency.

ASTIGMATISM
In this condition, the cornea is slightly out of shape. The effect is that, when one line is focused on clearly, any line at right angles to it seems blurred. Spectacles are necessary: a lens with a similar distortion is set at right angles to the distortion in the cornea. (If nearsight or farsight is also a problem, a compound lens can deal with both deficiencies.)

COLOR VISION DEFICIENCY
Also called "color blindness," this does not usually mean that no colors are seen but that some look the same as others or are seen less clearly. Usually it is reds or greens that are involved. It is an inherited disorder, and affects up to 8% of all boys (though only 0.4% of girls). But usually it is mild, unnoticed, and not very significant - though it may rule out certain careers later. Only in rare severe cases may it significantly handicap a child's learning or functioning.

STRABISMUS (CROSS-EYE)
Occasional strabismus in the first couple of months of life is normal, occasional strabismus after three months should be seen by a specialist as soon as possible. Strabismus is not a visual defect in itself, but it is often the cause or effect of one. For example, strabismus after three months is in most cases due to a simple imbalance of the eye muscles; but the result can be that the brain constantly receives two images, and learns to ignore one, so that one eye becomes effectively "blind." In other cases (usually at three or four years), strabismus is due to nearsight, farsight, or astigmatism.

BLINDNESS
Most blind children are blind from birth. German measles during the mother's pregnancy is the usual cause. The defect may be realized when a baby does not begin by the normal age to follow moving objects with his eyes or to recognize his mother before she speaks to him. Blindness later in childhood may be due to injury or to such infections as meningitis or encephalitis. Whatever the cause, "blindness" is seldom total but it can only rarely be cured. (For the special care of blind children see L06).

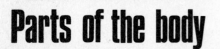

Parts of the body

J36 NEARSIGHT

A person who is "nearsighted" can see near objects clearly, but is unable to bring distant objects properly into focus.

This deficiency is due to the eyeball being too long, or to the eye's refractive power being too strong (for example, if the lens is too thick).

In each case the effect is the same: rays from distant objects need less refraction than rays from near objects (see J32), and are focused in front of the retina (a) instead of on it. As a result a blurred image is transmitted to the brain.

Concave correction lenses are used to bring distant objects into focus. They work by bending the light rays out slightly (b). More refraction is then demanded of the eye itself, and the rays are focused farther back, on the retina.

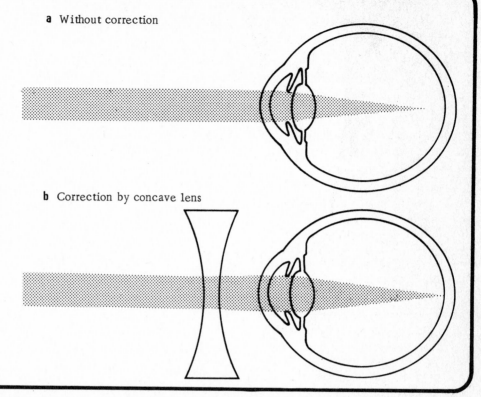

a Without correction

b Correction by concave lens

J38 EYE DISORDERS

INJURIES AND FOREIGN BODIES
For first aid, see N10 (black eye) and N24 (foreign body or chemical in the eye).

Any penetrating injury on or near the eye should receive medical attention as soon as possible.

STYES
A stye is a small boil on the eyelid, due to an infection in the follicle of an eyelash. The infection can be spread by rubbing the stye with the hands, or by way of a washcloth or towel. Home treatment involves:

1 applying lint or cotton soaked in hot water to the stye; and/or

2 using tweezers to pull out the eyelash at the stye's center, so that the pus can drain away.

STICKY EYE
In the first days of life this is usually due to debris entering the eye at birth. Hospitals give routine treatment for this. If at home, use cotton swabs, wiping gently outward from the inside corner of the eye. Later on, a sticky eye is usually due to infection.

PERSISTENT WATERING
Some babies have perpetually watering eyes, due to blockage or late development of the ducts that should carry away tear fluid. The ducts eventually open of their own accord, but in the meantime the eyes are liable to infection. Frequent swabbing with boiled water may help prevent this.

CONJUNCTIVITIS
This is inflammation of the conjunctiva (see J31), due to infection. The eye may look pink (though a pink eye may just be due to dust in the eye); or there may be a sticky yellow discharge. Proper medical treatment (usually with antibiotics) is needed.

1 Treating a stye: applying cotton soaked in hot water

2 Treating a stye: removing the eyelash at the stye's center

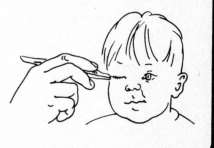

EARS

J39 EAR STRUCTURE

The ear is in three parts: the outer ear, middle ear, and inner ear. The outer ear includes the external flap of cartilage, or "pinna" (**a**), and the ear canal (**b**).

The middle ear includes the eardrum (**c**); three small bones called the ossicles (**d**), and known individually as the hammer ("malleus"), anvil ("incus"), and stirrup ("stapes"); and the eustachian tube (**e**), which links the middle ear and the back of the throat, keeping air pressure in the middle ear equal to that outside.

The inner ear includes the oval window (**f**); the organ of balance (**g**), the cochlea (**h**) - a spiral filled with fluid and containing the "organ of corti"; and the round window (**i**).

The auditory nerve (**j**) passes from the organ of corti to the brain.

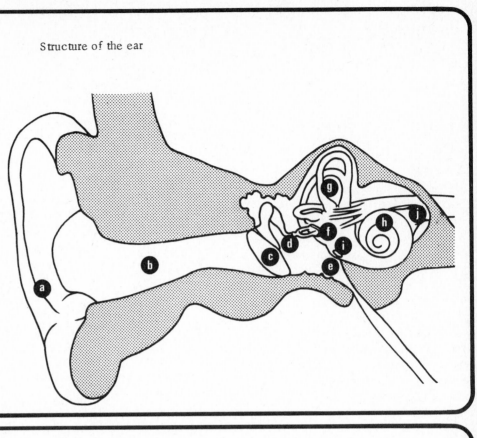

Structure of the ear

J40 HEARING MECHANISM

THE OUTER EAR Sound waves are collected by the ear flap and funneled into the ear canal (**1**).

THE MIDDLE EAR The eardrum (**2**) vibrates in time with the sound waves. This vibration is passed on along the three ossicles (**3**) to the oval window (**4**). The lever action of the ossicles increases the strength of vibration, so it can be passed to the fluid of the inner ear.

THE INNER EAR The vibration of the oval window makes the fluid in the cochlea (**5**) vibrate. The pressure changes in the fluid are picked up by special cells in the organ of corti (**6**). This organ converts the vibrations to nerve impulses, which pass along the auditory nerve (**7**) to the brain (J41). Meanwhile, the vibrations pass on through the cochlea and back to the round window (**8**), where they are lost in the air of the middle ear and eustachian tube (**9**).

The hearing mechanism

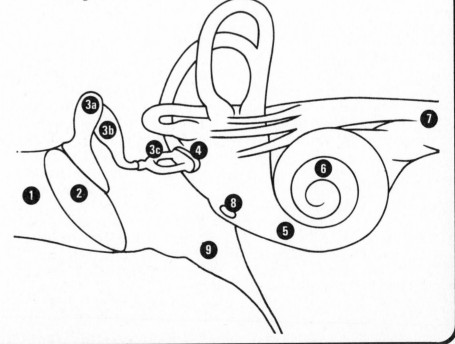

Parts of the body

J41 RECEIVING SOUNDS

The auditory nerves (**a**) transmit impulses from the ears (J40) to the brain, where they are interpreted as sounds. Auditory crossovers (**b**) in the brain stem allow signals from each ear to reach both of the auditory centers (**c**). On their way to the auditory centers impulses pass through relay centers (**d**), which process them and cut out unwanted or very loud sounds.

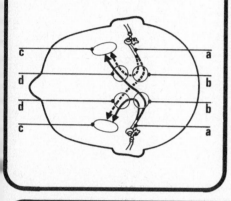

J42 BALANCE

The organ of balance is in the inner ear next to the cochlea. It consists of three U-shaped tubes ("semicircular canals"), at right angles to each other. They are filled with fluid, which is set in motion when the person moves. Hairs at the base of each canal sense this movement and send messages to the brain, which are interpreted and used to maintain the person's balance.

The organ also contains two other structures, the saccule and the utricule. These have specialized cells which are sensitive to gravity, and so keep a check on the body's position.

Balance mechanism
a Canal (back-and-forward movement)
b Canal (side-to-side movement)
c Canal (up-and-down movement)
d Saccule
e Utricule

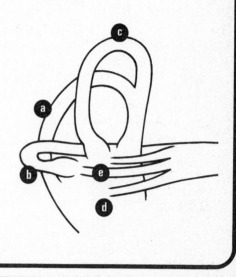

J43 EAR DISORDERS

Ear disorders are mainly due to infection, and are fairly common in children. Nevertheless, if a child has any ear discharge, earache, deafness, giddiness, or ringing in the ears, contact a doctor without delay.

OUTER-EAR INFECTION
Frequent causes of infection and inflammation of the outer ear are physical damage, foreign bodies in the ear, infection picked up in swimming pools, spread of inflammation from the middle ear, and scratching the ear with unclean fingers after visiting the toilet. Symptoms include itching, redness in the canal, and often pain and a discharge, with temporary deafness if the discharge blocks the canal.

Wipe away any surplus discharge, and see a doctor. Do not wash out the ear. You should never try to clean inside a child's ear canal in any case (only wipe wax from the entrance); and water in the ear, though not normally significant, may help spread infection.

MIDDLE-EAR INFECTION
Infection here can cause fever, vomiting, and diarrhea. There are three typical causes.
a) Foreign matter can enter via the eustachian tubes (for example, milk can dribble in from the throat if a baby's head is not kept raised during feeding).
Similarly, material from the nose can be forced back into the tubes if the nostrils are blown together rather than in turn.
b) Infection can spread up the eustachian tubes from the nose or throat, for example during measles or a cold.
c) Infected adenoids or tonsils can block off drainage down the eustachian tubes, so that stagnant material in the middle ear may generate infection there.

Treatment of middle-ear infection is with antibiotics and nose drops. Always see a doctor: pressure of pus in the middle ear can cause permanent damage to the eardrum.

MASTOIDITIS
Middle-ear infections can spread to the mastoid bone - the part of the skull just behind the ear. Infection swells the skin around the bone, causing pain and fever. Treatment is by antibiotics, or the surgical removal of the infected bone (mastoidectomy).

DEAFNESS
Deafness can be temporary or permanent, caused by obstruction or disease. Congenital deafness can be due to genetic defect or to infections (eg German measles) during the mother's pregnancy. If deafness is suspected in a baby, help should be sought at once (see L05).

J

NOSE AND MOUTH

J44 NOSE AND MOUTH

THE NOSE

The nose is made of tissue and cartilage, supported by bone at the top. The nostrils lead to a large nasal cavity inside the skull. Air entering the nose is filtered by tiny hairs, and warmed by the blood vessels of the nasal lining.

THE MOUTH

This is designed for digestion and speech. Its teeth break up food, its salivary glands supply digestive fluid, its taste buds judge the food's acceptability, its tongue kneads the food till it is ready to swallow. Tongue, teeth, hard palate, and uvula are all used in speech.

TONSILS AND ADENOIDS

The body's lymph system helps to remove bacteria and impurities from the bloodstream. Two special collections of lymph tissue guard the air passages: the tonsils at the back of the mouth, and the adenoids at the back of the nasal cavity. They enlarge when infection occurs. Repeated infection may make them useless.

SINUSES

These are air cavities in the skull, opening off the nasal passages. Without them the skull would be much heavier. They also help to warm and moisten the air during inhalation. Infection ("sinusitis") causes pain and catarrh.

J45 SECTION THROUGH NOSE AND MOUTH

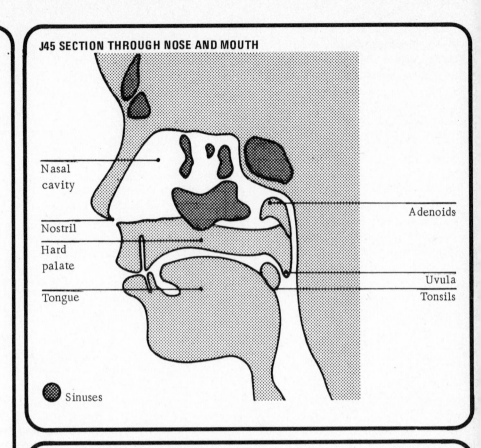

Nasal cavity

Nostril

Hard palate

Tongue

Adenoids

Uvula

Tonsils

⬤ Sinuses

J46 CLEFT PALATE/HARE LIP

A cleft palate occurs if the two sides of the roof of the mouth fail to join before birth, leaving a gap into the nasal cavity. It occurs in one in 750 live births - often together with a "hare lip," which is a split between the two halves of the upper lip.

Surgery improves, and often cures, both conditions, leaving only tiny scars. Surgery for hare lip can be at three months, but an operation for cleft palate must wait until 15 months. Until then the baby may need a special plate fitted in the roof of the mouth to encourage each half of the palate to grow to the same size. Special nipples or feeding by spoon may be necessary. Speech therapy may be needed later.

J47 TASTE AND SMELL

Before it can be tasted, a piece of dry food must be partly dissolved in the mouth by saliva. The taste buds on the tongue then send signals to the brain: different areas of the tongue register different tastes, as shown on the diagram.

Information from smell, however, is also important in "tasting": people who have lost the sense of smell through injury also lose much of the sense of taste.

The organ of smell consists of tiny hair-like nerve endings, in the roof of the nasal cavity. These detect odorous molecules in the air, and send signals to the brain via the "olfactory bulbs" and a system of nerve fibers. The actual process of smelling is, however, still a mystery.

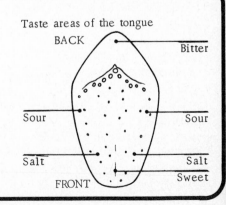

Taste areas of the tongue

BACK

Bitter

Sour

Sour

Salt

Salt

Sweet

FRONT

Parts of the body

J48 RESPIRATORY SYSTEM

Every organ in the body needs oxygen to keep it working. This oxygen is taken into the body during breathing, and carried around the body in the blood. Carbon dioxide, a waste product of body activity, leaves by the same route. (Also see J51.)
The nasal cavity and mouth lead by way of the pharynx, trachea, and bronchi to the lungs. (When swallowing, this route is closed off by a flap of cartilage.)
The lungs are pink, spongy organs lying in the chest cavity, bounded by the ribs, chest muscles, back muscles, and beneath by a muscular wall called the diaphragm.
Within the lungs the bronchi divide repeatedly into branches called bronchioles, each of which ends in an air sac surrounded by tiny blood vessels.

The respiratory system

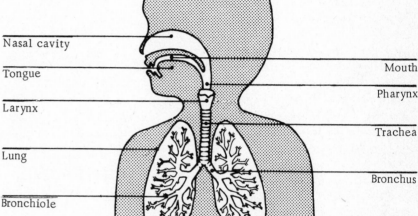

Nasal cavity

Tongue

Larynx

Lung

Bronchiole

Mouth

Pharynx

Trachea

Bronchus

J49 BREATHING MECHANISMS

During breathing in - inspiration - the diaphragm is pulled down and the ribs move forward and outward, enlarging the chest cavity. This threatens to create a vacuum in the cavity, so air rushes into the lungs under atmospheric pressure. During breathing out - expiration - the diaphragm rises, pressure in the chest cavity increases, and air is forced out of the lungs.

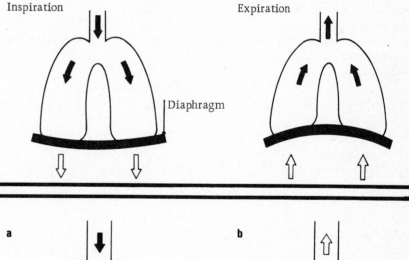

Inspiration

Expiration

Diaphragm

J50 EXCHANGE OF GASES

Gases pass easily through the thin walls of the air sacs and tiny blood vessels in the lungs:
a oxygen enters the air sac during inspiration; carbon dioxide is brought to the lungs in the blood vessels;
b oxygen has entered the bloodstream to travel around the body; carbon dioxide has entered the air sac to be breathed out.

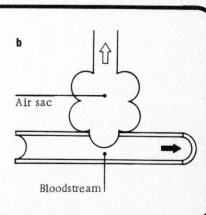

a

b

Air sac

Bloodstream

➡ Oxygen
⇨ Carbon dioxide

J

© DIAGRAM

CIRCULATORY SYSTEM

J51 HEART AND CIRCULATION

The blood (also see J54-56) is the transport system by which oxygen and nutrients reach the body's cells, and waste materials are carried away. The heart, a muscular organ positioned behind the rib cage and between the lungs, is the pump that keeps this transport system moving.

Before birth, oxygen and nutrients are obtained from the mother via the placenta (see A14), and most waste passes back the same way. After birth, oxygen enters the blood via the lungs (see J48-50), and nutrients via digestion (J60-62). Carbon dioxide leaves via the lungs, while most other waste is filtered out of the blood by the kidneys (J58).

These fundamental differences in supply and disposal require the circulatory system to be different before and after birth. (The fetal circulatory system is described in J52.)

Once a baby is born, circulation starts to function as it will throughout the rest of life.

In the lungs, blood takes in oxygen from the air sacs (J50), becoming "oxygenated." This blood is then transported to the left side of the heart for distribution around the body, entering the left atrium. When the atrium contracts, blood is forced into the left ventricle. The left ventricle then contracts, forcing blood along blood vessels called arteries to all organs except the lungs. (Within the heart, backflow of blood is prevented by one-way valves.)

In the organs of the body, oxygen from the blood is used up and waste products collected - the blood becomes "deoxygenated." This blood travels back to the heart in blood vessels called veins. Deoxygenated blood is dark,

bluish red compared with the bright red color of oxygenated blood. Blood from the veins enters the right side of the heart to be pumped to the lungs to be oxygenated. It passes from the right atrium to the right ventricle, and from there to the lungs. The blood has now completed its full circuit - lungs, heart, body, heart, lungs - as shown in the small diagram (right).

Diagram showing the flow of blood through the heart's chambers

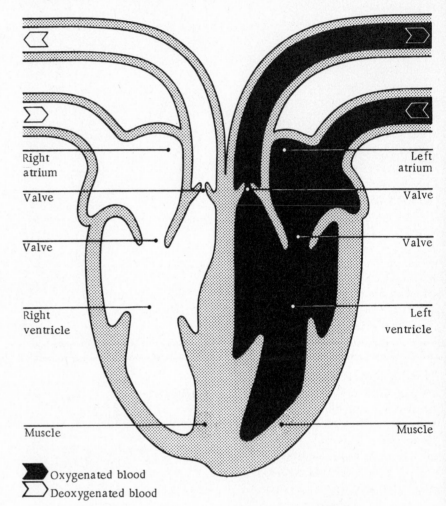

Right atrium

Valve

Valve

Right ventricle

Left atrium

Valve

Valve

Left ventricle

Muscle

Muscle

◤ Oxygenated blood
◁ Deoxygenated blood

Normal circulation

Lungs

Heart

Body

◤ Oxygenated blood
◁ Deoxygenated blood

Parts of the body

J52 FETAL CIRCULATION

Circulation before birth differs from later because the lungs are not functioning, and oxygen and nutrients arrive from the mother by way of the placenta.

Because blood has been diverted via the placenta, blood entering the heart is already oxygenated. Only a little of this blood is sent to the lungs: just enough to keep the cells there supplied. The rest is diverted back toward the body - some to supply the body cells and take away their waste, and some back to the placenta to dispose of waste and pick up more supplies.

Diversion of blood from the lung route in the heart is by way of two short circuits: a hole between the two sides of the heart, and a tube the ductus arteriosus - between the route to the lungs and the route to the body. Blood flows through these short circuits away from the route to the lungs because the unexpanded lungs restrict bloodflow. At birth, the first breaths expand the lungs, and so lower their resistance to blood flow. As a result, blood tries to flow in the opposite direction through the hole in the heart. But, since this is a flap opening, the effect is only to close it up (and within a few days the hole has sealed).

The tube short-circuiting the lung and body routes closes by muscular contraction.

Circulation to the placenta ends when the umbilical cord is cut.

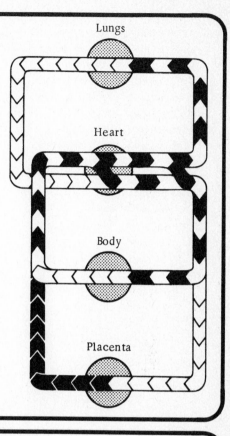

Fetal circulation
▰ Oxygenated blood
▱ Deoxygenated blood

J53 CONGENITAL DEFECTS

Congenital heart disorders are not uncommon, and all babies are checked for them. They may be due to: fetal development stopping too soon, as in some holes in the heart; failure of the circulation to adapt correctly at birth, eg as in patent ductus arteriosus (a), in which the tube between the blood route to the lungs and the route to the body fails to close (see J52); and maldevelopment, as in eg Fallot's tetralogy (b), in which there are multiple defects. Disorders are grouped according to whether the baby looks "blue" (cyanotic disorders: most cases of maldevelopment) or a more normal color (acyanotic disorders: most holes in the heart). The blue appearance in cyanotic disorders is due to deoxygenated blood (J51) flowing into vessels that should only be carrying oxygenated blood. Surgical advances have greatly improved the survival rate, while many minor holes in the heart close of their own accord.

a Patent ductus arteriosus (acyanotic)

Lungs

Heart

Body

b Fallot's tetralogy (cyanotic)

Lungs

Heart

Body

©DIAGRAM

THE BLOOD

J54 THE BLOOD

The blood transports oxygen, nutrients, and waste around the body (J51), and is also vital in fighting infection (K06). It is made up of red cells, white cells, platelets, and plasma.

RED BLOOD CELLS - also called red "corpuscles" - are rounded disks, dented on each side. They measure about three ten-thousandths of an inch in diameter, and have no nucleus. Hemoglobin, a pigment in the cells, gives them their color and, through a chemical reaction, allows oxygen and carbon dioxide to be transported.

WHITE BLOOD CELLS - or white corpuscles - are roughly spherical in shape. They are slightly bigger than red blood cells, but less numerous (about 500 red cells to each white one). There are three basic types - neutrophils, lymphocytes, and monocytes - with nuclei of different shapes. They devour bacteria (K06).

PLATELETS - or "thrombocytes" are tiny colorless cells that can clump together and so make the blood clot.

PLASMA is an almost colorless liquid that is mostly water. It transports the blood cells and many dissolved substances. Proteins in the plasma include disease-fighting antibodies (K07).

Red blood cells:
a front view **b** side view

Types of white blood cell:
c neutrophil **d** lymphocyte **e** monocyte

Platelets

J55 BLOOD MANUFACTURE

Before birth, red blood cells are made in the blood vessels, liver, and bone marrow. After birth, they are made only in the bone marrow. In a young child blood cells are formed in the marrow of most bones, but in an adult they are usually formed only in the marrow of the spine, ribs, breastbone, pelvic bones, and part of the upper arm and leg bones. Lymphocytes are formed in the lymph nodes, spleen, and the thymus of a child. Other white cells are made in the bone marrow. Platelets, too, are made in the bone marrow. Most of the proteins in the blood are formed in the liver (J66).

A red blood cell typically lives for 120 days, a lymphocyte for over a year, other white cells for only 10 hours, and platelets for about 10 days.

Worn-out cells are broken down in the liver and spleen.

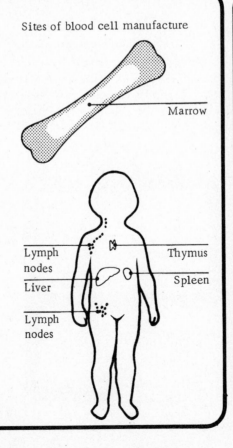

Sites of blood cell manufacture

Marrow

Lymph nodes

Liver

Lymph nodes

Thymus

Spleen

J56 BLOOD DISORDERS

Inherited disorders of the blood include the following.

HEMOPHILIA In this disorder, a deficiency of one of the factors that causes the blood to clot means that special treatment is needed even for minor injuries. Treatment includes transfusions of fresh plasma, and injections of concentrated clotting factor.

SICKLE-CELL ANEMIA is commonest among Negroid people. Red blood cells become sickle-shaped when deprived of oxygen. These sickle cells impair circulation. Over-exertion produces severe pains in the abdomen and joints. Blood transfusions may be needed.

THALASSEMIA, or Mediterranean anemia, is an inherited disorder in which red blood cells are broken down more quickly than the body can replace them. It is treated by blood transfusions, and sometimes by removal of the spleen.

Parts of the body

J57 URINARY SYSTEM

The urinary system is responsible for removing waste products from the blood, and for regulating the body's salt and fluid levels.

The system comprises a pair of kidneys, two tubes called ureters linking the kidneys with the bladder, the bladder, and another tube called the urethra. In a male the urethra leads to the tip of the penis; in a female to an opening in front of the vagina.

Urine produced by the kidneys (J58) drips down the ureters to the bladder, which acts as a reservoir. A muscular ring surrounds the exit from the bladder into the urethra. When this is contracted, it prevents leakage of urine out of the bladder. Relaxation of the muscular ring causes urination as the urine passes into the urethra and out of the body.

Male urinary system

Female urinary system

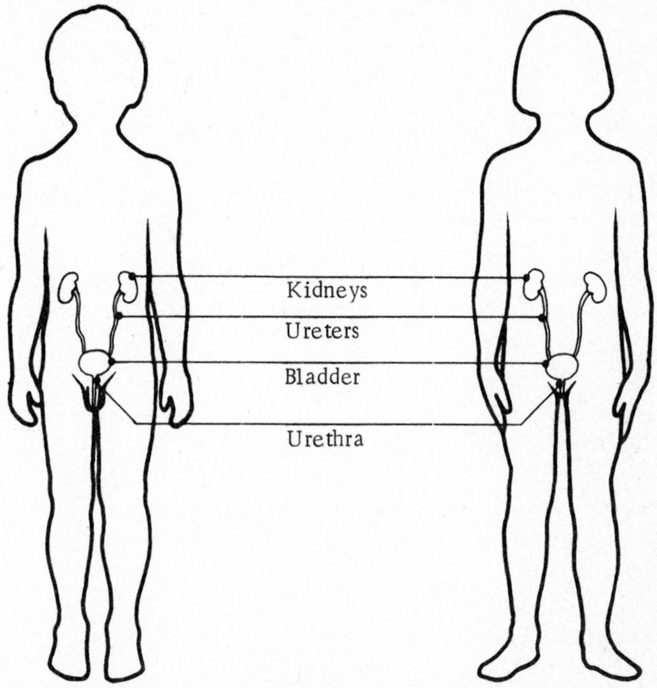

Kidneys
Ureters
Bladder
Urethra

J58 KIDNEYS

The kidneys are dark red, bean-shaped organs that purify the blood and regulate salt and fluid levels in the body.

Each kidney is composed of tiny tubular filter units called nephrons, which are coiled in the outer cortex of the kidney and straight in the inner medulla. Nephrons open into pyramids that project into the expanded end of the ureter.

As the blood flows through the kidneys, water, salts, and urea (a waste product formed in the liver, J66) pass into the nephrons through the thin walls of the blood vessels and the nephrons. Farther along the nephron tubes, water and salts needed by the body pass back into the blood. Surplus water and waste products become urine, which passes via the pyramids into the ureter for elimination from the body (J57).

Cross section of a kidney
a Cortex
b Medulla
c Renal artery
d Renal vein
e Pyramid
f Ureter

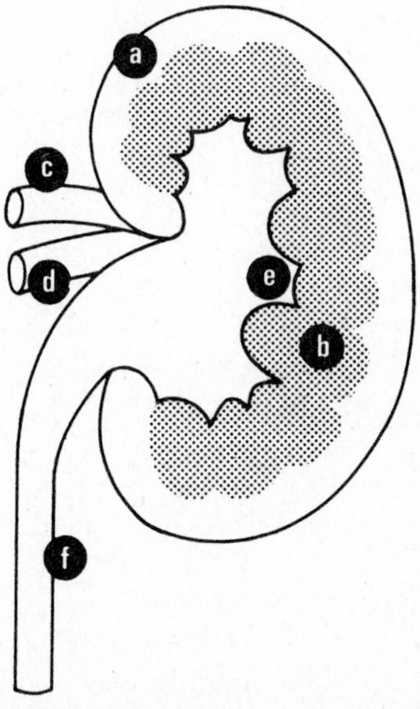

J59 KIDNEY ABNORMALITIES

Abnormalities such as double kidneys or a single horseshoe kidney are quite common (2-3% of the population have double kidneys). Usually they cause no trouble, and are discovered in a general check-up. Surgery is rarely needed.

Double kidneys

Horseshoe kidney

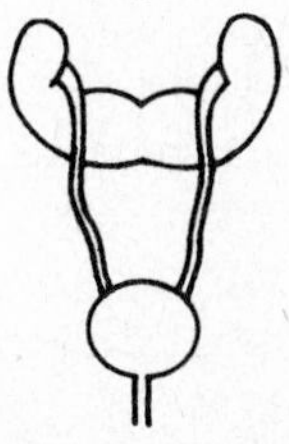

DIGESTIVE SYSTEM

J60 THE DIGESTIVE TRACT

The digestive tract forms a long tube, beginning in the mouth and ending in the anus. Between these it includes the esophagus (or gullet), the stomach, the small intestine (the first part of which is called the duodenum), and the large intestine. It is also joined by small tubes from the pancreas and gall bladder.

Food is passed through the digestive tract by "peristaltic action," that is by rhythmic squeezing movements that flow along the muscles of the tract wall.

Food usually takes at least 15 hours to pass through the whole system. It generally stays in the stomach 3-5 hours, the small intestine $4\frac{1}{2}$ hours, and the large intestine (where the sequence of meals may be jumbled) for 5-25 hours or more.

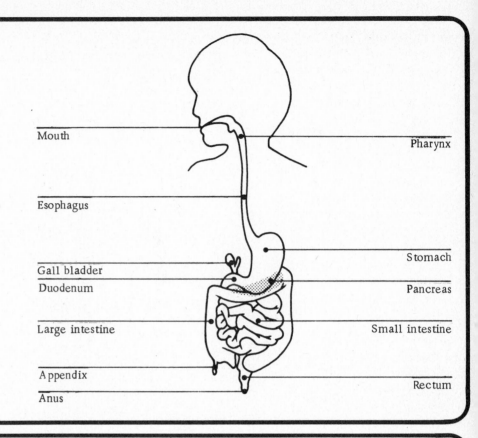

Mouth
Pharynx
Esophagus
Stomach
Gall bladder
Duodenum
Pancreas
Large intestine
Small intestine
Appendix
Rectum
Anus

J61 THE DIGESTIVE PROCESS

Digestion breaks food down so it can be absorbed by the body. The process is partly mechanical: food eaten is chewed and churned to a mushy consistency. But it is mainly chemical: the complex chemicals taken in as food are worked on by enzymes and other chemicals made by the body, and so broken down to simple substances that the body can absorb. Absorption itself occurs almost entirely in the small intestine: the nutrients pass through the intestinal wall into thousands of tiny blood and lymph vessels. The remaining waste matter is a mixture of indigestible remnants, unabsorbed water, and millions of bacteria, and it passes out of the body via the anus.

The digestive tract of a newborn baby finds fluids easier to cope with than solids. But it rapidly adapts, and does not function differently from that of an adult.

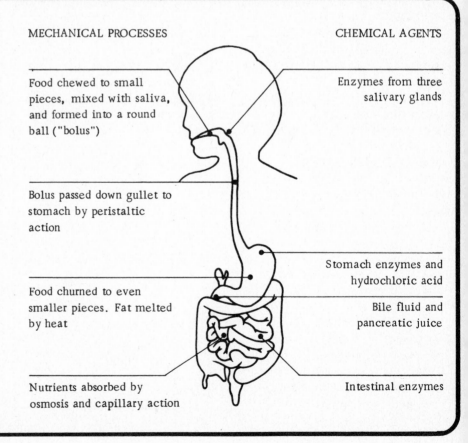

MECHANICAL PROCESSES

CHEMICAL AGENTS

Food chewed to small pieces, mixed with saliva, and formed into a round ball ("bolus")

Enzymes from three salivary glands

Bolus passed down gullet to stomach by peristaltic action

Food churned to even smaller pieces. Fat melted by heat

Stomach enzymes and hydrochloric acid

Bile fluid and pancreatic juice

Nutrients absorbed by osmosis and capillary action

Intestinal enzymes

Parts of the body

J62 DIGESTION AND ABSORPTION

CARBOHYDRATES Digestion begins in the mouth, and continues in the stomach and duodenum. The simple sugars that result are absorbed into the bloodstream in the small intestine.

FATS Some are digested in the stomach, but others need to be emulsified with bile fluid in the duodenum before digestion can begin. Resulting fatty acids are absorbed by blood and lymph vessels in the small intestine.

PROTEINS Digestion begins in the stomach, and continues in the duodenum. In the small intestine the resulting amino acids are absorbed into the bloodstream.

WATER is not digested. In the large intestine it is absorbed into lymph vessels and the bloodstream.

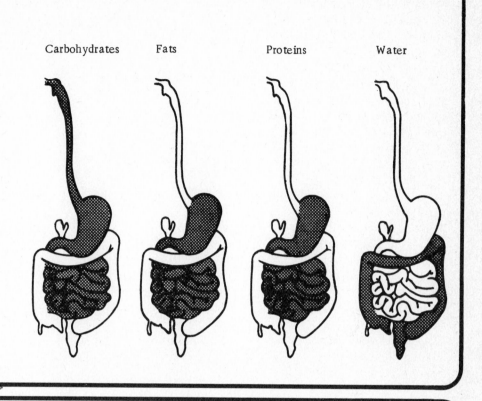

Carbohydrates   Fats   Proteins   Water

J63 CONGENITAL DISORDERS

ANATOMICAL ABNORMALITIES Abnormalities of the digestive tract occur in one in 500 live births. The diagram gives examples. Most can now be corrected by surgery.

OTHER CONGENITAL DISORDERS
a) Celiac disease: fats and some other elements of food are not digested. There is diarrhea and weight loss, and stools passed are fatty. The cause is unknown, but recovery is usual if gluten is kept out of the diet. (Gluten is a protein found in wheat and oats.)
b) Cystic fibrosis: an inherited disorder found in one in 1,000 live births. All mucous glands are affected - including digestive ones, causing diarrhea and loss of weight (though the main danger is from bronchitis and pneumonia due to excessive lung mucus, see K20). Treatment is still being developed.

Diagram showing possible congenital disorders of the digestive tract

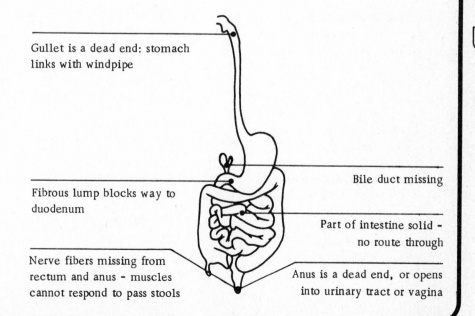

Gullet is a dead end: stomach links with windpipe

Bile duct missing

Fibrous lump blocks way to duodenum

Part of intestine solid - no route through

Nerve fibers missing from rectum and anus - muscles cannot respond to pass stools

Anus is a dead end, or opens into urinary tract or vagina

J

GLANDS AND HORMONES

J64 GLANDS AND HORMONES

The word gland is sometimes used to refer to lymph nodes - as when we speak of "swollen glands" in the neck, armpits, or groin. But in medical terms the glands are those body organs that make and put out liquid chemical substances, and that through these have an effect elsewhere in the body. There are two types of gland.

EXOCRINE GLANDS
Glands of this type have tubes to carry their output to a nearby point where it will act. They include the liver (see J66), the salivary glands in the mouth, and the sweat glands in the skin.

ENDOCRINE GLANDS
These glands release their chemicals directly into the bloodstream. The chemicals they produce are called hormones and play a vital role in controlling many body processes.
The endocrine system is made up of the following glands: pituitary (see J65), thyroid, parathyroids (embedded in the thyroid), thymus, pancreas, adrenals (lying against the upper end of each kidney), and the sex glands or gonads (ovaries in a female and testes in a male, see M04 and M05).

HORMONAL RELATIONSHIPS
The action and interaction of hormones in the body is far from simple. In the first place, most endocrine glands consist of two or more separate parts, and each part may produce several different hormones with different roles in the body. Second, hormones from several different glands may play a part in a single role. For example, childhood growth depends on hormones from the pituitary, the thyroid, and the testes or ovaries. Third, and most important, pituitary hormones regulate the hormone production of other glands in the body (see J65).

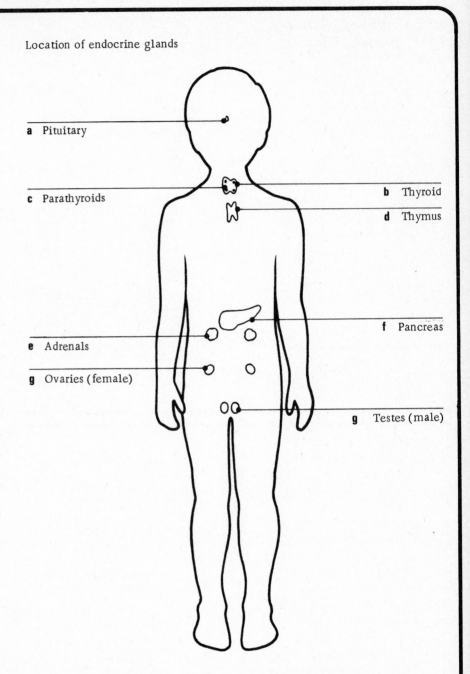

Location of endocrine glands

a Pituitary

c Parathyroids

b Thyroid

d Thymus

f Pancreas

e Adrenals

g Ovaries (female)

g Testes (male)

SUMMARY OF HORMONAL ACTION
Although the endocrine system is extremely complex, some of the processes affected by hormones from the various glands can be listed briefly, as follows:

a pituitary - growth;

b thyroid - energy level, and rate of growth and sexual development;

c parathyroids - use of calcium and phosphorus in the body;

d thymus - production of agents to combat infection early in life;

e adrenals - physical effort, use of glucose, inflammatory response to infection, and use of fat;

f pancreas - level of sugar in the body;

g testes or ovaries - production of sex hormones.

Parts of the body

J65 PITUITARY GLAND

The pituitary is a two-lobed gland connected by a thin stalk to the base of the brain. It is about the size of a pea.

Some of the hormones produced by the pituitary act directly on body processes. These include a hormone that regulates the growth of bones and other tissues, two hormones thought to affect body pigmentation, and a hormone that regulates the amount of water absorbed by the kidneys (J58).
Other pituitary hormones affect body processes indirectly - by regulating the production of hormones in the thyroid gland, adrenals, and sex glands.
Hormone production within the pituitary itself is regulated in two ways - directly by the brain, and by feedback mechanisms from elsewhere in the body.

Action of the pituitary gland

Direct action

Action through thyroid

Action through adrenals

Action through sex glands

J66 THE LIVER

The largest gland in the body, the liver is a wedge-shaped mass of tissue containing a great many blood vessels. Its glandular liquid is called bile, which is stored in the gall bladder until needed and then flows into the duodenum (J60). Bile allows the body to digest fats and helps it take in vitamins A, D, E, and K.
Other important functions of the liver are the production of blood proteins, the production of heparin (a substance that in normal circumstances prevents the blood from clotting), the breaking down of worn-out red blood cells to be excreted in the bile, the storing of iron in a fetus, the regulation of the sugar content of the blood under the influence of the hormone insulin from the pancreas, and the conversion of waste into urea for excretion via the urinary system (see J57).

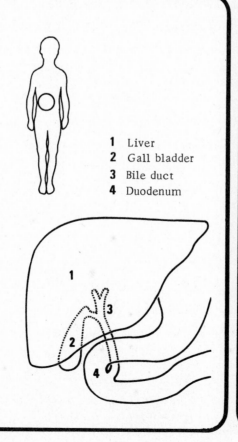

1 Liver
2 Gall bladder
3 Bile duct
4 Duodenum

J67 HORMONAL DISORDERS

Various disorders result from too much or too little of a hormone. Examples include abnormal growth, and diabetes (diabetes mellitus).
DWARFISM
Deficiency of pituitary growth hormone produces a type of dwarfism in which proportions are normal but body size is extremely small. Mental ability is not affected. This type of dwarfism (unlike hereditary dwarfism) can sometimes be prevented if growth hormone is supplied before the normal growth period has ended.
GIGANTISM
Excessive length of the long bones of the arms and legs may be due to overproduction of pituitary growth hormone. Such overproduction is often caused by a non-cancerous pituitary tumor, which can be treated by irradiation or surgery.
DIABETES
This fairly common condition is due to a deficiency of the hormone insulin, made in the pancreas and vital to the body's use of sugar. Insulin deficiency, which may have a variety of causes, sets up a complex chain of reactions.
a) Unused glucose builds up in the bloodstream. It is filtered out by the kidneys but extra urine is needed to carry it away. This increases thirst.
b) Since the body cannot use glucose, it burns fat and protein instead. Weight is lost. Burning fat without glucose results in a build-up of waste products that can cause a coma.
c) Another chain of effects may gradually lead to degeneration of small blood vessels, especially in the eyes and kidneys.
Treatment checks these effects. It involves limiting carbohydrates (sugars) in the diet, and in some cases tablets that act like insulin, or daily insulin injections.

NERVOUS SYSTEM

J68 NERVOUS SYSTEM

Except for certain nerve sheaths that develop during infancy and childhood, the nervous system is fully developed at birth. It is made up of three different units: the central, the peripheral, and the autonomic nervous systems.

CENTRAL NERVOUS SYSTEM This consists of the brain and spinal cord, and is concerned with central control and coordination.

PERIPHERAL NERVOUS SYSTEM This consists of the nerve connections to all the different parts of the body; it receives information and sends out instructions.

AUTONOMIC NERVOUS SYSTEM Comprising nerve centers alongside the spinal column, this controls elementary functions such as heartbeat (and is involved in responding to the stress of feelings and emotions).

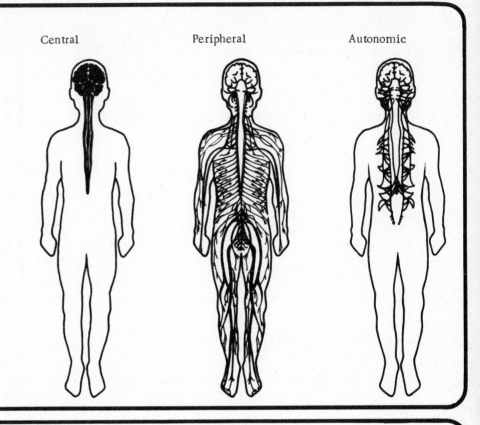

Central   Peripheral   Autonomic

J69 THE BRAIN

The brain is a convoluted mass of nerve cells and fibers, protected by the skull and by a cushion of fluid. It is the coordinating center of the nervous system.

FOREBRAIN Including the cerebral hemispheres, the thalamus, and the hypothalamus, the forebrain is the center of memory, intelligence, and voluntary actions. The cerebral hemispheres, one on each side, are linked by bridges, of which the corpus callosum is the largest. The right hemisphere controls muscles on the left side of the body, and the left hemisphere those on the right.

MIDBRAIN This consists mostly of connecting nerve fibers. Its roof is formed by the optic lobes.

HINDBRAIN The hindbrain includes the cerebellum, which coordinates balance and movement, and the medulla oblongata, which directs involuntary actions such as heartbeat and breathing.

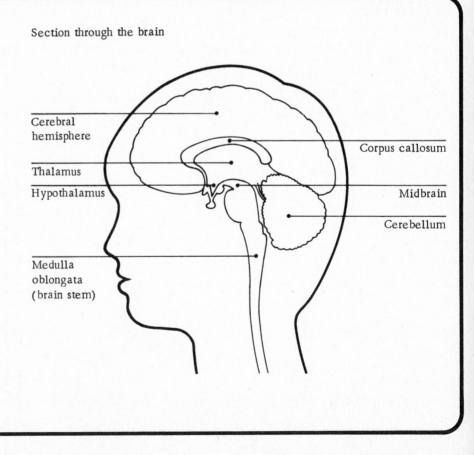

Section through the brain

Cerebral hemisphere

Corpus callosum

Thalamus

Hypothalamus

Midbrain

Cerebellum

Medulla oblongata (brain stem)

Parts of the body

J70 MALDEVELOPMENT AND DAMAGE

Maldevelopment of the brain may be due to spontaneous chromosome abnormality, as in Down's syndrome (mongolism), or to an infection such as German measles during the mother's pregnancy.

Mental retardation (L08) or problems of nervous control may also result from damage to a normal brain, because damaged brain cells, unlike other cells in the body, can never be replaced. Possible causes of damage include the following.

The brain may sometimes be damaged during birth, if the head strikes hard against the mother's perineum (the muscular outlet of the pelvis) during a too rapid birth, or if the brain is starved of oxygen through constriction of the umbilical cord. Modern obstetric techniques have greatly reduced such risks (B09-14). In a baby that is very premature, physical immaturity can result in glucose deficiency and subsequent brain damage.

Thyroid deficiency is responsible for cretinism, in which brain damage is accompanied by lack of activity, chronic constipation, slow growth, and distinctive coarsening of the features. Prompt treatment is essential to prevent severe mental retardation.

In hydrocephalus, often associated with spina bifida (J72), the head becomes swollen because of inadequate drainage of the fluid around the brain. Untreated, the condition produces brain damage as the fluid presses on the brain. Treatment is by the insertion of plastic drainage tubes.

Other causes of brain damage include severe head injury, and poisoning, for example with lead.

J71 EPILEPSY

Epilepsy is a disorder of the nervous system. It is usually due to brain damage but may also be inherited. Mental ability is not affected. There are two main types: petit mal and grand mal. Both can be controlled with drugs.

PETIT MAL is characterized by momentary lapses of attention, sometimes with blinking or slight twitching. Attacks last only a few seconds, but may occur several times in a day. In many cases the sufferer is unaware that anything has happened.

GRAND MAL is a more severe form of epilepsy in which actual fits occur: the sufferer loses consciousness and has convulsions in which he thrashes about and may foam at the mouth. A fit usually lasts one or two minutes, followed by sleep (see N16 for first aid).

J72 SPINA BIFIDA

In a normal backbone (a), each bone (vertebra) forms a closed ring around the spinal cord. In spina bifida (literally, split spine) one or more vertebrae are open at the back. Genetic and other factors may be responsible.

Approximately 5% of the population have a mild form of the disorder, which causes no problems and usually remains unnoticed.

In other cases, spinal fluid passes through the gap to form a bulging bag at the back (b) although the spinal cord is not affected. Such cases are usually cured by an operation soon after birth.

In the most severe form of spina bifida the spinal cord is deformed or damaged before birth, producing varying degrees of paralysis and deformity in the lower body. An operation only sometimes succeeds, and physiotherapy and special treatment will be needed (L01-03).

Section through trunk

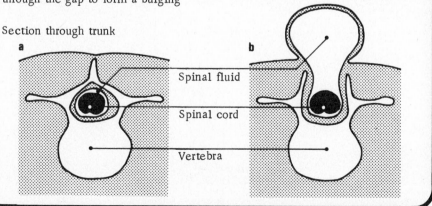

Spinal fluid

Spinal cord

Vertebra

J73 CEREBRAL PALSY

Cerebral palsy is a disorder in which brain damage sustained before or around the time of birth interferes with muscular control. There are three main forms:
a) spasticity, characterized by stiff and difficult movements;
b) athetosis, in which pronounced involuntary movements interfere with normal body movements;
c) ataxia, in which a disturbed sense of balance and depth results in an unsteady gait.

The degree of disability varies considerably. Associated defects include impaired speech and hearing, and - in about 50% of cases - reduced intelligence. Treatment involves training healthy muscles to take over the work of affected ones as far as possible. Drugs, surgery, and special equipment may help in this. (For details of special care see L01-03).

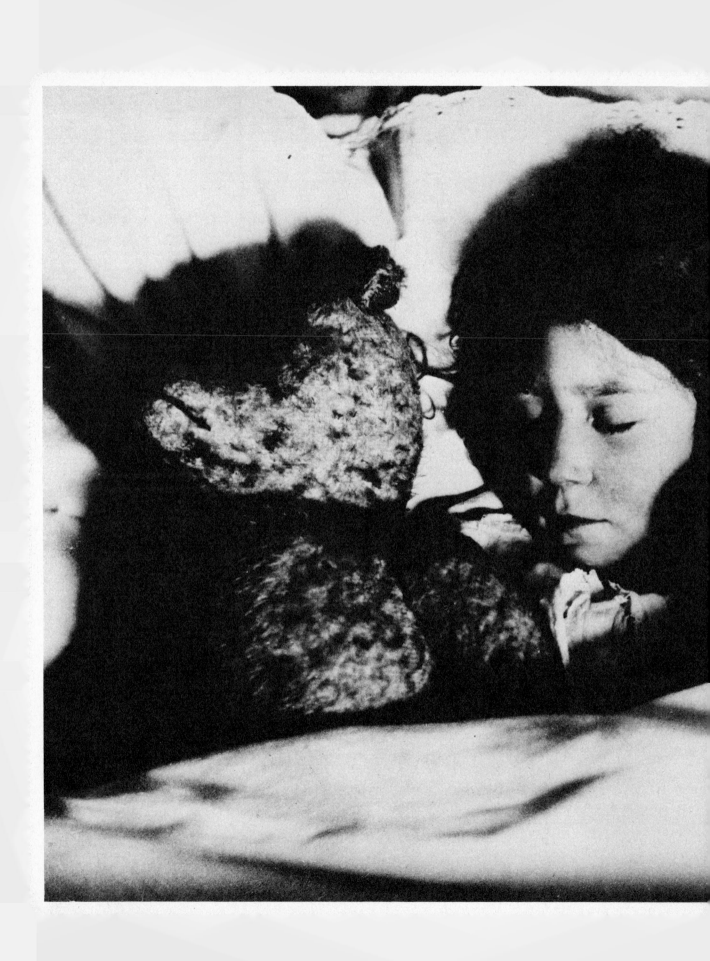

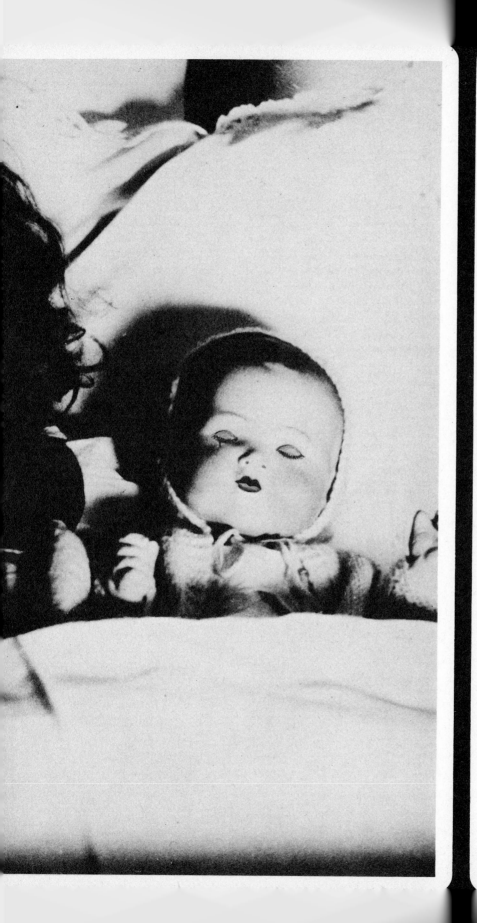

The sick child

A variety of illnesses are common in childhood — most of them mild, others more serious.

Left: Sleep, the great healer
(The Mansell Collection)

THE ONSET OF ILLNESS

K01 CHRONIC OR ACUTE

An illness may be described as being either acute or chronic. An acute illness is one that comes on suddenly, intensifies sharply, and usually lasts a short time. Such an illness is not necessarily serious - the common cold is a good example.

A chronic illness is one that lasts for a considerable time without any rapid developments in the patient's condition. In a chronic infectious illness the unaided body is unable or slow to destroy the agent of infection. Most chronic illnesses, however, can be cured or helped by medical treatment. As is the case with acute illnesses, the term chronic has no bearing on the severity of the disease or its symptoms.

K02 CONGENITAL OR LATER

BEFORE BIRTH
Some conditions are inherited: hemophilia and sickle-cell anemia (J56) for instance. Others are acquired during fetal development or during birth, for instance some kinds of brain damage (J70) and deafness due to German measles in the pregnant mother. Both groups are termed congenital if present at birth. (Other congenital disorders are described in J06, J07, J22, J46, J53, J63, J72, J73.)

IN LIFE
Most diseases arise during life. These include nutritional diseases; diseases due to environmental factors such as cold, heat, damp, or fog; allergies; infestation of skin, hair, or internal organs by parasites; and infection of the body by disease micro-organisms. Most infections result from hostile micro-organisms entering the body through nose, mouth, ears, eyes, urogenital openings, or broken skin.

K03 SYMPTOMS AND SIGNS

Disturbing symptoms and signs accompany some of the ailments common among children. Many result from poisons released by agents of infection in the body before its defenses can crush them. In many infections a child sweats, shivers, runs a high temperature, and is tired, flushed, apathetic, and lacks appetite. Rashes or spots appear in scarlet fever, measles, and German measles. Diarrhea and vomiting may stem from a variety of causes. Sore throats come with diphtheria, mononucleosis, and poliomyelitis. Aching and shivering come with mumps, chicken pox, German measles, and stress. But many of these symptoms and signs can also have trivial causes and vanish overnight.

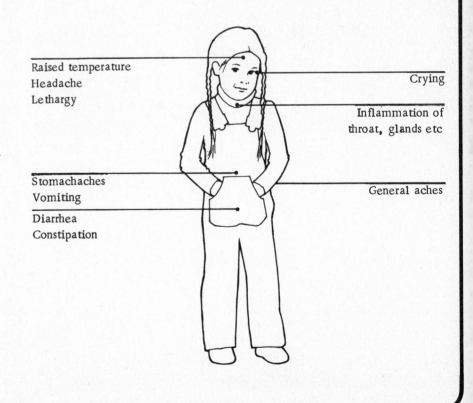

Raised temperature
Headache
Lethargy

Crying

Inflammation of throat, glands etc

Stomachaches
Vomiting

General aches

Diarrhea
Constipation

The sick child

K04 AGENTS OF INFECTION

Many diseases are due to one of six groups of infective agents: bacteria, viruses, rickettsias, fungi, and protozoan and metazoan parasites.

1 Bacteria are microscopic one-celled organisms, some of which normally live harmlessly on skin, in the nose, mouth, throat, and lungs, and in intestines. Reduced bodily resistance allows some to multiply and cause sore throats or other ailments. Illness can occur if bacteria normally in one part of the body get into another. But most disease bacteria enter the body from outside. Diphtheria, scarlet fever, tuberculosis, and whooping cough are bacterial diseases.

2 Viruses are smaller than bacteria and live as parasites, active and reproducing only in other living cells, which they break down. Viral diseases include the common cold, chicken pox, influenza, measles, mumps, and smallpox.

3 Rickettsias are germs found in certain fleas, lice, mites, and ticks. Rickettsias cause typhus, scrub typhus, and Rocky Mountain spotted fever.

4 Fungi are non-green plants. Tiny fungi cause ringworm and some lung diseases.

5 Protozoan parasites are one-celled animals some of which can get inside the body to cause diseases including amebic dysentery, malaria, and sleeping sickness.

6 Metazoan (many-celled) parasites include tapeworms, roundworms, fleas, and lice.

K05 SPREADING DISEASE

1 Disease is often spread by bacteria or viruses airborne in droplets breathed, coughed, or sneezed out by infectious people and breathed in by others. (A sneeze can hurl 20,000 droplets 15ft:4.6m.) People sometimes contract anthrax and tuberculosis by breathing in dusty air bearing old, dried bacterial spores.

2 Some skin conditions spread by skin-to-skin contact.

3 Infected soil or dust entering a cut can cause tetanus or gangrene.

4 Pets may harbor and transmit diseases, for example: dogs, tapeworms; parrots, psittacosis; guinea pigs, encephalitis; turtles, salmonella poisoning; horses, glanders; goats, brucellosis; cats, toxoplasmosis; various mammals, rabies.

5 Food or water contaminated by germs at source, or by poor personal hygiene, can cause diseases such as brucellosis, cholera, typhoid, dysentery, and poliomyelitis.

6 Flies can infect food with bacteria if it is left uncovered.

7 Bites by parasitic insects can also transmit disease.

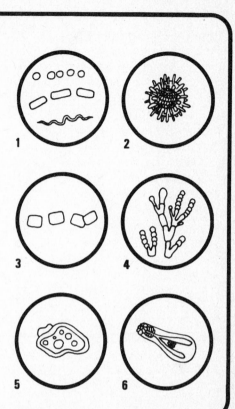

K

THE FIGHT AGAINST INFECTION

K06 DEFENSE MECHANISMS

The body fights infection in three ways: preventing the entry of foreign organisms; attacking those that get inside the body; and neutralizing those it cannot kill.

The body's main outer barrier is the skin, a sheath that guards underlying tissues. Antiseptic substances in sweat exuded from the skin kill many germs.

Different openings in the skin have special defenses. For instance, lacrimal fluid containing bacteria-combating lysozyme bathes the eyes at each blink. Tears also wash out foreign bodies from the eyes.

Salivary glands help to combat infectious substances entering the mouth. Adenoids and tonsils make lymphocytes (J54).

The body's openings and internal passages are lined with mucous membranes. Coated with antiseptic substances in a layer of mucus, these act as physical barriers and traps.

Inside the body certain organs produce special defenses.

The stomach secretes acids that attack bacteria in swallowed food.

The liver filters harmful substances from blood flowing through it, and creates clotting substances that help wounds heal.

Spleen, bone marrow, and lymph glands all make white blood cells that circulate around the body and attack invading organisms (see J54).

Neutrophils produced in bone marrow are white cells that engulf, kill, and digest bacteria.

Macrophages – large, bacteria-engulfing cells – turn the lymph nodes in armpits, neck, and groin into bacterial traps and filters. Local infection may trigger blood inflow, creating swelling, pain, and pus (white blood cells and bacteria).

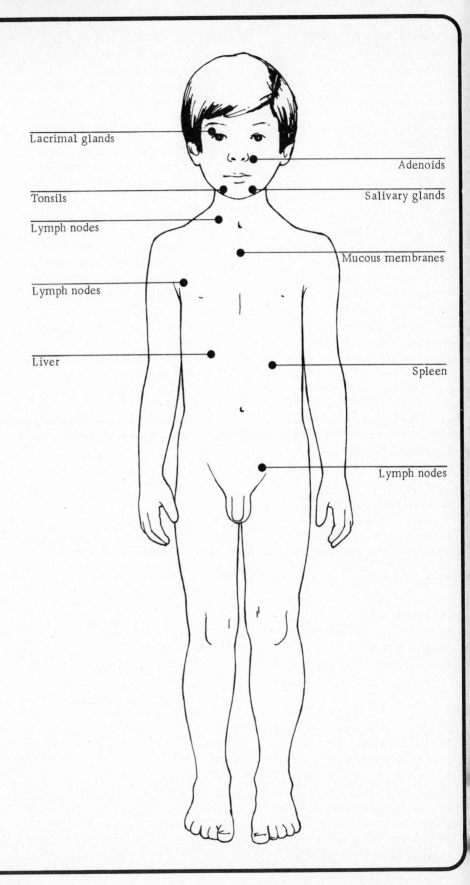

Lacrimal glands

Adenoids

Tonsils

Salivary glands

Lymph nodes

Mucous membranes

Lymph nodes

Liver

Spleen

Lymph nodes

The sick child

K07 NATURAL ANTIBODIES

Antibodies are large, complex protein molecules produced by plasma cells (see J54). They combat antigens (alien proteins that have invaded body fluids). Antibodies attack the protein sheaths of bacteria and viruses by interlocking with and thus inactivating them. Antibodies that neutralize the toxins (poisons) produced by alien bacteria are known as antitoxins.

In early life, production of antibodies is concentrated in the thymus gland. Later, spleen, lymph nodes, and bone marrow become the chief producers. Antibodies are specific in their actions: in most cases, one type of antibody will react only to one type of germ.

K08 TREATING INFECTION

The body's defenses do not easily subdue all infections, but many can be crushed by antibiotics and sulfonamide drugs.
Antibiotics are chemicals made by micro-organisms. They halt the growth of or kill bacteria, fungi, and rickettsias by interfering with nutrient absorption and cell formation. Some act against only a small group of microbes: others (broad spectrum antibiotics) attack a wide range of targets. Much used antibiotics include penicillin, streptomycin, and tetracycline.
Diseases susceptible to antibiotics include dysentery, endocarditis (bacterial infection in the heart), scarlet fever, tularemia, tuberculosis, typhoid, and many minor infections.
Sulfonamides (or sulfa drugs) are synthetic chemicals all of which contain the elements sulfur, hydrogen, nitrogen, and oxygen. They work by blocking the production of certain chemicals that bacteria need in order to grow.
Some sulfa drugs are used against general infection of the body, others for local action in the intestinal tract and for certain bladder infections.
Sulfa drugs have proved useful against blood poisoning, dysentery, meningitis, pneumonia, and some other diseases. But for most purposes, antibiotics have replaced sulfa drugs. Neither attacks viruses, and some bacteria have evolved resistance to antibiotics.

K09 IMMUNITY

Immunity is the body's original or induced ability to withstand invasion by disease organisms such as certain fungi, bacteria, and viruses.
The chief source of immunity is the lymphatic system, including the spleen and lymph nodes which manufacture antibodies attacking specific alien proteins.
Other sources include interferons - special proteins that curb the spread of viruses inside the body. Unlike antibodies, interferons are not restricted to a single type of target.
The body's production of antibody or white blood cells to combat an alien, antigenic substance is known as an immune reaction. Someone protected by antibodies against a particular disease is said to have immunity to that disease.

NATURAL IMMUNITY
The human body is naturally immune to many plant and animal diseases. But natural immunity to human disease largely varies with inherited differences in individuals' antibody output.

ACTIVE IMMUNITY
This is the immunity the body builds by making antibodies to fight invading organisms. One attack by a disease may produce lifelong immunity against fresh attacks by that disease.

Active immunity to some diseases can be artificially induced by vaccination: introducing weakened agents of disease. Vaccination using live germs is known as inoculation.

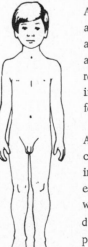

PASSIVE IMMUNITY
An unborn child acquires some antibodies from his mother, and after birth receives antibodies in her milk. The result is a passive natural immunity. This lasts only a few months.

Artificial passive immunity can be given to protect instantly against an established disease. Serum with antibodies against the disease is injected into the patient's bloodstream.

K

VACCINATION AND IMMUNIZATION

K10 WHY VACCINATE?

Vaccination can protect children against many once-common killing and disabling diseases. Vaccination against smallpox, tuberculosis, and diphtheria alone has saved millions of lives.

But the resulting decline in such diseases has persuaded many parents that vaccination is unnecessary. Others, worried by suggested links between whooping cough vaccine and encephalitis, think vaccination risky. In fact the risk of death or bodily damage from whooping cough far outweighs that from vaccination.

If the proportion of unvaccinated children rises, the risk of grave epidemic disease among them increases too. So, unless doctors advise against it, seek a full vaccination program for your child.

K11 MEDICALLY OBTAINED IMMUNITY

Chief sources of artificial immunity are vaccines, specific kinds conferring protection against specific diseases. They work by exploiting the same natural process in which the body builds natural immunity against disease organisms that get in by chance. Hostile substances in a vaccine provoke the body to make antibodies against them. Some vaccines cause usually trivial and transient symptoms.

Vaccines may be made in various ways to employ:

1) an organism akin to one that causes disease (eg cowpox virus to immunize against smallpox);
2) dead organisms of the disease, or inactivated disease organisms (eg in influenza, Salk polio, and whooping cough vaccines);
3) weakened live disease organisms (BCG, German measles, Sabin polio vaccines);
4) A toxoid - a non-poisonous substance derived from a toxin (poison) produced by the disease organism (eg a toxoid that persuades the body to make antitoxins against diphtheria).

Some vaccines give lifelong protection. Less effective and less durable immunity may be won by injecting a ready-made antibody or antitoxin (eg against tetanus or diphtheria).

Vaccination for diseases other than those named may be needed where they prevail, eg yellow fever, typhoid, and cholera in certain tropical countries. Influenza vaccines are available but not urged for general use.

K12 IMMUNIZATION PROGRAM

Illustrated here is a typical program of vaccinations during childhood. German measles vaccination is particularly recommended for girls, to prevent damage to an unborn child if the disease is contracted during a future pregnancy.

DPT — Diphtheria, whooping cough, and tetanus
DT — Diphtheria and tetanus
BCG — Tuberculosis
— Injection
— Oral vaccine

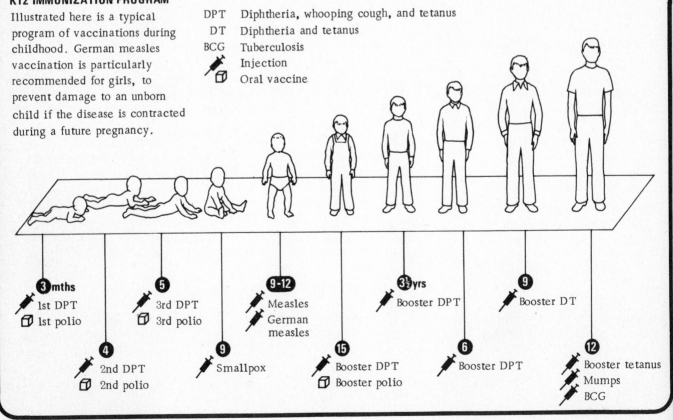

3 mths 1st DPT / 1st polio
4 2nd DPT / 2nd polio
5 3rd DPT / 3rd polio
9 Smallpox
9-12 Measles / German measles
15 Booster DPT / Booster polio
3½ yrs Booster DPT
6 Booster DPT
9 Booster DT
12 Booster tetanus / Mumps / BCG

The sick child

K13 IMMUNIZATION   🖉 Injection   🖉 Possible injection   ▱ Oral vaccine

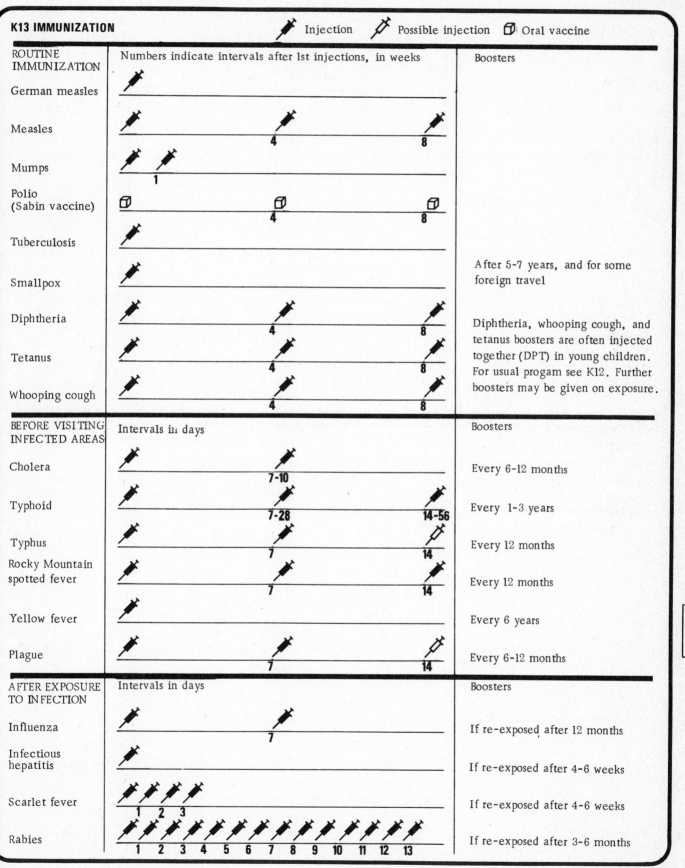

ROUTINE IMMUNIZATION	Numbers indicate intervals after 1st injections, in weeks	Boosters
German measles		
Measles	4 ⋯ 8	
Mumps	1	
Polio (Sabin vaccine)	4 ⋯ 8	
Tuberculosis		
Smallpox		After 5-7 years, and for some foreign travel
Diphtheria	4 ⋯ 8	Diphtheria, whooping cough, and tetanus boosters are often injected together (DPT) in young children. For usual progam see K12. Further boosters may be given on exposure.
Tetanus	4 ⋯ 8	
Whooping cough	4 ⋯ 8	

BEFORE VISITING INFECTED AREAS	Intervals in days	Boosters
Cholera	7-10	Every 6-12 months
Typhoid	7-28 ⋯ 14-56	Every 1-3 years
Typhus	7 ⋯ 14	Every 12 months
Rocky Mountain spotted fever	7 ⋯ 14	Every 12 months
Yellow fever		Every 6 years
Plague	7 ⋯ 14	Every 6-12 months

AFTER EXPOSURE TO INFECTION	Intervals in days	Boosters
Influenza	7	If re-exposed after 12 months
Infectious hepatitis		If re-exposed after 4-6 weeks
Scarlet fever	1 2 3	If re-exposed after 4-6 weeks
Rabies	1 2 3 4 5 6 7 8 9 10 11 12 13	If re-exposed after 3-6 months

K

© DIAGRAM

SKIN CONDITIONS

K14 COMMON EARLY RASHES

Rashes are common in the first few months of life. These rashes are usually insignificant and reflect the reaction of the young baby's skin to external conditions. Treatment may be needed, however, if the rash looks infected.

PRICKLY HEAT appears on the neck and shoulders of babies in hot weather, and may spread to the chest, arms, and face. It forms a rash of pink pimples surrounded by blotches of pink skin. The pimples may blister. It is usually caused by the baby being dressed too warmly.

MILD FACE RASH may occur as tiny white pimples, small red pimples that take longer to go away, or as rough red patches. The cause is unknown. Such rashes will clear up in time without treatment.

DIAPER RASH (see E15).

K15 DISEASE RASHES

Many rashes in childhood are insignificant, but others are signs of infectious diseases. To avoid mistakes in identification the doctor should always be consulted if a child with a rash appears in any other way unwell (also see K23).

1 MEASLES rash develops on the third to the fifth day of the illness, after which the child usually begins to feel better. The rash is of dark red spots that merge into blotches. It usually begins behind the ears and then spreads over the body.

2 GERMAN MEASLES produces a light pink rash that begins on the neck and face and gradually spreads over the body. Often the spots merge to give a flushed appearance. The rash is often the first sign of illness and lasts only a few days.

3 CHICKEN POX rash is often the first sign of illness. Commonest on face, scalp, and chest, and sometimes found in the mouth, spots appear over a three-day period. The rash consists of dark red pimples on which blisters develop a few hours after appearance. These burst easily and scabs form. Unless they are scratched - when permanent scars may result - the scabs fall off to leave pink scars that soon fade. Calamine lotion reduces itching.

4 SCARLET FEVER rash appears on the second day of illness, spreading over the body from damp areas like the groin, armpits, and sometimes the back. The rash is made up of tiny red spots on a flushed skin. The area around the mouth remains white. After a week, the skin over the spots begins to peel.

K16 SKIN INFECTIONS

RINGWORM is a very contagious fungus infection affecting the skin and sometimes the nails. Scaly, crusted lumps form circular patches that clear in the center and spread out from the site of the infection. On the scalp, ringworm often causes the hair to break off short. Ringworm can now be effectively treated with drugs.

ATHLETE'S FOOT is caused by a fungus that thrives in wet, warm conditions. The skin between the toes becomes white, soft, wet, and and itchy. The condition is made worse by perspiration. Good general foot care is essential, and fungicide ointments should be used.

IMPETIGO is a highly contagious bacterial infection. It usually starts on the face with a pimple that develops into a brown crusty scab. Impetigo spreads very rapidly, and antibiotics may be needed.

COLD SORE is a virus infection that tends to recur. A stinging sensation gives rise to clusters of blisters that dry up in about 10 days. Commonest near the mouth, it may occur in the genital area.

WARTS are small harmless growths caused by a virus. On the hands they often disappear without treatment, but on the feet (verrucas) they should be treated, by cutting or chemically, since they are painful and easily spread to others.

BOILS are painful, pus-filled lumps caused by bacterial infection of a hair follicle, a sebaceous or sweat gland, or a break in the skin. They are most common where the skin is rubbed by clothing, and usually burst after several days. Most need only a protective dressing, but a doctor should be consulted if the child is very young or if several boils occur.

ACNE is an infective skin condition common in adolescence (see M10).

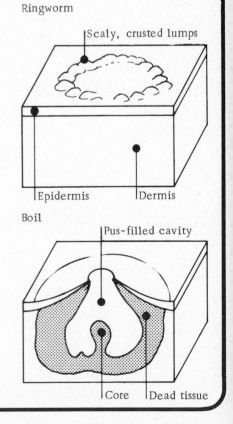

Ringworm

Scaly, crusted lumps

Epidermis   Dermis

Boil

Pus-filled cavity

Core   Dead tissue

The sick child

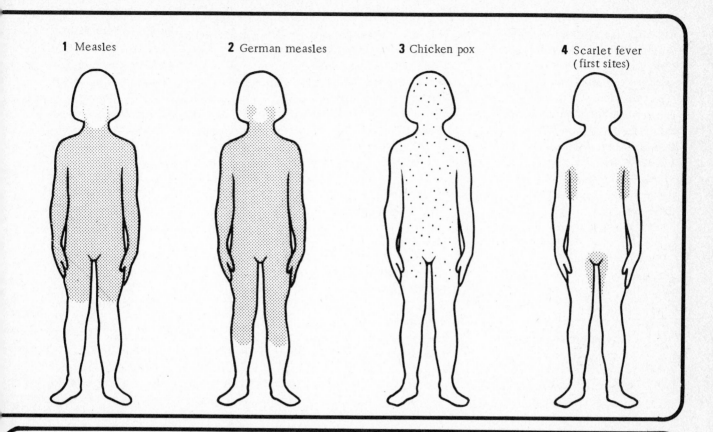

1 Measles

2 German measles

3 Chicken pox

4 Scarlet fever (first sites)

K17 SKIN CONDITIONS

ECZEMA is an allergic skin condition in which patches of rough, red, scaly skin cause intense irritation. It is most common in children with a family history of eczema or other allergic conditions such as hay fever or asthma. Causes include foods, and external irritants such as soap or wool. It may be aggravated by nervous tension.

In a young baby, eczema most often begins on the cheeks or forehead. Later, it may occur anywhere on the body, especially in the elbow creases and behind the knees. The condition often improves or disappears as the child gets older. Cortisone ointment may be prescribed in severe cases.

HIVES, or nettle rash, is another form of allergic skin reaction. Characterized by painful, itchy skin wheals, it may be caused by certain types of food, drug, or insect bite. Hives may also result from emotional tension.

The condition is not normally serious, and soothing lotions will ease the child's discomfort. Medical attention must, however, be sought if swellings that may affect breathing occur in the area of the mouth and throat.

CHILBLAINS are itching, red swellings that occur on the extremities as a result of poor circulation in cold weather. Scratching may lead to infection. Warm clothing is the best form of protection. Treatment may be with drugs, or by improving circulation through exercise.

SWOLLEN RED HANDS may occur in babies in cold weather. The condition disappears once the baby is warm again.

SUNBURN, see N41.
FROSTBITE, see N42.

Possible locations

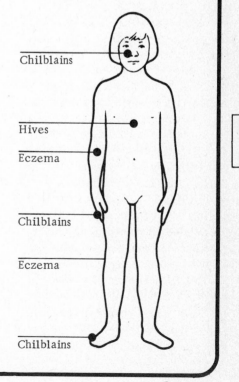

Chilblains

Hives

Eczema

Chilblains

Eczema

Chilblains

K

©DIAGRAM

INTERNAL DISORDERS

K18 DIGESTIVE PROBLEMS

Digestive problems in children have many causes. Signs include vomiting (see K35), stomachache, diarrhea, and constipation. (For problems in babies see E18, F26, F27, F29, F30.)

In general, the doctor should be consulted if the parent is at all worried by the child's condition, particularly if warning signs occur together, if the child has a fever, or if abdominal pain is at all persistent.

STOMACHACHE Many young children complain of a stomachache when they really mean that they feel unwell, perhaps if they are about to vomit. Other children develop a quite genuine stomachache when they are tense or worried. A common cause of stomachache in children is the onset of another illness such as a cold, throat infection, or influenza. Other causes are appendicitis (K19), and intestinal infections that also cause sickness and diarrhea.

DIARRHEA is seldom significant in itself. If it occurs with vomiting, however, there is a danger of dehydration if the condition persists. The doctor should be called at once to a baby, or to an older child who is unable to take fluids.

CONSTIPATION may sometimes be a sign of illness - if the child is eating or drinking less, or if fluid has been lost through fever or vomiting. One problem, usually a passing phase, is that young children "hold back" their bowel movements until they are hard and difficult to pass. More usually, however, constipation is a condition imagined by parents.

K19 APPENDICITIS

The appendix is a small closed tube leading off the large intestine. In appendicitis it becomes inflamed, usually as a result of a blockage. Sometimes the condition develops very rapidly, becoming critical in 24 hours or so. Often the first symptom is pain around the navel, which then changes to a pain in the right of the abdomen. Tenderness in the area over the appendix - McBurney's point - is a distinctive feature. Nausea is common, and vomiting and fever may occur.

It is important to call a doctor at once if appendicitis is suspected; without prompt medical attention the appendix may burst, causing peritonitis which can be fatal.

Do not give laxatives or treat for indigestion. Cases of acute appendicitis are treated by prompt surgical removal of the appendix.

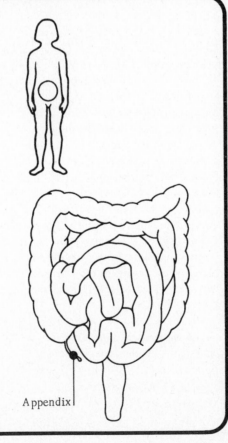

Appendix

K20 RESPIRATORY PROBLEMS

PNEUMONIA is acute inflammation of the lungs. Symptoms include fever, chest pains, and a harsh, dry cough. The infection may be patchy, usually around the bronchial tubes (bronchopneumonia), or may affect an entire lung (lobar pneumonia). When body resistance is low, pneumonia may be caused by bacteria usually present in the mouth and throat. Bronchopneumonia is often a complication of another illness, or may be caused by foreign matter such as food in the lungs. Treatment is with antibiotics or sulfonamide drugs.

BRONCHITIS is acute or chronic inflammation of the bronchi (J48), but other parts of the respiratory tract are often also affected. Mucus gathers and causes wheezy breathing and coughing. Sometimes bronchitis follows a cold, influenza, measles, whooping cough, or chicken pox. Bronchitis may itself lead to pneumonia. Drugs, inhalations, and physiotherapy are used in treatment.

CYSTIC FIBROSIS (also see J63) is a rare disease in which malfunctioning mucus-secreting glands cause severe respiratory problems. Antibiotics are used against infection, and breathing may be helped by physiotherapy and use of a mist tent or respirator.

ASTHMA is a chronic disorder of the bronchial tubes causing attacks of wheezing, coughing, and difficult breathing. It may be due to infection, but is more usually an inherited allergic reaction. Allergic asthma is made worse by emotional stress. Antibiotics may be used against infection, and desensitizing injections against allergies. An attack may be controlled with a special inhaler, and breathing exercises may be useful.

The sick child

K21 JAUNDICE

Jaundice is a sign of disorder rather than an illness itself. In jaundice the skin and sometimes the whites of the eyes appear yellow due to the presence in the blood of an excess of bile pigment. This pigment is produced in the liver by the normal breakdown of red blood cells (J66). The excess bile pigment in the blood in jaundice may be due to a number of causes, requiring different types of treatment. For this reason it is important to consult a doctor as soon as jaundice is suspected. Other signs of jaundice are dark urine and pale bowel movements. Jaundice is quite common in newborn babies, when the most usual cause is simple inefficiency of the liver. Jaundice of this type usually disappears after a few days, but special treatment is sometimes needed. In very rare cases jaundice in a baby is due to congenital defect: the baby is born with no duct to carry bile away from the liver. A further cause of jaundice in infants is erythroblastosis fetalis, resulting from rhesus incompatability between mother and baby (see A09 for details).

Rare in infants but more common in older children is jaundice due to infection. Most common is infectious hepatitis, transmitted by food or drink handled by a carrier of the hepatitis virus. It may occur in epidemics, especially where hygiene is poor. Preventive vaccination may be given (K13). Less common is serum hepatitis, transmitted by infected blood used in transfusion or by contaminated medical instruments.

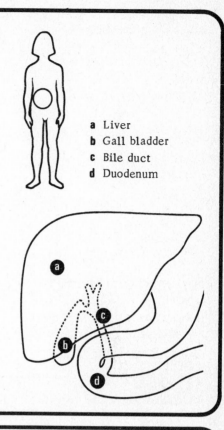

a Liver
b Gall bladder
c Bile duct
d Duodenum

K22 URINARY TRACT PROBLEMS

Infections may occur anywhere in the urinary tract - kidneys, ureters, bladder, or urethra. They are fairly common in young children, when they may be difficult to diagnose since it is not always apparent that the child is finding urination painful or is urinating abnormally often. Other symptoms - such as vomiting and fever - may have many causes. For this reason a urine test is usual whenever a child has an unexplained fever, or if any fever persists. In some cases infection of the urinary tract results from an infection elsewhere in the body, usually in the throat or ears. This type of urinary tract infection is, however, now less common than formerly because of the use of antibiotics before the initial infection has had a chance to spread. Urinary tract infections may also be caused by the entry of bacteria from below - most commonly in girls because the urethra is shorter than in boys and because the urinary tract opening is nearer the anus.

Infection of the urinary tract is more likely if there is any abnormality in the system. To avoid permanent damage to the kidneys it is important that any abnormality is discovered and treated as soon as possible. Any child who has had a urinary tract infection should be kept under careful observation for some months. A child who suffers from persistent or recurrent urinary tract infections should be X-rayed to find any abnormality.

Difficult urination - straining to urinate or a dribbling urine flow - indicates an abnormally narrow passage or small opening, and requires urgent treatment to prevent permanent kidney damage.

Possible sites of disorder in the urinary system

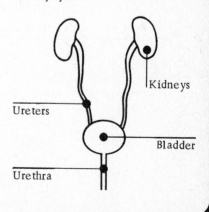

Kidneys

Ureters

Bladder

Urethra

K

INFECTIOUS DISEASES

K23 INFECTIOUS DISEASES

	INCUBATION	SYMPTOMS	TREATMENT	QUARANTINE
Gastro-enteritis	0-24 hours	Continual vomiting, diarrhea, irritability, dehydration.	In babies: reduce feeding, or give clear liquids, eg dextrose in water.	Isolation from infants
Bacterial meningitis	1-10 days	In young babies: lassitude, irritability, poor feeding, fits, fever, vomiting, possible increase in head size. In older children: headache, fever, vomiting, convulsions, neck rigidity, rash.	Immediate antibiotics.	Yes, until recovered.
Viral meningitis; Encephalitis	0-7 days	As for bacterial meningitis.	Supportive treatment. Antibiotics to prevent recurrence.	Yes, until recovered.
Coughs and colds	0-48 hours	Stuffy or runny nose, raised temperature, possibly vomiting.	In babies: supportive treatment and in severe cases antibiotics in liquid form to prevent pneumonia.	Isolation from infants
Rheumatic fever	1-6 weeks	Sore throat, temperature, diffuse rash, pains in limbs and large joints, may be small rheumatic nodules beneath the skin.	Bed rest, aspirin, prolonged use of penicillin in large doses, and occasionally steroid hormones.	Yes, for 2 weeks after start of treatment.
Diphtheria	2-5 days	Fever, sore throat, swollen neck glands, may be a dark, offensive-smelling membrane at the back of the throat.	Heavy doses of antitoxin, and sometimes antibiotics.	Yes, until free of symptoms.
Poliomyelitis (Polio)	10-12 days	Minor: fever, headache, diarrhea, vomiting (this stage lasts 1-2 days). Major (beginning 7 days later): fever, signs of meningitis, tender muscles, severe restlessness. May go on to paralytic stage: weak muscles, asymmetrical paralysis possibly affecting breathing. Improves after 7 days but may leave residual disability.	Bed rest and sedatives. In paralytic stage, massage of affected muscles and possibly use of a respirator.	Sufferers: 6 weeks isolation. Contacts: 3 weeks isolation.

The sick child

	INCUBATION	SYMPTOMS	TREATMENT	QUARANTINE
Chicken pox	4-7 days	Chill, fever, headache, malaise. Red spots - on face, chest, back - that later contain clear fluid, burst, and develop brown crusts.	For symptoms only: rest, and lotion for itching.	Yes, until appearance of crusts over lesions.
German measles	14-21 days	Malaise, fever, headache, inflamed mucous membrane. Fine pink spots first on face and neck, and then elsewhere.	Little or none. Lotion for itching.	Yes, until rash disappears.
Measles	8-13 days	Fever, cough, conjunctivitis. All-over rash appears later - white spots with red perimeter, along with inflamed background skin.	For symptoms: rest, cough syrup, soft diet, protection from cold, damp, and bright light. Treatment also for any complications.	Isolation from infants.
Mononucleosis (Glandular fever)	Not known	Headache, fever, sore throat, swollen lymph nodes. Loss of appetite.	For symptoms: rest, mouth wash, aspirin. Treatment for complications, if any.	Yes, until temperature has been normal for a week.
Mumps	12-20 days	Chill and fever, headache, temperature, swollen salivary glands (pain on chewing). Other glands may be swollen.	For symptoms: rest, soft diet, aspirin, perhaps sedatives. Also treatment for complications, if any.	Isolation from men and youths who have no immunity.
Roseola	4-7 days	High fever 3-4 days. Convulsions. Enlarged spleen. Later, purple-brown spots on chest, abdomen, face, and extremities.	For symptoms only: aspirin, water sponging to lower temperature.	No
Scarlet fever	1-3 days	Chills, fever, vomiting. Rash 24 hours after fever: small red spots join to form redness on whole body. Strawberry tongue. Sore throat.	Penicillin, rest, soft diet, water sponging to lower temperature, lotions for itching.	Yes, for not less than 7 days after onset.
Whooping cough	7-14 days	Sneezing, listlessness, and cough becoming convulsive with typical whooping breathing. Vomiting. May expel thick mucus.	Rest, fresh air, small meals, refeeding after vomiting. Mild sedatives and antibiotics. Hospital for serious cases.	Yes, for 21 days after onset of cough.

K

INFESTATIONS

K24 **K24 FLEAS, LICE, MITES**

Some types of parasite that live by biting the skin of animals and humans to suck their blood cause irritation and may spread disease.

a FLEAS The flea that usually lives on man (Pulex irritans) causes severe irritation. Some animal fleas also bite man - most serious are the bites of the rat flea, which spread typhus and bubonic plague. Eggs are laid in floorboard cracks, beds, and on pets. Fleas are best controlled by strict cleanliness.

b BODY LICE live and lay their eggs in the seams of clothing. Infested clothing should be washed and sterilized in boiling water. Body lice spread typhus, and bites may be sources of other infection.

c HEAD LICE live on the scalp, laying tiny, white, sticky eggs (nits) on the hair. It is easiest to detect head lice by finding the eggs. There may also be itching red spots where the hair meets the back of the neck. Head lice are not known to spread disease, but bites may become sites of infection. The scalp should be shampooed several times with medicated soap, and the hair combed with a fine-toothed comb. Insecticides should not be used.

d MITES Bites by the inch mite cause scabies - groups of scabbed pimples frequently occurring on the backs of the hands, the wrists, penis, and stomach. Scabies is contagious and requires medical treatment. The usual remedy is benzylbenzoate, painted on the skin. Chiggers, or harvest mites, are found in some countries and cause itching, blotching, and blisters. They can be removed with soap and water.

K25 PARASITIC WORMS

Several types of parasitic worm live in the intestines of humans.

a THREADWORMS, or pinworms, are fairly common in children. About $\frac{1}{4}$in (6mm) long, they resemble tiny white threads. They live in the intestine but come out at night to lay their eggs around the anus, where they cause itching. Mild stomach pains, nausea, and diarrhea may also occur, and worms can be seen in the feces. Eggs are spread on sheets and on the hands after scratching. Treatment is easy, but first consult a doctor.

b COMMON ROUNDWORMS invade intestines, liver, and lungs. They are up to 4in (10cm) long and look like earthworms. There may be no symptoms unless a great many worms are present, in which case an obstruction of the bile duct may occur. Microscopic eggs are passed in the feces, and are spread in contaminated food. A doctor will prescribe effective treatment.

c TAPEWORMS Several types of tapeworm are found in man, usually caught from inadequately cooked beef, fish, or pork. Tapeworms may grow 30ft (9m) long, and attach themselves to the intestinal wall by suckers or hooks on the head. Body segments break off and are passed in the feces. Only the larva of the pork tapeworm develops in man, producing severe complications. Effective drugs can be prescribed.

d HOOKWORMS Commonest in tropical countries, hookworms also occur in the southern states of the USA. About $\frac{1}{2}$in (1.27cm) long, they attach themselves to the wall of the intestine to suck blood. Symptoms are unusual appetite, constipation alternating with diarrhea, anemia, and malnutrition. Eggs are passed out in the feces. Larvae from contaminated soil enter the body by burrowing into bare feet. Treatment is by drugs, high-protein diet, and iron supplements.

The sick child

K26 GENITAL PROBLEMS

Genital problems that may occur in boys include the following.
HYPOSPADIAS is a congenital deformity of the penis in which the opening of the urethra is on the shaft and not at the tip. It is usually discovered at birth and to prevent infection can be corrected by a simple operation.
HYDROCELE In this condition an excess of fluid protecting the testes causes swelling of the scrotum, often on both sides. In babies, the swelling usually disappears without treatment. If it occurs later in life, it may be treated by drawing off some of the fluid, or by surgery.
UNDESCENDED TESTES The testes are formed in the abdomen and usually descend into the scrotum before birth or soon after. Sometimes, however, the testes fail to descend naturally until later, or surgery may be needed to bring them down.
It is not always easy to tell if the testes have descended because they are attached to muscles that can draw them back into the groin for protection against injury or cold. (The best time to check them is when the child is in a warm bath. Do not handle them, and avoid causing alarm.)
If one or both testes have never been seen in the scrotum when the child is two years old, a doctor should be consulted. Surgery is usual at age six if they remain undescended. If the testes are in the groin they can be brought down easily by surgery: if they are in the abdomen it may be necessary to remove them to prevent trouble in the future.

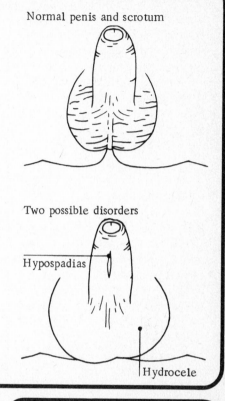

Normal penis and scrotum

Two possible disorders

Hypospadias

Hydrocele

K27 HERNIAS

A hernia occurs when an organ protrudes through a weak point in the muscle around it. Two types of hernia are common in children.
UMBILICAL HERNIA, visible as puffing out of the navel when the child cries, occurs when a small portion of the intestine protrudes through a gap in the abdominal wall left by the umbilical vessels. An umbilical hernia rarely causes trouble, and the gap usually closes after a few weeks or months. Surgery may be recommended if the hernia is still present when the child is two.
INGUINAL HERNIA is potentially more serious and is usually corrected by simple surgery soon after it is discovered, often in the first year. It is most common in boys, occurring when part of the intestine is pushed during crying or straining through the inguinal canal into the groin or scrotum.

In girls, inguinal hernia produces a swelling in the groin.
Occasionally an inguinal hernia becomes strangulated - trapped so that its blood supply is cut off, causing pain and vomiting. Immediate surgery is required in such cases because of the risk of gangrene or peritonitis.

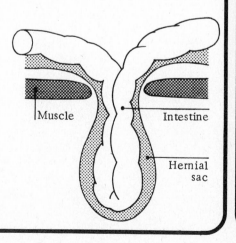

Muscle

Intestine

Hernial sac

K28 INFANTILE CONVULSIONS

Some young children are prone to infantile convulsions that have no connection with epilepsy (J71). Also called febrile convulsions, they are usually brought on by high fever. (They are best avoided by keeping fever down, see K31.)
A convulsion lasts at most for a few minutes, but may be alarming. The child loses consciousness, and starts to twitch and shake. His eyes roll, his teeth are clenched, his breathing is heavy, and he may froth at the mouth or wet himself. A convulsion always ends in sleep. The child must not be left alone until the convulsion ends, because of the risk of inhaling vomit (his head should be turned to one side if he vomits). His limbs should be kept away from danger but no attempt made to restrain him or to hold down his tongue. The doctor should be called after the child has gone to sleep.

K

HOME CARE 1

K29 GENERAL POINTS

These pages give simple hints about solving some of the basic problems likely to crop up in nursing a sick child. A few general points are included here.
1) Lethargy, loss of appetite, or slight fever indicate the onset of many childhood illnesses.
2) If such a condition develops, put the child to bed; if it worsens, consult a doctor, who may prescribe medicine, and advise on diet and overall care.
3) Some illnesses are infectious and require quarantine.
4) Sick children may need help with simple, everyday actions.
5) They need solicitude but not pampering.
6) Cheerful patients often recover faster than gloomy ones, so as far as possible keep your sick child occupied.

K31 LOWERING TEMPERATURE

Normal body temperature is said to be 98.6°F (37°C). But temperature fluctuates even in healthy bodies. In fact a temperature as high as 99.5°F (37.5°C) or as low as 97.7°F (36.5°C) may be normal for some individuals. Also body temperature varies during the day. Then, too, a child's temperature may be readily raised by excitement, an infant's by incessant crying. Thus a high temperature need not mean illness.
But a temperature above 100°F (37.8°C) indicates a fever. A temperature of 104°F (40°C) indicates a high fever.
To lower a child's temperature give aspirin (unless the child is allergic to it) and plenty of water or fruit juice. For high fever, a tepid sponge applied to the arms and face may help.

K30 TAKING A TEMPERATURE

The temperature can be taken in the mouth, rectum, or armpit (the latter gives a reading approximately 1°F:0.5°C below the others). Do not take the temperature soon after the child has eaten or drunk anything, or had a bath.
First rinse the thermometer in cold water, and wipe it dry. Place it in the appropriate position (for an oral reading the bulb should be under the tongue, and the mouth kept closed). Remove the thermometer after two minutes. Holding the end opposite the bulb, read the silver column of mercury against the scale. Make a note of the temperature. Shake down the mercury column. Rinse the thermometer in cold water, dry it, and stand it in antiseptic.

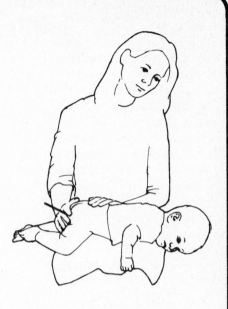

Taking the temperature with a rectal thermometer

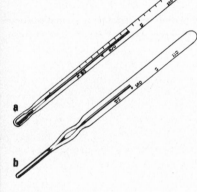

Types of thermometer:
a Oral
b Rectal

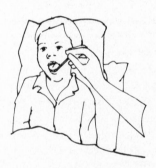

Taking the temperature with an oral thermometer in the mouth

Using a sharp wrist action to shake down the mercury column

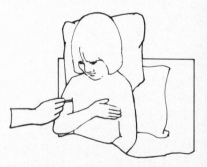

Taking the temperature with a thermometer in the armpit

The sick child

K32 PULSE RATE

The heart's pumping action makes arteries expand and contract as blood pulses through them. Heart rate can be easily judged by finding the pulse rate of the artery in the wrist just below the thumb. To feel a patient's pulse, press your finger tips lightly but firmly on the wrist and move them gently until you feel the artery beating. Because the ball of the thumb has a pulse avoid using your thumb.
The average pulse rate for an adult is is 65-80 beats a minute. This increases with exertion, during infection, or under emotional stress. Children always have a high pulse rate. A baby's may be 120-140 per minute. A six-year-old child's may be 90. Pulse rhythm may vary as the child breathes in and out.

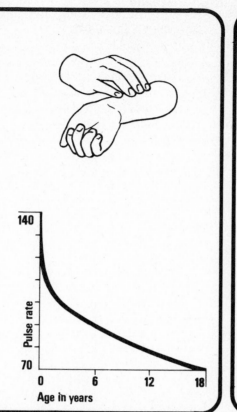

K33 RESPIRATION RATE

Respiration rate is discovered by counting the number of times the chest rises and falls in a minute. It is easily changed by emotion, and is best measured when a person is asleep or unaware that his respiration rate is being checked. Respiration rate, like pulse rate, decreases with age.

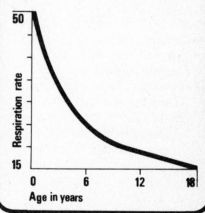

K34 GIVING MEDICINE

Medicines can be dangerous if they are misused, and it is vital always to use them with care. Never give a medicine to anyone for whom it was not prescribed.

POINTS TO REMEMBER
1 Adopt a matter of fact manner.
2 Check it is the correct medicine - always preserve labels.
3 Check correct times of dosage.
4 Measure dose correctly (5ml spoon).
5 Non-dissolving pills can be crushed and added to jelly or honey.
6 Make a checklist of doses given.
7 Make sure bottle tops are always replaced securely.
8 Finish course if told to do so.

K35 COPING WITH VOMITING

Vomiting can be due to motion sickness, obstruction of the digestive tract, food poisoning, indigestion, worry, tonsillitis, or infections including scarlet fever. Attacks occur most often in early infancy.
A vomiting attack is unpleasant to watch and can be frightening for the child. Deal with it calmly. Hold a bowl for the child and support him while the attack lasts. Then let him rinse his mouth with water. Wash his lips and face with a cloth. Change his bedclothes if they were soiled by the attack. Stay with him for a while in case he vomits again. Don't give him anything to drink for at least a couple of hours. Inform the doctor at once if the child is in pain.

K

HOME CARE 2

K36 INCREASING COMFORT

A sick child may easily become lonely, miserable, and bored. Try to make his room bright and attractive. If he is well enough to sit up, build a soft wall of pillows to support his back. Remove crumbs and wrinkles from his sheets. These need changing often, and if bedwetting is a problem, put a rubber sheet below them. A bedside table placed in easy reach should hold favorite books, magazines and games, a radio, and drinking water. If he is strong enough, a short period sitting on a chair or on the bed will help relieve monotony. Be solicitous but practical: resist continual attention seeking, but spend set times with him. In a long illness avoid showing too much concern.

K37 GIVING A BED BATH

The patient should be undressed and covered with a blanket. First wash face and neck, then arms and armpits. Roll the blanket to the waist and wash chest and belly. Cover the washed parts after drying thoroughly. Uncover one leg at a time and wash from feet to groin. Turn the patient on his side to wash his back. Let the patient wash whatever parts he is able to.

K39 INVALID'S PROGRESS

1 Rest and sleep are among the most effective medicines for the really sick body. At this stage a child wants little more than a comfortable bed, a noise-free bedroom, and understanding.

2 When the child is well enough to sit up and eat meals, provide them on a tray, one course at a time, the food pre-cut if necessary. Make sure the food is tasty and attractive.

3 Early on in his recovery a child prefers physically undemanding amusements: soft toys to hug; books or comics to glance at; a radio to listen to. His attention span may be brief.

The sick child

K38 DIET IN ILLNESS

In many illnesses appetite drops off and some foods are not readily digested. Ask your doctor's advice on feeding if possible. The following hints are only general guides and some illnesses need special diets.

At the start of a high fever frequently offer water, soft drinks, and (if wanted) milk with no cream. In a day or two, if he is hungry, even a feverish child may cope with cereal, toast, soft-boiled egg, custard, ice cream, or cookies. Children convalescing after fever can usually tackle meat, fish, and vegetables.

After vomiting, wait two hours before allowing a sip of water. Later give half a glass, and, after several hours, a cookie or a little cereal or skim milk.

In simple colds, extra fluid may be helpful to children with diminished appetites.

In convalescence the child's appetite returns as he recovers. Meanwhile, forcing him to eat everyday foods before his digestive system is disease-free may cause revulsion and can even trigger long-term food fads.

Strict dietary rules apply to some medical conditions. Children with celiac disease, for example, cannot absorb gluten and should not eat bread, cakes, sausages, ice cream, or other foods that contain gluten. Patients convalescing after a liver or kidney disease may need a high-protein diet. Adolescents need extra calcium for building bones.

Foods suitable for inclusion in the diet after one or two days of fever

4 Convalescence can be boring for a child and visits cheer him up. But they should not be too long and the visitors should not be exposed to infection. If in doubt about the risk, ask a doctor.

5 A child on the way to recovery enjoys constructive, imaginative play: model making, sewing, making scrapbooks. It is more fun if you can help. Some schoolwork can be done in bed too.

3 When the child can get up for a time, he enjoys leaving his bedroom to watch television or sit with other family members. Make sure he is not in a draft. Use a blanket for warmth.

K

CHILD IN THE HOSPITAL

K40 GOING TO THE HOSPITAL

Almost every child has to visit the hospital at some time, either as an outpatient, or for a longer stay for medical treatment or an operation. The unfamiliarity of the hospital and its staff, and the separation from his family, can make even the shortest visit a frightening experience for a child. Parents should therefore use every opportunity to familiarize the child with the idea of the hospital in advance by taking him there to visit a friend or relative.

A simple explanation of the equipment that may be used and the treatment that he is likely to receive can be helpful, and a young child can be encouraged to "act out" some aspects of the treatment on his toys.

K41 HOSPITAL ADMISSION

Admissions to the hospital fall into two broad categories - routine and emergency.

ROUTINE ADMISSIONS
In the case of routine admissions the hospital admission is arranged some time in advance - which has the incidental advantage of giving the parents sufficient time and opportunity to prepare the child. Among children, the commonest reason for routine admission to the hospital is for the correction of a congenital malformation such as cleft palate or a faulty heart valve. Where possible, doctors try to avoid admitting very young children to the hospital, but in some cases surgery has the best chance of success if it is carried out at a particular stage of the child's development.

EMERGENCY ADMISSIONS
An emergency admission to the hospital is potentially more disturbing for a child because of the lack of preparation time. Perhaps the most useful thing that a parent can do to help in these circumstances is to try and appear as calm as possible. Reasons for emergency admission include the diagnosis of an illness such as appendicitis that requires urgent treatment, or a particular development in a disease that requires the child to be kept under constant supervision.

An alarming number of emergency admissions among children, however, are the result of accidents - many of which could be avoided with better safety precautions at home and outdoors.

K42 ADMISSION PROCEDURES

A thorough examination is customary when a child is admitted to the hospital.

The child's weight, height, temperature, pulse, and blood pressure are normally recorded, and a urine test, blood test, and X-ray may be performed.

The parents will be asked routine questions about the child's earlier illnesses and previous visits to the hospital. This helps the doctor build up a general picture of the child's medical history.

If the child is to be admitted, he

should be allowed to take with him a few favorite toys, and, if he has one, his "comforter." When the child undresses, it may be less alarming for him if his clothes are left nearby even if he cannot wear them.

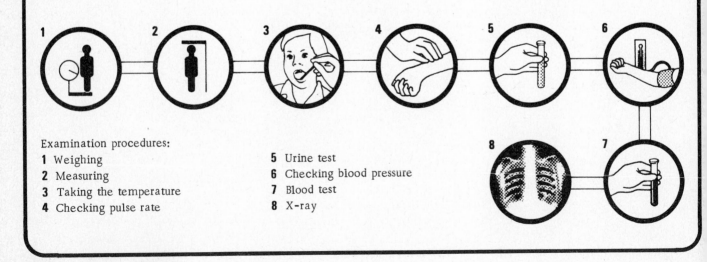

Examination procedures:
1 Weighing
2 Measuring
3 Taking the temperature
4 Checking pulse rate
5 Urine test
6 Checking blood pressure
7 Blood test
8 X-ray

The sick child

K43 VISITING

A hospital's visiting schedule depends on its organization and staff arrangements.

In some hospitals visiting is normally allowed only during special visiting hours arranged to fit in with the daily routine of each section of the hospital. These restricted hours may make visiting difficult for some parents because of their hours of work or commitments at home, so many hospitals are now introducing unrestricted visiting in children's sections. This enables parents to visit at times that suit their particular circumstances.

A small child left alone in the hospital may feel frightened, overwhelmed, and even abandoned, and his loneliness and confusion may be reflected in a rather indifferent or sulky reaction to his parents' first visit. In general, visits should ideally be kept short and frequent, and parents should if possible use the time to play with their child.

A visit from brothers and sisters will reassure a sick child and may also help them become familiar with the hospital situation.

Recognizing the severe emotional stress that a stay in the hospital can impose on a child, some hospitals now provide facilities for parents to remain with their child throughout his stay. If this is the case, a parent can help the child not just by playing with him and reading to him, but also by assisting in aspects of his day-to-day care such as bathing, changing, and administering medicine.

K44 OUTPATIENT VISITS

A short visit to a clinic or the hospital may be necessary for a variety of reasons.

Before admission to the hospital for surgical or medical treatment a visit to a specialist as an outpatient is usual.

Also, many routine tests or examinations, and some minor surgical procedures are frequently performed in the outpatients' department.

The child should be warned in advance of his visit to the hospital, and, as in the case of an admission, he should be given some idea of what to expect.

A favorite book, game, or toy should be taken, as delays between appointments are sometimes unavoidable even in the best-run sections.

K45 HOSPITAL PERSONNEL

The children's section of a hospital is staffed with personnel specially trained in child care.

The treatment of a child in the hospital is supervised by one doctor -either a pediatrician specializing in childhood disorders of every kind, or a specialist in a particular type of disorder.

Routine aspects of medical care and general welfare in a pediatric section are the responsibility of the nursing staff.

Physical and occupational therapists may be involved in the recovery program, and where X-rays are necessary, these will be studied by a radiologist.

A dietitian, a play supervisor, and a teacher are now employed in most pediatric sections, and a medical social worker is usually available to discuss problems with both the child and his family.

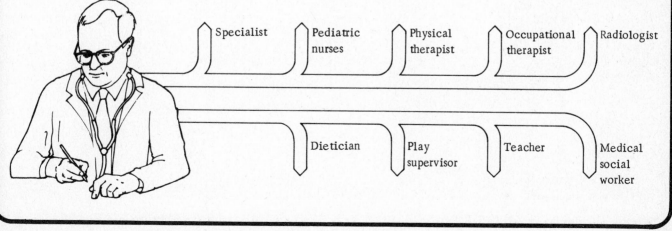

Specialist · Pediatric nurses · Physical therapist · Occupational therapist · Radiologist · Dietician · Play supervisor · Teacher · Medical social worker

© DIAGRAM

Children in need of special care

Some children need special care and attention — from their parents, from the community, and sometimes also from professional personnel.

L

Left: Suppertime in a French orphanage at the turn of the century (The Mansell Collection)

PHYSICAL HANDICAP 1

L01 RESTRICTED MOBILITY

Restricted mobility may be a temporary or a permanent condition, or the degree of handicap may vary with the occurrence of remissions in some illnesses. The nature of the disorders that result in restricted mobility is very varied. The biggest single cause of restricted mobility in children is cerebral palsy (J73), although the number of children surviving with handicaps due to spina bifida (J72) has increased in recent years. Other causes of restricted mobility in children include muscular dystrophy, limb abnormalities, and some types of arthritis. Thanks to effective immunization programs, however, poliomyelitis is now uncommon. In addition to illnesses, accidents can result in either temporary or permanent problems of mobility.

L02 HELPING THE HANDICAPPED CHILD

A wide range of help has been developed to meet the needs of children with physical handicaps that restrict mobility.

In some cases, such as certain bone malformations and injuries, surgery can ease or even cure the cause of the mobility problem.

In others, notably cerebral palsy, drugs may be used to check some of the symptoms of disorder.

Very often, however, help for the child with restricted mobility must be concentrated on helping him to make the best possible use of whatever movement he has, through medical services such as physical therapy (L03), occupational therapy, special schooling, and the use of various types of aid (L04).

Ultimately the amount of controlled movement that a child with a mobility handicap will be able to achieve depends on the nature and severity of his particular problem. But specialized help can produce striking results.

Many children with a mobility handicap benefit from attending a special school, equipped with a full range of specialized facilities and equipment. In other cases it may be possible and preferable for a child to attend the regular neighborhood school.

Coping with the needs of a physically handicapped child in the home can place a severe strain on other members of the family. Help and advice is available from social workers, and from charity organizations associated with particular disabilities. In some areas, excellent community support schemes are now in operation.

L04 SPECIAL AIDS

With the needs of the physically handicapped in mind, various aids have been developed to simplify some routine tasks which might otherwise prove impossible.

An appropriately designed wheelchair can make a significant difference to a handicapped child's life, but many different designs are available and a doctor's advice is essential to avoid an expensive mistake.

For certain types of handicap, feeding equipment such as suction-based plates, dishes with lips, and specially-shaped cutlery encourage valuable independence. Devices that can be operated with minimal movement - perhaps only a toe - have been perfected and are now applied to a wide range of equipment such as page-turners, typewriters, and tape recorders.

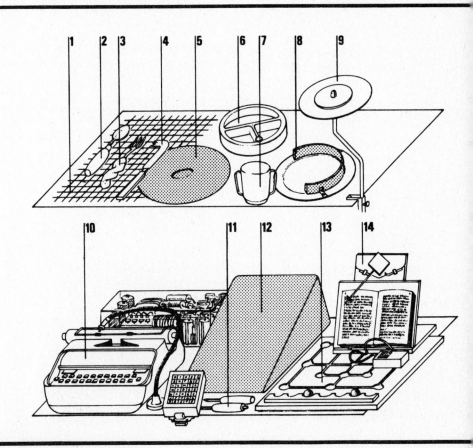

Children in need of special care

L03 PHYSICAL THERAPY

Physical therapy can help a child with restricted mobility in two important ways.

First, it can teach him to make good use of existing movement, and perhaps help him to cope with routine tasks such as feeding and dressing that might otherwise prove impossible.

Second, it can teach him to use certain aids appropriate for his needs which may help compensate for lack of mobility or control of particular parts of the body. For example, the crawler (1) has been developed to enable a physically handicapped small child to improve muscle control while getting around and exploring his environment. Many older children enjoy and benefit from riding a tricycle (2) or, with the aid of a special saddle and supports, a pony (3). Swimming, too, is a valuable and enjoyable form of exercise for the physically handicapped, while a variety of other sporting activities, such as fencing (4) and archery, can be enjoyed by children in wheelchairs.

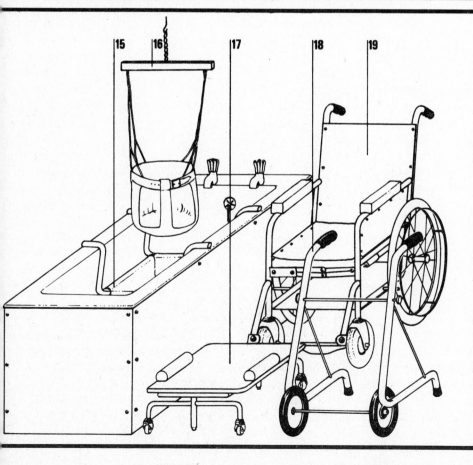

Selection of aids suitable for children with different disabilities.

1 Non-slip place mat
2 Large-handled spoon
3 Fork with malleable handle
4 Knife with curved blade
5 Non-slip mat for plate
6 Suction-based deep divided dish
7 Double-handled cup
8 Detachable lip for plate
9 Adjustable rotating feeding plate
10 Electronic typewriter controlled by "suck and blow" input
11 Thick-grip pencils
12 Foam rubber play wedge
13 Game with deeply recessed board
14 Page-turner
15 Bath seat
16 Hoist
17 Crawler trolley
18 Walking frame
19 Wheelchair

PHYSICAL HANDICAP 2

L05 IMPAIRED HEARING

Impaired hearing in an infant can result from a genetic defect, from damage caused by an infection such as German measles early in pregnancy, from the effect of some drugs, or from brain damage.

Since a hearing defect interferes with the development of language it is vital that the problem is identified as soon as possible. There are a number of warning signs. A child with impaired hearing continues to "babble" long after others are using recognizable words. Also, he may be later than average in walking, less adventurous and imaginative in his play, and often very noisy. If the child is able to hear anything at all he will be fitted with a hearing aid. At home, parents can do a great deal to supplement the work of experts. The child's hearing aid must be in good working order, and should be worn for as much of the day as possible. Constant aural stimulation is vital, and to make it effective the child should be encouraged to pay attention to the sound source. Good "watching" conditions should be created, and there should be as few visual distractions as possible. When talking to the child about an object a parent should if possible hold the object near his own face so that the child can see the object and his parent's facial movements at the same time. The child will also benefit from feeling the vibrations of his parent's chest or throat during speech, and from the sensation of breath against his hair while the parent sings gently in his ear.

SPECIAL TEACHING
Special pre-school groups, special schools, or special classes in regular schools will help the child with impaired hearing to communicate with confidence.

L06 VISUAL HANDICAP

Among the the causes of visual handicap in infancy are an infection such as German measles early in pregnancy, brain damage at the time of delivery, or an infection in the post-birth period. A child who is blind (with no sight at all) or partially sighted (with some residual vision, however little) will need a great deal of special care and attention to help him cope in a world where there is such dependence on sight.

HELP AT HOME
A visually handicapped child will benefit from added stimulation from the earliest age. Crawling, walking, and talking must be strongly encouraged by parents and skilled workers because of the lack of visual incentive. All the objects in daily use such as feeding implements and clothes should be identified by the parents by name as the child handles them, and investigation by feeling should also be encouraged.

Independence can be developed by ensuring that feeding equipment and clothes are simple enough for the child to manage for himself. Conversation based on reality is invaluable to a visually handicapped child, preventing him from feeling isolated and helping him to learn. If possible, he should be told of an impending loud noise or sudden action to prevent him from being startled.

SCHOOLS
Excellent special schools cater for the needs of visually handicapped children. They aim to encourage the effective use of any residual vision, to teach the use of various aids, to help with any additional handicap, and to ease the child's social adjustment by fostering his sense of personal worth.

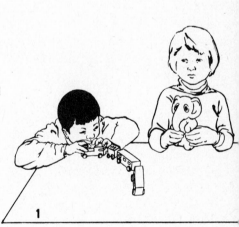

AIDS
A visually handicapped child particularly enjoys and benefits from "noisy" toys and those with hard edges or an intriguing shape (1). A special drawing frame (2) has been developed to enable the child to feel a shape or word that

Children in need of special care

Speech reading (lip reading) and special signs are often taught as valuable aids to comprehension and communication.
Among the equipment used in the teaching of children with impaired hearing are simple objects like mirrors (**1**) and balloons (**2**) that help the child to see or feel his developing powers of speech, as well as more complex aids like tape recorders and headphones (**3**).

he has created: a series of raised dots appears as the child gently presses on the board with a ballpoint pen. Learning to type (**3**) allows the visually handicapped child to communicate by letter with sighted friends, and may also help him find employment later.

Braille books (**4**) allow a blind child to read for himself; large-type books are available for partially sighted children. A tape recorder (**5**) is invaluable in education and for entertainment. Special "talking books" are also much appreciated.

L07 OTHER PROBLEMS

In addition to children needing special care because of a more obvious physical handicap affecting mobility, hearing, or sight, there exists another broad group of children who must also be singled out for particular attention. Included in this group are children with chronic physical conditions that require medical attention and special care over a prolonged period of time.

A variety of conditions require regular visits to a hospital for check-ups or treatment, and in some cases of congenital disorder a series of operations may be needed over a period of years.

The regular administration of drugs plays an important part in controlling conditions such as epilepsy (J71), and daily injections may be needed to correct hormonal deficiencies as in the case of diabetes (J67).

Certain conditions require that special attention be paid to diet – for example restricting the carbohydrate intake of diabetics, and excluding gluten from the diet of sufferers of celiac disease (J63). Other children require what may be called a cushioned environment. A child with hemophilia (J56), for example, must be protected from situations in which he may become cut or bruised, and over-exertion can be dangerous for children with sickle-cell anemia (J56). Children with heart disorders (J53), however, are generally allowed to do as much as they feel is possible.

Caring for a child with a chronic physical problem such as those outlined here involves the parent in added responsibilities – not least in helping the child to lead as normal a life as possible in the circumstances.

MENTAL HANDICAP

L08 MENTAL HANDICAP

Some degree of mental retardation occurs in approximately three per cent of the population. Causes of this type of handicap include chromosomal abnormalities, as in Down's syndrome (mongolism), and brain damage, due to a variety of causes before, during, or after birth (see J70). Over 200 causes of retardation have in fact been discovered by researchers, but in the majority of cases it remains impossible to discover the precise cause of mental handicap.

The term mentally retarded is used to describe persons with a wide range of ability. A person who is only mildly retarded will very probably be able to lead a normal, independent life as an adult. Someone who is profoundly retarded, however, may be unable to perform even quite simple everyday tasks. Between these two extremes are persons in need of varying degrees of special care either in the home or sometimes in special centers or institutions. Whatever the nature and degree of a child's handicap it is preferable for it to be diagnosed as soon as possible. Some types of mental handicap are evident at birth because there are distinguishing physical characteristics, as in the case of mongolism. Other types of handicap become apparent only when the child is older, perhaps when he starts school and finds it impossible to cope without the help of special teaching.

It is even more difficult to test the intelligence level of a child who is mentally retarded than it is to test that of a child who has no handicap. Careful observation over a considerable time should, however, lead to the development of a program of care and training that will help each child achieve his maximum potential.

L09 CARE AND EDUCATION

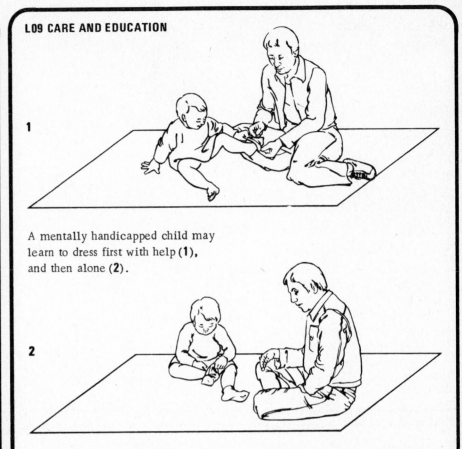

A mentally handicapped child may learn to dress first with help (1), and then alone (2).

It is essential that a mentally handicapped child should be treated in accordance with his own particular needs - emotional, educational, and social.

A child who is only mildly retarded should be able to cope at a normal school, possibly spending some time in special classes where the emphasis is on developing social, educational, and vocational skills needed to live independently as an adult.

Until comparatively recently it was common practice for more severely retarded children to enter an institution at an early age, and to remain there for the rest of their lives. The last two decades, however, have seen a shift away from institutionalized care - with its risk of emotional deprivation - toward care for the mentally handicapped within the family and the community as a whole. Within this general picture, it is obvious that recommendations for individual cases must depend both on family circumstances and the degree of a particular child's handicap.

Caring for a severely mentally handicapped child in the home obviously places considerable strain on other members of the family. Effective professional and community support are essential if the child's best interests are to be taken into account.

Many moderately retarded children benefit from attending a special day school or training center, where they will if possible be prepared for future employment in a sheltered work situation.

In severe cases expectations will be lower, but systematic training programs can often teach basic skills such as self-feeding, dressing, language development, and social responsiveness.

Children in need of special care

L10 EMOTIONAL DISTURBANCE

An emotionally disturbed child is not likely to complain openly about his worries. Instead he may become depressed - losing interest in activities, seeing few friends, and being unusually quiet. Other children become overanxious - crying a lot, sleeping badly, and clinging to their parents. Unruly behavior, too, may be a sign of disturbance, as the child tries to draw attention to his problems. Children with phobias transfer their real fears to situations or objects with symbolic value. Other children suffer from hysterical illnesses - converting an emotional problem into a physical one. Often parental understanding is sufficient to help a child through a difficult period, but in prolonged or severe cases the child may be in need of professional help.

L11 AUTISM

Autism is an uncommon mental condition in which the child is completely absorbed in himself. He appears indifferent to other people, rejects affection, and refuses to communicate. Often he will sit for hours, lost in a world of fantasy, perhaps playing with his fingers or a scrap of paper. At other times he is hyperactive, behaving in an unruly and difficult manner. Many autistic children can go for days with very little food or sleep.

The cause of autism is unknown, but research suggests that the problem may be biochemical. Special education and therapy have brought dramatic improvements in some cases; the first requirement is usually to break down the child's barrier to communication, so helping prepare the way for the development of more normal patterns of behavior.

L12 TREATMENT

Therapy for a young child usually includes play (**1**) and painting (**2**).

Specialists in the treatment of emotionally disturbed children include psychiatrists (medical doctors with additional training in psychiatry), psychologists (nonmedical professionals with graduate and postgraduate training in psychology), social workers, and nurses involved in mental health programs. Occasionally an emotionally disturbed child will be admitted into a hospital or residential unit for treatment, but in most cases it is preferable for the child to receive treatment while continuing to live at home. Special centers providing day care and treatment of various kinds have been set up in some areas to cater for the needs of emotionally disturbed children. Other children continue to attend their regular school, but visit a child psychiatrist or psychologist for treatment sessions at intervals depending on their own particular needs.

Many disturbed children benefit from psychotherapy. In the case of a young child, the emphasis is on play and painting; the therapist interprets these activities as the child's personal language, and through them helps the child to face and work through his problems. With an older child whose use of language is more developed, the therapist encourages the child to talk freely; in this way the therapist coaxes the child's problems to the surface so that the child can be helped to understand and come to terms with his difficulties. Sometimes a child's emotional problems are part of a general picture of difficulties within his family, and family counseling and other help from social workers may be needed.

© DIAGRAM

FAMILY PROBLEMS

L13 FAMILY PROBLEMS

Children can be deeply affected by family problems. Sometimes the family is under pressure from social problems such as poverty, poor housing, and prejudice (see L19-22). In other cases the problems have their origins within the family itself - in individual personalities, or in difficult relationships between family members. Very often, pressures from outside the family cause pressures within it. One-parent families (L17) have their own particular problems, as do families who foster or adopt a child (L18). In general it is useless and potentially harmful to pretend that all is well when this is obviously not the case. Families under pressure need support from friends, and perhaps also from professional agencies.

L14 NEGLECT

Neglect may be physical or emotional, immediately obvious or more difficult to recognize. In any case it is likely to have a profound effect on the child - many neglected children grow up to neglect their own families. Very often, neglect is part of a more general picture of family difficulties. In some cases the parents were emotionally unprepared for raising a family, or are confused by the economic demands of running a home. These same stresses may lead to physical violence against their children as well as chronic neglect. Parents who are in need of help themselves are often unable to care properly for their children, even though they want to. Support from social workers is essential in all cases of child neglect.

The diagram shows trends in US dependency and neglect cases (based on US Department of Health, Education, and Welfare statistics).

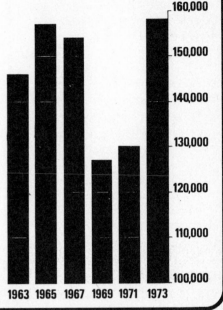

160,000 — 150,000 — 140,000 — 130,000 — 120,000 — 110,000 — 100,000

1963 1965 1967 1969 1971 1973

L16 DIVORCE

In a great many countries the number of children whose parents divorce is increasing every year. Special care is needed to ensure that these children suffer as little as possible from the break-up of their parents' marriage.
Many of the parents who now choose divorce would once have opted to "stay together for the sake of the children." In practice, the children rarely benefited. An atmosphere of tension in the home can easily be detected by a child, and there is a strong temptation for parents to draw the children into their own quarrels.
Divorce does not have to mean the loss of a parent; most couples make arrangements for sharing time with their children. If a parent remarries, the child may, after a period of readjustment, come to enjoy and benefit from his new "extended" family.

The diagram (based on US divorce statistics) shows the increasing number of children whose parents are obtaining a divorce.

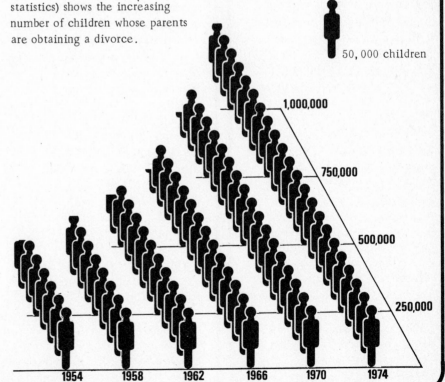

50,000 children

1,000,000

750,000

500,000

250,000

1954   1958   1962   1966   1970   1974

Children in need of special care

L15 CHILD ABUSE

Every year courts handle many cases in which children have been physically injured by their parents. The problem is not a new one, but its survival into modern, more enlightened times is cause for serious concern. Child abuse, or "battering" as it is now commonly called, occurs in every community. It is found in families at all economic and educational levels, occurring in homes that are clearly in chaos and in others that are apparently well-regulated. Very often, cases of child abuse are discovered when a child is brought to the doctor after an "accident" - and increased medical awareness has helped in this respect. Child battering rarely results from willful cruelty - but is rather a sign that the parent needs urgent community help.

Based on a study by the Children's Division of the American Humane Society, the diagram below shows the proportions of persons brought into court for causing physical injury to a child.

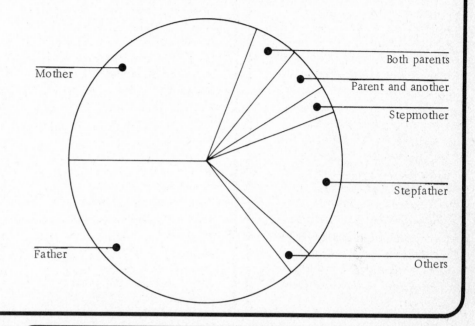

L17 ONE-PARENT FAMILIES

A parent who for whatever reason must bring up a child alone has many additional problems to face. Even problems common to any parent can be an extra strain when there is no partner to give support. Many one-parent families have money problems - the physical and emotional needs of the children may make it difficult to take a well-paid job, or it may prove impossible to do any work outside the home. More nurseries and playgroups for young children are urgent requirements, and provision is needed for older children after school or during vacations. Lone parents also face emotional problems - feelings of isolation, or behavior problems in their children caused by insecurity. Support from friends, self-help organizations, and the community can prove of tremendous value to lone parents and their children.

L18 FOSTERING, ADOPTION, RESIDENTIAL CARE

Sometimes family problems are such that it is impossible or undesirable for children to remain, either temporarily or permanently, in the homes of the natural parents. FOSTERING If the period of separation is to be temporary, attempts will be made by social workers to place the child in a foster home. Foster parents are carefully screened, and every effort made to unsettle the child as little as possible. Problems arise if the child is moved too often, or if he becomes too attached to his foster parents at the expense of his natural parents to whom he must return. ADOPTION When the separation from the parents is to be permanent, the child is usually taken first to a reception home. Every effort will then be made to find an adoptive home for him. Adoption of a child is a permanent arrangement, and great care is taken to do everything possible to ensure that the adoption will be a success: the physical and mental health of the child is assessed, and the prospective parents will be searchingly questioned. After the adoption, support will be given by social workers. An adopted child should always be told early on of his adoption - a chance discovery of the fact is much worse than being told the truth at some suitable natural moment. RESIDENTIAL CARE Only if it is impossible to place him in a suitable family is a child likely to spend much time in a residential children's home. Within these homes, every effort is made to provide as natural a family environment as possible - with small groups of children in the care of residential houseparents.

SOCIAL PROBLEMS

L19 SOCIAL DISADVANTAGE

Some children are in need of special care, from within the family and without, to prevent them from suffering from the effects of social disadvantage - effects that may last for the rest of their lives.

In many cases family poverty is the key problem. Inadequate diet may lead to poor health, which in turn may cause absences from school and poor academic performance. Poor housing, too, has physical and social effects (L21). Parents who are forced to work long hours have less time and energy to devote to their children, while unemployment can strain all family relationships. Many disadvantaged children grow up to lead successful and happy lives, but numerous difficulties must first be overcome.

L20 INTEGRATION

Mutual understanding and respect are needed to hasten the integration of different national, racial, and religious groups within the community as a whole. Differences in social customs can prove confusing to a child, who may encounter different sets of rules at home and elsewhere. Dietary regulations are an obvious example of this type of problem; harder to cope with, perhaps, are different views on polite or impolite behavior. Encouraging children to respect the cultural traditions of others is one of the simplest, most positive ways for parents to help fight destructive prejudice.

Language is one of the major barriers to integration, but in general children tend to cope better than their parents with this

particular problem. Most young children manage to pick up a new language comparatively easily, although special language teaching may be needed at first.

L21 HOUSING PROBLEMS

Inadequate housing can affect the health and happiness of children as well as their parents.

Children who are brought up in slum dwellings obviously face greater risk to health from cold, damp, and vermin. Overcrowding frequently makes matters worse. Ambitious rehousing schemes - often involving moves to large apartment blocks in different parts of town - have not, however, been an unqualified success.

Separation from old friends and difficulty making new ones can cause problems for children and parents, and the lack of community feeling in many new housing developments is a major social loss. Very often the greatest single problem for children is inadequate provision of play space - both indoors and out - and to avoid serious social problems planners must take this into account.

L22 POVERTY

The inhabitants of the United States are among the richest in the world. But here, as in other countries, a great many people live in poverty.

The diagram below shows the proportion of US children aged under 18 who in 1973 were members of families in poverty. The "poverty index" on which it

is based was developed by the US Social Security Administration. This index takes into account family income, family size, farm or nonfarm residence, and changes in the Consumer Price Index. In 1973, 13.1% of children in metropolitan areas were in poverty, compared with 16.6% of children in nonmetropolitan areas.

The diagram shows proportions of US children in poverty in 1973 (based on US Bureau of the Census statistics).

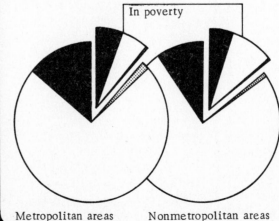

In poverty

Metropolitan areas   Nonmetropolitan areas

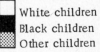

White children
Black children
Other children

Children in need of special care

L23 JUVENILE CRIME

Recent years have seen alarming increases in the incidence of juvenile crime in many countries. Sometimes delinquent behavior is no more than an isolated incident in a child's normal pattern of development. In other cases, the problem is more deeply rooted - with incidents of varying severity occurring over a period of time. Very often, delinquent behavior is a response to unsatisfactory family or social circumstances, and this must be taken carefully into account by the authorities when deciding the best course of action in each particular case.

Many juvenile offenses stem from boredom, and one positive way in which a community can help tackle the problem of juvenile crime is to see that adequate entertainment facilities are provided.

L24 DELINQUENCY TRENDS

The number of delinquency cases handled in juvenile courts in the USA has shown a marked increase over the past 20 years. Especially striking is the increase in the number of girls now appearing in the courts. Similar increases are to be found in other countries.

The diagram shows cases handled by juvenile courts (from statistics published by the US Department of Health, Education, and Welfare).

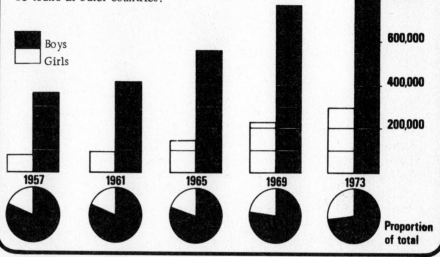

Proportion of total

L25 TYPES OF CRIME

The majority of crimes committed by juveniles are crimes against property. In the USA in 1975, property crimes - including burglary, larceny-theft, and motor vehicle theft - accounted for 42% of arrests among persons under 15 years of age. In the same year, violent crime - including murder, forcible rape, robbery, and aggravated assault - accounted for only 3% of the total number of arrests within this same age group. Runaways accounted for 11% of arrests in this age group in 1975, and violations of local curfew and loitering laws - another specifically juvenile category - for a further 4%.

The diagram shows principal causes of arrest among those aged under 15 (based on FBI statistics for 1975).

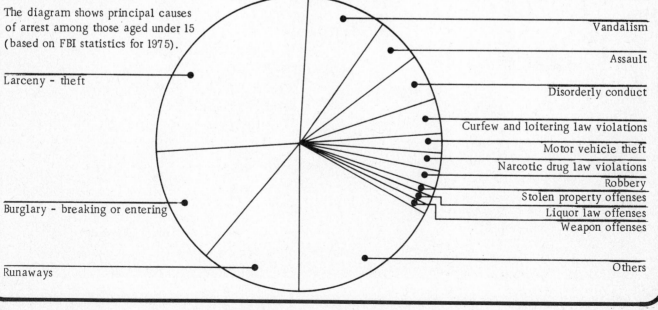

The end of childhood

As well as the physical changes that transform a girl into a woman and a boy into a man, there are significant emotional adjustments to be made as childhood comes to an end.

Left: On the steps – a city scene from the 1950s (Photo Roger Mayne)

PHYSICAL ASPECTS 1

M01 CHANGES AT PUBERTY

The physical changes of puberty transform the body of a child into that of an adult. These changes take place over a number of years, and occur in response to the production of sex hormones (testosterone in the male and estrogen in the female). The age at which puberty occurs varies, but in general it starts and finishes earlier in girls than in boys.

The most significant development of puberty is the maturing of the sex organs (see M04, M05). Girls begin to menstruate and, after the first few periods, begin to produce mature ova during the menstrual cycle (see M06). Usually, a single ovum is produced from one of the ovaries each month. Maturing of the male sex organs during puberty results in the production of sperm, which are sometimes emitted from the penis during sleep ("wet dreams"). It is important that adolescents should be fully informed of these developments before they occur.

Male and female hormones are also responsible for the development during puberty of what are called secondary sexual characteristics. Before puberty, except for very obvious genital differences, the physical appearance of boys and girls is fairly similar. During puberty, differences betweeen the two sexes are emphasized. Girls generally do not grow as tall as boys. Girls develop rounded contours and broad hips, compared with the angular, more muscular male physique. Both sexes develop body hair during puberty but it occurs in different areas and is heavier in males. Also at this time, a boy's larynx grows more than a girl's, making his Adam's apple more pronounced and his voice deeper (see M09).

M02 DEVELOPMENT: GIRLS

Before puberty the breasts are undeveloped, there is no pubic or underarm hair, and the body shape is boyish. In early puberty - perhaps from age 11 to 13 - the face becomes fuller, the pelvis widens, fat is deposited on the hips, the breasts start to develop and the nipples stand out, pubic hair begins to grow, the vaginal walls thicken, and menstruation may begin. Later in puberty - perhaps from 14 to 17 - growth of the breasts continues, pubic hair thickens, menstruation begins if it has not already done so, the genitals mature, skeletal growth ends, and body shape becomes more rounded. Further rounding, breast development, and weight gain continue into the early twenties.

Illustrated here is a typical development pattern for a girl during puberty - obviously individuals vary considerably.

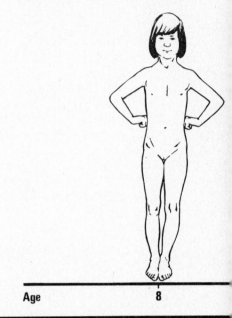

Age   **8**

M03 DEVELOPMENT: BOYS

In a boy before puberty the penis and scrotum are small, and there is no pubic, underarm, or other coarse body hair. In early puberty - perhaps from 12 to 15 - the testes begin to enlarge, pubic hair appears at the base of the penis, the penis begins to grow, and there is a sudden, rapid increase in height. As puberty continues - perhaps from 15 to 18 - the shoulders broaden, the voice deepens (M09), hair grows in the armpits and on the upper lip, penis growth continues, sperm are produced, pubic hair coarsens and spreads and other body hair grows, the prostate gland enlarges, height and weight increase and there is a sudden gain in strength. Height and weight typically continue to increase into the early twenties, and there is also further growth of coarse body hair.

A typical developmental pattern for a boy during puberty is illustrated here - as with girls, considerable individual variations obviously occur.

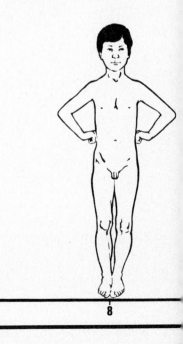

Age   **8**

The end of childhood

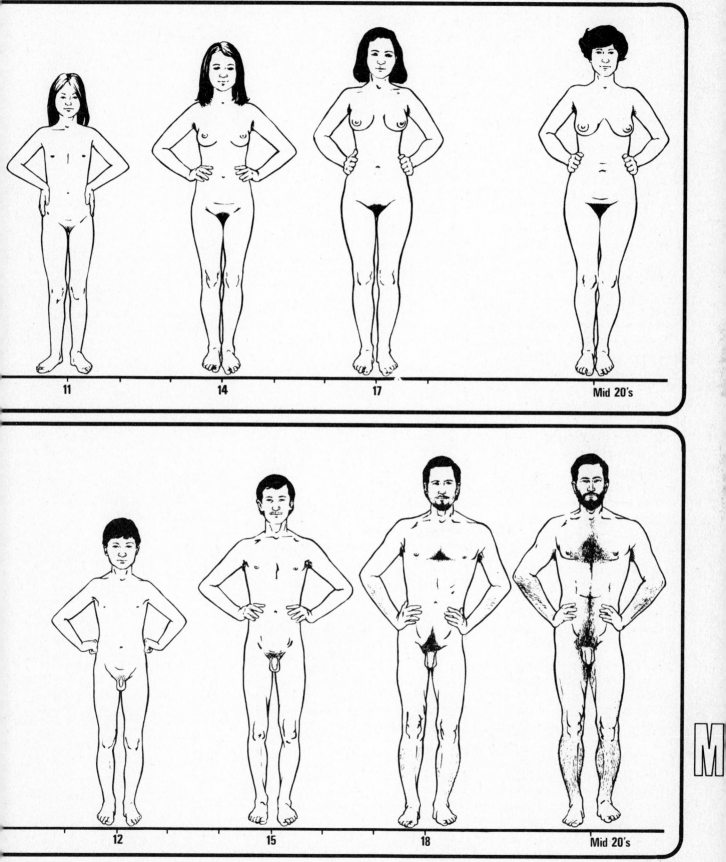

11   14   17   Mid 20's

12   15   18   Mid 20's

M

© DIAGRAM

PHYSICAL ASPECTS 2

M04 FEMALE SEX ORGANS

The two ovaries are egg-shaped organs situated in the abdominal cavity. Immature ova (eggs) are present in the ovaries at birth, but do not begin to mature until puberty (see M01).

Close to each ovary is the open end of a Fallopian tube (also illustrated in A02-03), along which ova travel to the uterus (womb). The uterus is a pear-shaped organ in the center of the pelvis, where the fetus develops during pregnancy.

The vagina is a muscular tube linking the cervix (neck of the womb) to the female external genitals, or vulva.

The vulva is a vertical cleft, on each side of which are the labia, lip-like folds of skin that meet at the clitoris, the female equivalent of the male penis.

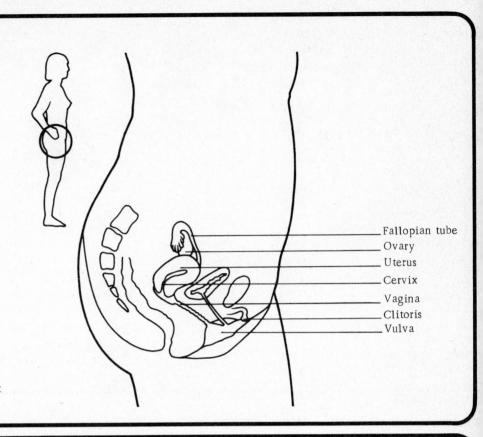

Fallopian tube
Ovary
Uterus
Cervix
Vagina
Clitoris
Vulva

M05 MALE SEX ORGANS

The male reproductive glands, the testes, hang in an external pouch called the scrotum.

At puberty, the testes begin producing the male sex hormone, testosterone, and sperm, the male reproductive cells. Until his death a man then produces millions of sperm every day.

After being stored in the epididymides, mature sperm swim along the vas deferens, tubes linking each testis with the prostate gland. Here they are mixed with seminal fluid made in the prostate gland and in the seminal vesicles.

The urethra is the tube that carries urine from the bladder to the penis. It is also the route by which seminal fluid leaves the body during ejaculation.

The penis is mostly spongy tissue, which fills with blood to produce an erection in sexual arousal.

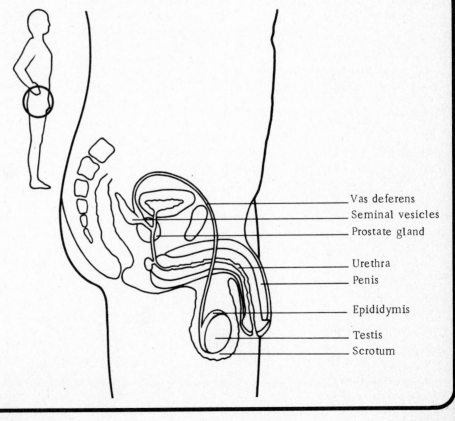

Vas deferens
Seminal vesicles
Prostate gland

Urethra
Penis

Epididymis

Testis
Scrotum

The end of childhood

M06 EXPLAINING MENSTRUATION

It is important that a girl should be told about menstruation before she is likely to have her first period (see M07).

During menstruation blood and mucus is discharged from the vagina, and pads or tampons are worn to absorb it. The period may last from two to eight days, but four to five days is most usual. Menstruation is the outward sign of the routine cycle of hormone change and ovum (egg) production that occurs in females from puberty to the menopause. During the first part of each cycle the lining of the cervix swells with blood and tissue in preparation for receiving a fertilized ovum (see A03). If the ovum is not fertilized, all but the deepest layers of the uterine lining are discharged, with the ovum, as the menstrual flow. The cycle then repeats itself.

The usual cycle is 28 days but varies from woman to woman, and sometimes from month to month. Adolescents in particular are prone to irregular periods.

The diagram below shows the typical 28-day cycle.
Day 1: Start of menstruation
Day 5: End of menstruation
Day 14: Ovulation
Day 28: Last day of cycle
▨ Menstrual period

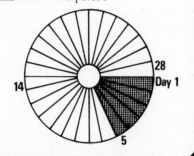

M07 ONSET OF MENSTRUATION

Some girls start to menstruate as early as nine, whereas others may be 16 or 17. Most begin between the ages of 12 and 14. A medical examination is needed if the first period has not occurred by age 18. The diagram illustrates the general fall in the average age of onset during the 20th century.

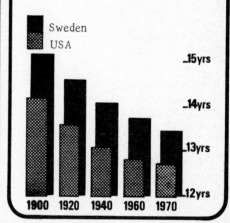

■ Sweden
▨ USA

M08 HAIR GROWTH

The growth of hair on different parts of the body is one of the characteristic developments of puberty. Girls develop pubic and underarm hair (see M02). Boys also develop hair on their faces and chests (see M03).

At first a boy's facial hair is soft and downy, and grows only slowly. Over a period of time it becomes heavier and darker, and shaving becomes necessary. The age at which a boy first needs to shave varies a great deal: some boys may shave for the first time at 12, others do not start shaving until they are 17 or 18.

Interest in head hair generally increases during adolescence as more attention is paid to personal appearance. Greasy hair - a common problem - is caused, like teenage acne (M10), by increased activity of the sebaceous glands during puberty.

M09 DEEPENING VOICE

A girl's voice deepens slightly during adolescence, but the change is much less marked than the voice change in males.

The transition from a boy's to a man's voice may take several years, and is caused by pubertal enlargement of the larynx (J48). Like other developments at adolescence voice-breaking occurs at different ages, and a boy whose voice breaks earlier or later than those of his contemporaries may be a target for teasing. Growth of the larynx spurts ahead about the same time as the penis is finishing its final growth - often between 13 and 15 years old. While his larynx is growing a boy often loses control over his voice, causing strange croaking sounds or sudden changes of pitch. But once the teenager has mastered it, his developed voice will be much deeper and more manly.

M10 SKIN PROBLEMS

Skin problems are extremely common in adolescence, and can cause great heartache at a time when physical appearance is thought to be vitally important. Acne is an infection of the oil-producing sebaceous glands (J19). It results in pimples, blackheads, whiteheads, and sometimes boils and cysts. Face, neck, shoulders, chest, and back are often affected. At adolescence the sebaceous glands are extremely active, producing greater quantities of sticky sebum that clogs the pores and makes infection more likely. Most cases of acne clear up in time. Meanwhile attention should be paid to diet, hygiene, and choice of cosmetics. Treatments include lotions and creams to reduce the spread of infection, make the skin peel, and unblock the pores. Antibiotics may be needed in severe cases.

M

TOWARD EMOTIONAL MATURITY

M11 TOWARD MATURITY

Physical developments during adolescence bring a child's body to maturity. Inside his body the child will also have to mature emotionally, and leave behind a time when he was cared for by others. Soon he will have to care for himself, and then perhaps for his own family. This is exciting, but it can be frightening too. Interests and abilities may suddenly change. A boy who was small and physically weak may develop and shine on the sports field. Academic ability may rush ahead, or suddenly halt.

In their teens, young people no longer feel that their parents must be respected or obeyed without question. Quarreling is common; the teenager is testing his parents to find out if he really accepts their attitudes.

Above all, adolescence is a time when the opposite sex must be met in a new way. Traditionally boys and girls do not think highly of each other in the years before puberty. This now changes. A girl who was happy and confident in her pre-teen years may become shy with boys, feel that she is unacceptable to them, and become miserable. Boys, too, need support. There are new social customs to be learned and new sexual needs to be coped with. In adolescence young people test themselves. Only in this way can they learn who they are and what they will become. They are not sure yet if they are extroverted or shy, lighthearted or serious. Will their abilities and temperament draw them to practical work, a profession, business, or the arts? The late teens see the formation of moral and political views; young people conceive the sort of ideal world in which they would like to live.

Before the changes and turmoils of adolescence the pre-teen child is characteristically happy and self-confident.

Teenagers' exploration of their own opinions and identity may lead to family rows as parental standards are challenged.

When their friends seem to be developing faster than they are, teenagers can often feel deeply uncertain of themselves.

Young teenagers often have a strong sense of togetherness. They need each other's support, and dress alike to win this.

The end of childhood

Teenagers also challenge school authority. In this way they test their strength and show that they will soon be adults.

Growing up can be frightening. Teenagers go through periods of lethargy and depression, wishing that changes were not so rapid.

Mixed in with the rebellion of adolescence is often a strong concern for others and a need to help them in the tasks of life.

Teenagers want to know if forbidden things are really dangerous and shocking. Many try drink, smoking, and drugs.

Through dating, boys and girls meet each other on a more serious level. It is an essential part of getting to know the opposite sex.

Emerging from the trials of adolescence, the young adult seeks to make the world a better place for everyone.

First aid

With a first aid kit and a knowledge of basic first aid techniques, a parent can cope with numerous emergencies.

Left: Red Cross aid for Persian Gulf children (Central Press Photos Ltd)

HOME MEDICAL KITS

N01 FIRST AID KIT

Every home should have this kit: close at hand, in a portable box or can, and unlocked - but out of reach of children. It should be complete in itself - not dependent on kitchen scissors, for example.

Its medicines and lotions should be clearly labeled, its dressings kept well wrapped. A basic first aid pamphlet (or copies of this chapter) and a notepad and pencil should be kept inside, and

emergency phone numbers pasted to the lid. It should be sealed with adhesive tape, to keep it clean and dry and help keep out children. Similar kits should be kept in cars, boats, and campers.

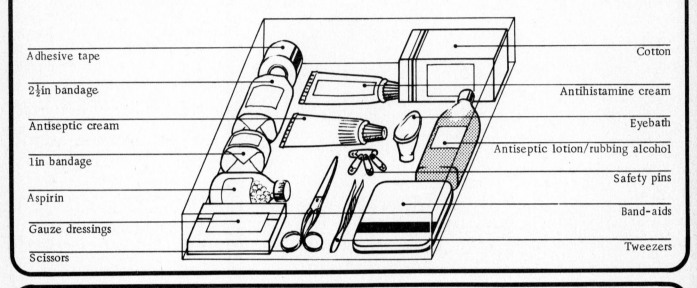

Adhesive tape
2½in bandage
Antiseptic cream
1in bandage
Aspirin
Gauze dressings
Scissors

Cotton
Antihistamine cream
Eyebath
Antiseptic lotion/rubbing alcohol
Safety pins
Band-aids
Tweezers

N02 EMERGENCY ITEMS

Here are shown some common home articles that may be useful in an emergency. It is a good idea to have all of them near at hand. Towels, handkerchiefs, and tissues are useful for cleaning or

covering wounds. Vinegar may be applied to wasp stings, and bicarbonate of soda to other stings and burns. Salt and water is a useful antiseptic. Olive oil may

be used for insects in ears. A needle can be quickly sterilized by holding over a lighted match before using to remove stones from wounds.

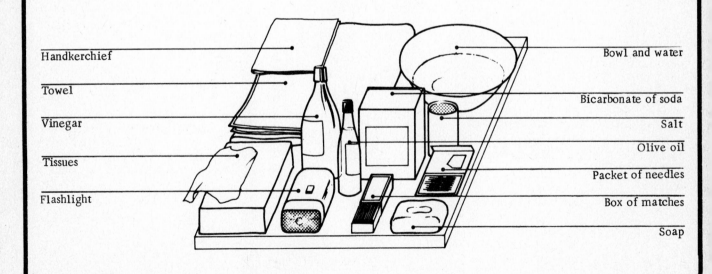

Handkerchief
Towel
Vinegar
Tissues
Flashlight

Bowl and water
Bicarbonate of soda
Salt
Olive oil
Packet of needles
Box of matches
Soap

First aid

N03 HOME TREATMENT KIT

This includes all the contents of the first aid kit, plus additional items (mainly medicines and lotions). It can be divided into compartments: one for wound cleaning and dressing, one for bandages and instruments, one for medicines and creams. (Do not include any prescribed medicines, though: these should be locked away separately.) As with a first aid kit, all items should be clearly labeled and first aid instructions and notepad and pencil added. But you should still have a separate – more portable – first aid kit, as shown in N01.

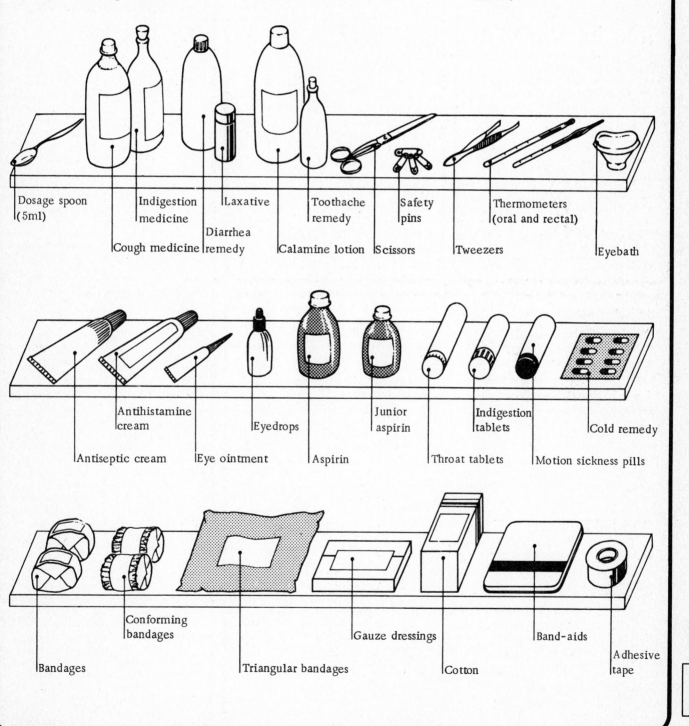

Dosage spoon (5ml)

Indigestion medicine

Laxative

Diarrhea remedy

Cough medicine

Toothache remedy

Calamine lotion

Safety pins

Scissors

Thermometers (oral and rectal)

Tweezers

Eyebath

Antihistamine cream

Antiseptic cream

Eye ointment

Eyedrops

Aspirin

Junior aspirin

Indigestion tablets

Throat tablets

Motion sickness pills

Cold remedy

Bandages

Conforming bandages

Triangular bandages

Gauze dressings

Cotton

Band-aids

Adhesive tape

N

©DIAGRAM

WOUNDS

N04 STOPPING BLEEDING

Press a pad of clean cloth against the wound. If bleeding continues, add thicker cloths on top, and use more pressure. Keep the injured area still, and calm the child. If a limb is badly cut (but not broken), it helps to raise it above the level of the rest of the body.

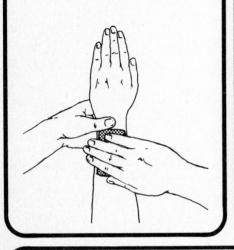

N05 WASHING A WOUND

Wash your own hands first. Clean the skin around the wound (wiping away from the wound), then the wound itself. Use soap, running water, antiseptic, and several fresh swabs (preferably of sterile gauze). Get out all loose dirt, etc; but anything embedded should be left for expert attention.

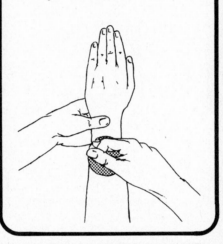

N07 BANDAGING A FINGER

Use sterile gauze as dressing, then cover with a long roll of narrow bandage. Run the bandage from base to tip of the finger, and back down the other side (1). Then wrap it around the finger (2), split the end (3), and tie (4). A finger stock (5) helps keep the bandage clean and secure.

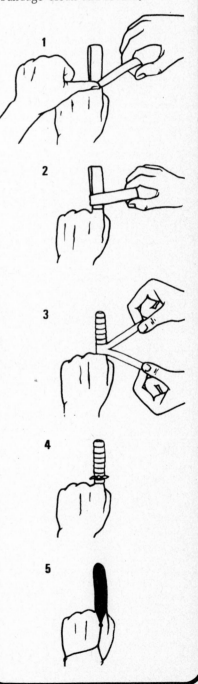

N06 DRESSING A WOUND

Apply mild antiseptic, using sterile gauze. When dry, cover wound and surrounding skin with a piece of sterile gauze, handling it only by the corners. Add surgical cotton on top, and keep this dressing in place with bandage or adhesive tape. Alternatively, use a prepacked sterile dressing and bandage.

When bandaging, start at the narrowest point (1). Overlap the first few turns, then work up. Bandage firmly but not too tightly. Finish with a safety pin (2) or adhesive tape, or split and knot the bandage end. In an emergency, a clean handkerchief or other cloth can be used.

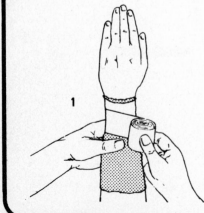

First aid

N08 ELBOW OR KNEE BANDAGE

Place the bandage against the elbow (or knee), point upward (**1**). Then wrap one of the bottom ends around the joint (**2**), and repeat with the other bottom end (**3**). Tie these two ends together, not too tightly (**4**), and finish by tucking the bandage point down over the knot (**5**).

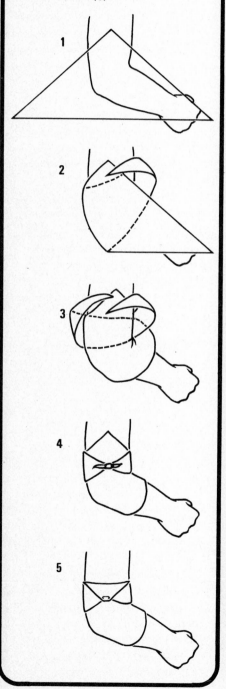

N09 INTERNAL BLEEDING

This can result from broken bones or ruptured internal organs. Blood may be coughed or vomited up, or be visible in the urine or feces, or trickle from nose or ear. Often, however, it is trapped in body tissues (which may swell) or in body cavities like the abdomen or chest (which may become painful). In any case of internal bleeding the victim shows rapidly developing symptoms of "shock" (pale face, cold, clammy skin, restlessness, rapid pulse, etc – see N19). Urgent medical attention is needed. Meantime take the measures against shock, and at intervals make notes for the doctor of the patient's pulse. Also note the color of any blood from the mouth (bright red, frothy blood is probably from the lungs, dark red or black from the stomach).

N11 WHEN TO CALL A DOCTOR

In the case of wounds, get urgent medical help for:
a) any internal bleeding;
b) any external bleeding that will not stop;
c) any external bleeding that only stops after considerable blood loss;
d) a bleeding nose or ear after a blow on the head.
Keep the patient still and quiet, and reassure him, till help comes. Also get medical attention without undue delay for:
a) any wound that has something embedded in it;
b) any puncture wound – one that is deeper than it is long (eg one made by a nail or knife point);
c) any wound from an animal bite;
d) any other wound that you think may be a tetanus risk.

N10 BRUISES AND BLACK EYES

A cold wet cloth on the damaged area should reduce pain and swelling. The cloth can be kept in place with waterproof material and a bandage. If after some days pain persists, see a doctor (for example, a black eye may conceal a fractured brow).

N12 BLEEDING NOSE

Make the child sit quietly as shown, nostrils held pinched together. Tell him to dribble any saliva in the mouth – swallowing movements can disturb blood clotting in the nose. After 10 minutes, if there is still bleeding, try plugging the nostrils with sterile gauze. Slight nosebleeds are common in childhood, but see a doctor if they become persistent.

N

RESUSCITATION

N13 ARTIFICIAL RESPIRATION

Mouth-to-mouth respiration can be used in almost any case where breathing has stopped.

1) Lay victim on his back. Turn his head to one side, and clear any debris from his mouth (**a**).

2) Turn his head up again, and put a folded coat under his shoulders. With one hand under the neck, and the other on the crown of the head, tilt the head back as far as possible. Then pull the chin up till the head is fully tilted back (**b**). This position ensures that the tongue does not obstruct the windpipe.

3) Put your mouth firmly over the victim's mouth, pinch his nostrils shut, and blow hard enough to make his chest rise (**c**). (With a small child, put your mouth over his nose and mouth, and use shallow breaths.)

4) Remove your mouth and listen for exhaled breath (**d**). Then repeat the blowing in: once every 3 seconds for children (once every 5 to 6 seconds for adults).

5) If no air is exhaled, check the victim's head and chin position, and check that his tongue is not blocking his throat. Try again.

6) If still no exhalation, put the victim's head down for a moment over your lap, and slap him sharply between the shoulder blades, to dislodge any blockage. Wipe the mouth clear.

a

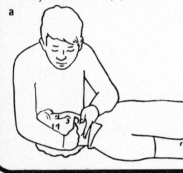

b

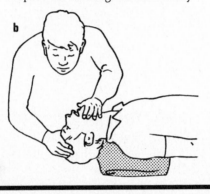

c

N14 DROWNING

Start artificial respiration at the earliest possible safe moment (eg in shallow water, in a boat, or at the water's edge). Do not try to drain water from the lungs: any that comes up will probably be from the stomach. Just clear the mouth of water, seaweed, etc, and give artificial respiration till breathing starts.

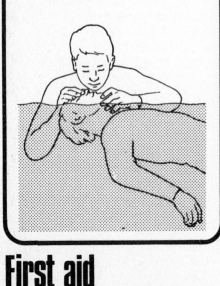

N15 FAINTING

If someone feels faint, make him lie down or sit as shown, and breathe deeply till he feels better. If he faints, lay him down on his back, head low, legs raised. Loosen tight clothing (especially at the neck), and let him come round in his own time. If the fainting lasts more than a minute or two, keep him warm and get medical attention.

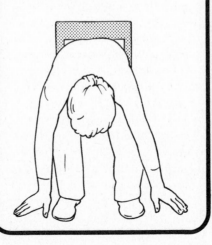

N16 FITS (CONVULSIONS)

In a fit, the victim's body seems jerked by uncontrollable spasms. His head may be thrown back, his lips turn blue, his eyes roll up, his mouth froth. Do not try to restrain him, or throw cold water over him, or pick him up to rush for help. But do guide his movements, remove furniture, and lay him on the ground so that he cannot hurt himself. (If it can be done without force, put a rolled handkerchief between his teeth to stop him biting his tongue.) Also keep his airway clear by loosening clothing at the neck and turning his head to one side so saliva drains out. If you can, guide him into the recovery position (see N18). A fit usually lasts only a few minutes. Afterward, put him to bed and get medical advice. Give no food or drink. A single fit in a child is commonly a sign of fever (K28), and sponging with tepid water may help.

First aid

7) Don't give up till the victim starts to breathe. Many have revived after hours of artificial respiration.

8) When he is breathing strongly, keep him warm and get help. Don't let him get up. Put him in the recovery position (N18) if you think he may vomit.

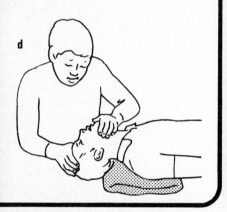

N18 RECOVERY POSITION

Death following unconsciousness is often from suffocation or pneumonia, due to the victim inhaling his own saliva or vomit. To prevent this, if someone is unconscious but breathing, place him in the recovery position shown: stomach down; head turned to one side; and arm and leg on that side pulled up till the thigh is at right angles to the body, and the hand level with the jaw. Pull the chin forward and up, so that the tongue cannot block the throat.

Loosen the collar, and see the mouth is clear of debris, blood, or mucus; remove false teeth. Do not put a pillow under the head. In fact, if possible, raise the legs and body slightly above head level, so fluids drain away from the lungs. Look for hidden bleeding beneath clothes or body; deal with any external wounds. Then cover with one blanket and watch closely till help comes. Give nothing to drink even if consciousness returns.

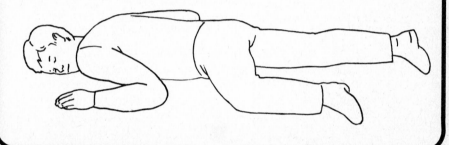

N17 ELECTRIC SHOCK

ELECTRIC SHOCK

Act fast - every second counts.

1) Break the victim's contact with the current in the quickest SAFE way (see below).

2) Check his breathing, and use artificial respiration if necessary (continue for hours if need be: recovery is still possible).

3) If breathing but unconscious, put in recovery position (see N18).

4) Give first aid to any burns.

5) Get help urgently.

BREAKING ELECTRIC CONTACT

a) Pull out plug, turn off current at fuse box, or pull away appliance by cord; or

b) pull at a DRY, LOOSE part of the victim's clothing; or

c) push or pull at the body with any dry non-metallic object. But DO NOT touch the victim's body; and be sure you are standing on a dry surface and touching only dry materials.

N19 SHOCK

Shock is of two kinds:

a) nervous shock, due to emotional trauma or severe pain; and

b) surgical shock, due to loss of body fluid (eg from bleeding, burns, or repeated vomiting or diarrhea). The second is much more dangerous. The victim is pale, with a cold or clammy skin, or rapid pulse, and rapid shallow breathing. He is often restless and apprehensive, with nausea and thirst. He may faint.

You should act quickly.

1) Lay the casualty down. Use the recovery position (N18) if vomiting seems likely. Otherwise keep his head slightly raised and turned to

one side, as shown.

2) Deal with the physical cause of shock (eg try to stop any bleeding).

3) Get medical help.

You can also loosen the patient's clothing at neck, chest, and waist, and cover him with a sheet or thin blanket. Moisten his lips if he is thirsty, and if possible note his pulse and breathing rates.

Do not:

a) warm the patient;

b) move him unless forced to;

c) give him anything to drink until he has been seen by a doctor.

FOREIGN BODIES

N20 CHOKING

Put the child over your knee, or over a chair back; or, if he is small enough, pick him up bodily. Then give three or four firm slaps between the shoulder blades. If this does not work, get medical help at once, and give artificial respiration (N13) if necessary.

Also – but only as a desperate measure – try reaching in and pulling the object out with your fingers.

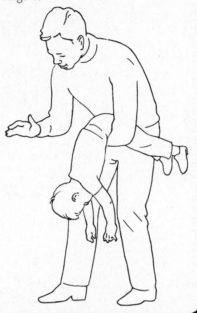

N21 FOREIGN BODY SWALLOWED

If the object is smooth, small, and rounded, it should cause no trouble. Just give normal diet, and examine the child's bowel movements for a few days, to make sure that the object has passed through. See a doctor, though, if the child is under two, or if he seems to become unwell. But if the object is sharp or pointed; or if there is any chance that it might have been inhaled into the lungs, not swallowed; then give nothing to eat or drink, and get medical help.

N22 REMOVING RINGS

Rings can get stuck because they are too small, or because the finger has swollen due to injury or infection. Smearing the finger liberally with soap (a) may allow the ring to be pulled off. If not, try binding thread tightly around the forefinger (b) for a short distance above the ring. Pull the ring up onto the bound part, unwind the thread behind it, and bind again above where the ring now is. Continue until you have worked the ring off the finger. But do not leave the binding on for any length of time, or else the blood supply to the finger will be affected.

a

b

N23 GRAZES

Remove any loose dirt, etc, with moist sterile swabs, or with tweezers sterilized in boiling water for five minutes. Then treat as a wound (N 05-06). But do not try to get out anything that is stuck or embedded: just wash the surrounding area, dry, put on a sterile dressing, and get medical attention.

First aid

N24 FOREIGN BODY IN THE EYE

Stop the child from rubbing the eye. If the object is sharp or hot, or if the eye is bleeding, do nothing, but get medical attention at once. But if it is probably just a speck of dust, bring the upper eyelid down over the lower, as shown (**a**), while the child turns his eye upward, or wash the eye, using an eyebath or eyedropper.

If these fail, look for the speck, and try to remove it with a moist cotton swab, or the moistened corner of a handkerchief (**b**). But if the foreign body does not move with the gentlest touch, stop, and get medical attention. Bandage the eye meanwhile to ease pain.

If any chemical gets in a child's eye, immediately flush it out with large amounts of water, making sure that the eye is wide open and the lids pulled back (**c**). Keep the child's head turned, so any chemical washed out does not run into the other eye. Do this for 15 minutes, then get medical help.

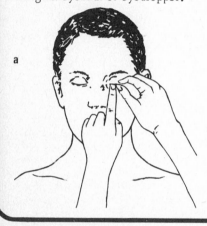

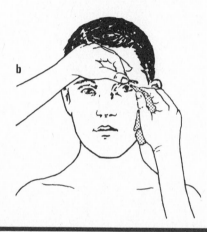

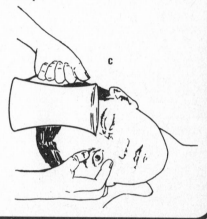

N25 SLIVERS (SPLINTERS)

If the sliver protrudes, wash your hands, wash the area well, and pluck out the sliver with sterilized tweezers, needle, or knife point. Press the skin so that a spot of blood comes from the wound, then wash well or apply a mild antiseptic. Cover with sterile dressing if necessary. Deeply embedded slivers or inflamed wounds need medical attention.

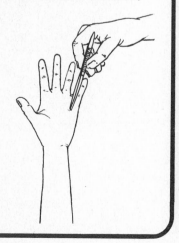

N26 FOREIGN BODY IN THE NOSE OR EAR

FOREIGN BODY IN THE NOSE
If the object is small and smooth, a sneeze will usually dislodge it: use pepper to set off sneezing (**a**). If this does not work, get medical advice. Do not try violent nose-blowing, or probe into the nostril, or pour water or oil into the ears.

FOREIGN BODY IN THE EAR
If the child has an insect in his ear, put in a few drops of lukewarm olive or mineral oil. This will stop the frightening buzzing, and may even wash the insect out. However with any other object in the ear, do nothing, except to tilt the head to one side, as shown (**b**), to see if the object falls out. If not, get medical help; any probing may damage the ear.

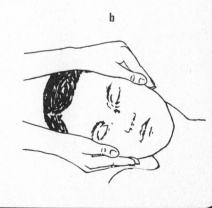

POISONING

N27 DANGEROUS ITEMS

a Some household chemicals, eg insecticide, rat poison, and weedkiller; kerosene, gasoline, benzine, turpentine, and any cleaning fluid; liquid furniture and auto polish; lye, and alkalis used for cleaning drains, bowls, etc; oil of wintergreen, ammonia, bleach, washing soda, and detergents; mothballs, and lead-based paint (which should never be used on indoor surfaces).
b Some grooming articles, eg perfume, cosmetics, hair tonics, nail polish and remover.
c Many prescription and some non-prescription drugs.
d Alcohol.
e Food containing bacteria; and misused food (eg salt given to a baby in mistake for sugar).
f Some common house plants (and water they stand in), eg soleander, diefenbachia, poinsettia.

N28 POSSIBLE SIGNS

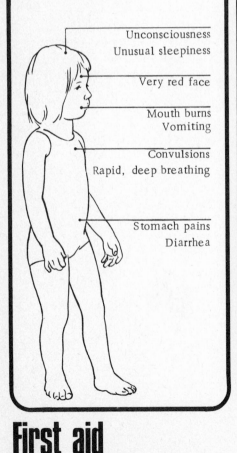

Unconsciousness
Unusual sleepiness

Very red face

Mouth burns
Vomiting

Convulsions
Rapid, deep breathing

Stomach pains
Diarrhea

N29 WHAT TO DO

1) If breathing is failing, give artificial respiration (see N13). (NB: use mouth to nose respiration if there is any chance of poison still in the mouth.)
2) If breathing but unconscious, put in recovery position (see N18).
3) If conscious but likely to vomit, put in recovery position (see N18).
4) Question the victim, if possible, and look for evidence of the poison (empty bottles, scattered pills, an odor, pills in mouth).
5) Call emergency help.
6) Decide whether to make the patient vomit; see N30.
7) Keep the patient warm till help comes. Do not leave.
8) Keep a sample of the poison and any vomit.
Still get attention even if: the patient vomits, and then seems all right; the poison seems to have had no effect; you are not sure if any poison was taken.

N30 INDUCED VOMITING

Make the patient vomit ONLY if:
a) he is fully conscious; and
b) he is not convulsing; and
c) you know for certain that the poison is not an acid, alkali, or liquid petroleum product.
To induce vomiting: either tickle the back of the throat with your fingers; or give two tablespoons of salt or mustard in a glass of warm water. Before he vomits make the patient lie on his front, with his head lower than his body and over a bowl. Induce repeated vomiting if possible.
If it is safe to induce vomiting, it is also safe to give bland fluid (eg water or milk) afterward to dilute any remaining poison.

First aid

BITES AND STINGS

N31 ANIMAL BITES

Calm the victim. Use running water on the wound to flush out saliva. Then wash wound well for five minutes with sterile swabs, using soap and water (not strong antiseptics such as iodine). Rinse, dry, and dress the wound, and get immediate medical attention. Animal bites are seldom serious, but anti-tetanus and/or anti-rabies injections may be needed. (If possible, catch the animal so it can be watched for rabies symptoms.)

N32 PLANTS AND JELLYFISH

NETTLE STINGS Relieve with calamine lotion or antihistamine cream.
POISON OAK OR POISON IVY Wash at once with soap and water. Then wash with rubbing alcohol to relieve itching.
JELLYFISH STING Treat with calamine lotion or antihistamine cream. But if the victim gets short of breath, or faints, get emergency medical attention.

N33 MOSQUITOES, GNATS, ANTS

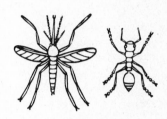

Wash with soap and water. Apply calamine lotion, antihistamine cream, or a paste of bicarbonate of soda and water. Cover any swelling with a cold wet cloth. Do not let the child scratch the bite - this can damage the skin and increases the risk of infection. Mosquitoes and gnats can carry disease so if any complications develop within a few days get medical advice, especially if in a tropical or subtropical country.

N34 FLEAS, LICE, TICKS

Isolated lice and ticks can be loosened by covering them with oil, grease, turpentine, or nail polish. They can then be removed with tweezers (with ticks make sure that you remove the head as well as the body). Crush the creature, and flush away or burn. Clean flea, louse, or tick wounds with soap and water or a mild antiseptic, and apply calamine lotion or antihistamine cream. Get advice about the possibility of transmitted diseases such as tick fever. (For treatment of infestations of fleas and lice, see K24.)

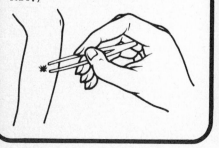

N35 BEES, WASPS, HORNETS

If the sting is still in the skin, scrape it out with a sterilized needle. (Do not pull it out with tweezers or fingernails: you may squeeze more poison into the wound.) If the sting has just occurred, apply antihistamine cream. If not, run cold water over the area, dry, and then apply surgical spirit or a solution of bicarbonate of soda. For a sting in the mouth, give a mouthwash of bicarbonate of soda solution. Get medical help if:
a) the victim shows signs of general distress, eg skin rash, pallor, weakness, nausea, or tightness in chest, nose, or throat;
b) there is a dangerous swelling (eg from a sting in the mouth); or
c) the victim has been stung many times.

N36 SNAKE BITES

If non-poisonous, treat as an animal bite. If poisonous or unknown, tie a tourniquet above the bite, cut two $\frac{1}{4}$in crossed incisions over the fang marks, and suck out the bite well (swallowing the poison is dangerous only if you have an abrasion in the mouth or digestive tract). Get urgent medical help. Keep the victim lying down and quiet, with the bitten area in ice or cold water. Loosen the tourniquet for 2-3 minutes every 15 minutes; suck the wound every 5 minutes. If possible, kill the snake for identification.

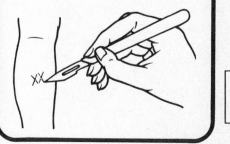

BURNS

N37 TYPES OF BURN

There are three main types:
a) dry burns, caused by fire, over-hot material (eg metal or rubber), electricity, or friction;
b) scalds, caused by over-hot liquid or fat; and
c) chemical burns, caused by acids, alkalis, and some other chemicals.

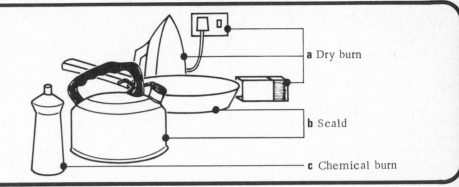

a Dry burn

b Scald

c Chemical burn

N38 SERIOUSNESS OF A BURN

This depends on its area and depth. The area will be obvious. Degrees of depth include:
a) skin reddened, but not blistered;
b) skin blistered;
c) layers of skin destroyed.
The first two are "superficial," the last "deep."
Any deep burn, however small, needs medical attention. But a large superficial burn can be more dangerous, for shock due to loss of body fluid (see N19) depends on the area of a burn, not its depth. Pain is no guide to a burn's seriousness: a deep burn can destroy nerve ends, so no pain is felt.

N39 CHEMICAL BURNS

Chemical burns are caused by acids (eg hydrochloric acid), alkalis (eg caustic soda), and some other chemicals. With chemical burns, always wash the burn with large amounts of water for up to 10 minutes. Also remove any affected clothing, with gloves if necessary. Then treat as for other burns.

N40 TREATMENT OF BURNS

SMALL SUPERFICIAL BURNS (ie smaller than the size of the victim's palm). Run cold tap water over the burn for a few minutes (a). Wash own hands well; also wash the burn gently if dirty. Dry the burn. If there is no blistering of the skin, a mild, soothing ointment may be applied. If there is blistering, apply nothing, and do not pierce the blisters, simply cover the burn with a sterile non-fluffy dressing and bandage (b).
ALL OTHER BURNS As above, but keep under water longer, apply nothing except a dressing, give liquid to drink, then get medical attention. Do not breathe on the burn or touch it, and do not pull away clothing stuck to it. If large areas are involved, also give treatment for shock (N19), and get help urgently. With very large burns, immerse till help arrives (c).

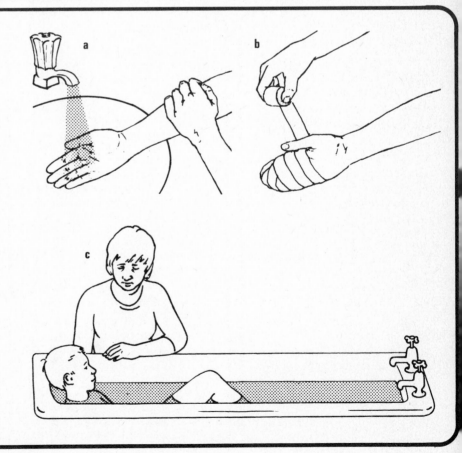

First aid

N41 SUN AND HEAT

SUNBURN

Treat as a burn. If there is no blistering and the burned area is small, apply ointment or lotion. If more severe, apply only a sterile dressing, and get medical advice.

HEAT EXHAUSTION

This develops gradually in very hot and humid conditions, when the body sweats profusely. Loss of body fluid and salt produces shock (N19). Symptoms include muscle cramps, exhaustion, restlessness, a pale face, and cold, clammy skin. Often there is dizziness, headache, nausea, loss of appetite, rapid breathing, and a rapid pulse. Make the victim lie down in a cool darkened area, fan air over him, and apply wet cloths to the head and body. Get him to drink a glass of water containing $\frac{1}{2}$ teaspoon of salt, and repeat this

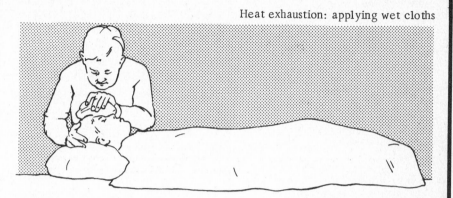

Heat exhaustion: applying wet cloths

three times at half-hour intervals. If the child is young, or does not recover quickly, get medical help. If fainting or unconsciousness occur, treat immediately as heatstroke.

HEATSTROKE

This is similar to heat exhaustion but more sudden and severe. The victim is red-faced, with hot, dry skin and a high temperature (eg 104°F: 40°C). Breathing is noisy, the pulse strong but fast. Stupor or unconsciousness are common. The urgent need is to get the body temperature down. Strip the victim, and immerse in cold water - or keep pouring cold water over him. Once temperature is below 102°F (38.8°C), wrap in cold wet sheets in the recovery position (N18). Fan air over him. Get medical help.

N42 COLD

FROSTBITE

Warm the victim gradually at room temperature, and give warm food and drink (not alcohol). Thaw out the frostbitten parts slowly: eg cover frostbitten ears or nose with a gloved hand, place frostbitten fingers in the armpits under the clothing. Do not apply heat directly to the frostbitten part, or rub it, or immerse it in hot water, or apply snow. Finally, begin to move the frostbitten part very gently. Get medical attention.

EXPOSURE

Remove wet clothing, wrap the victim in dry blankets, and get him to warm conditions. If possible, place him in a tub of warm water (not too hot). Dry, place in a warm bed, give warm drinks, and get medical help.

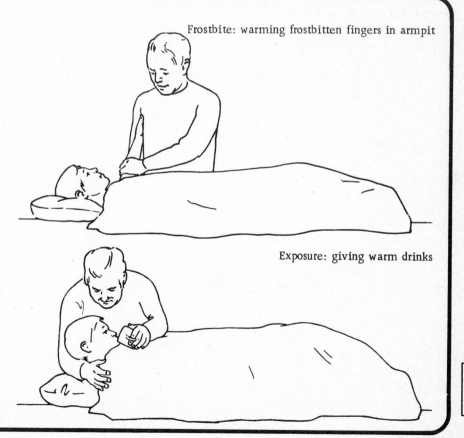

Frostbite: warming frostbitten fingers in armpit

Exposure: giving warm drinks

© DIAGRAM

JOINT AND MUSCLE PROBLEMS

N43 SPRAINS

Sprained ankles are common. The ligaments of the joint are stretched or torn, causing swelling and pain, which increase if the foot is used. A cold compress may reduce the swelling, and firm bandaging relieve pain, but it is best to get medical attention as well in case of fracture. To bandage, surround the joint (**a**) with a thick layer of cotton (**b**) and then bandage firmly as shown (**c**). On top, apply a second layer of cotton (**d**) and bandage again (**e**). Rest foot until swelling goes down.

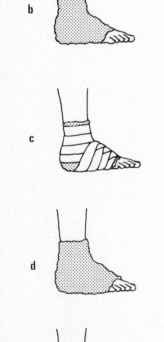

N44 PULLED MUSCLE

This is overstretching or tearing of muscle fiber, due to a sudden movement or to handling heavy weights. There is a sudden sharp pain, then pain whenever the damaged part is moved. Make the victim comfortable, with the injured part supported, and get medical attention.

N45 CRAMP

This is sudden painful contraction of a muscle, brought on by chilling (as in swimming), or badly coordinated movement, constriction, or loss of salt and body fluid (eg through sweating). If it occurs, treatment involves forcibly contracting the opposite set of muscles, so that those causing trouble relax by reflex. The drawings show correct procedures for cramp in foot or calf (**a**) and hand (**b**).

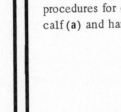

N46 DISLOCATION

The joint is immovable and very painful, and looks deformed. Do not use force, or try to put the bone back in place. Support the limb in a comfortable position (a dislocated leg can be bound to the good leg, in a lying position). Get medical attention. Watch the limb for impaired circulation.

a Normal joints

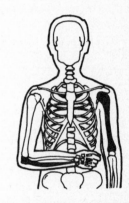

b Dislocated joints

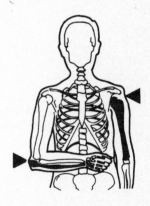

c Signs of dislocation

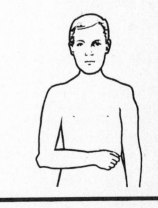

First aid

FRACTURES

N47 FRACTURES

Childhood fractures sometimes go unnoticed and untreated. This can be because a child's nervous system may not register the pain very acutely. Also children's fractures are often "greenstick" ones (see N48), with no complete break in the bone. So watch for other signs of a fracture: tenderness, swelling, and bruising. A broken limb is also often misshapen and uncontrollable. If you do suspect a fracture:

a) do not let the child use or move the affected part, and do not move or straighten it yourself;

b) stop any bleeding (see N04), and lightly cover any protruding bone with sterile dressings;

c) keep the child warm, and treat for shock (N19) if necessary; and

d) get medical help.

Do not try to push a protruding bone back in, or clean its wound. And do not move the child, except to avoid further immediate danger - in which case use a stretcher. Moving someone with a broken neck or back is especially dangerous. The only exceptions to the rule about moving are for a broken wrist, arm, or collarbone, when you can move the child to transport or to a warm place. But first support the arm well with a sling.

N48 TYPES OF FRACTURE

The main types are:

a) closed - the skin surface is not broken;

b) open - the bone is exposed to the air (ie it protrudes, or there is a deep wound over it);

c) "greenstick" - the bone is bent or not completely broken;

d) splintered - part of the bone is shattered;

e) complicated - some other part of the body (eg a blood vessel, or a nerve) has also been damaged in the fracture.

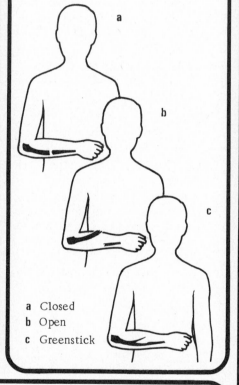

a Closed
b Open
c Greenstick

N49 ARM SLING

Using a triangular bandage:

a put the bandage between the chest and forearm, with the point out beyond the elbow and the top round behind the neck;

b bring the bottom up in front, tie to the top, and fasten in the point.

IMPROVISED SLINGS can be made with belts (**c**), scarves, neckties, or pinned-up sleeves.

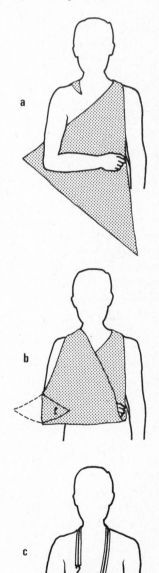

N50 SPLINTS

A splint is used to immobilize a broken limb, if medical help is not quickly available. Wood, metal, or stiffly rolled newspaper can be used, and the splint is bound to the limb above and below the break - firmly, but not too tightly. Alternatively, a broken leg can be bound to the good leg to steady it, and a broken arm to the chest.

N

© DIAGRAM

BIBLIOGRAPHY / ACKNOWLEDGMENTS

BIBLIOGRAPHY

Anderson, L., Dibble, M., Mitchell, H., Rynbergen, H. NUTRITION IN NURSING J. B. Lippincott

Bailey, Rosemary E. OBSTETRIC AND GYNECOLOGICAL NURSING Bailliére Tindall

Best, C. H. and Taylor, N. B. THE LIVING BODY Chapman and Hall

Bourne, Gordon PREGNANCY Pan Books

Charlton, C. A. C. THE UROLOGICAL SYSTEM Penguin Books

Comer, James P., and Poussaint, Alvin F. BLACK CHILD CARE Pocket Books

Cox, James FUN AND GAMES OUTDOORS Pan Books

Davidson, S., Passmore, R., Brock, J. F., Truswell, A. S. HUMAN NUTRITION AND DIETETICS Churchill Livingstone

De Kok, Winifred YOUR BABY - AND YOU Pan Books

Diagram Group MAN'S BODY Paddington Press

Diagram Group THE WAY TO PLAY Paddington Press

Diagram Group WOMAN'S BODY Paddington Press

Dubos, Rene, and Pines, Maya HEALTH AND DISEASE Time-Life Books

Dunn, Judy DISTRESS AND COMFORT Fontana/Open Books

Egan, D. F., Illingworth, R. S., and MacKeith, R. C. DEVELOPMENTAL SCREENING 0-5 YEARS Heinemann

Ellis, R. W. B. HEALTH IN CHILDHOOD Penguin Books

Fleck, H. INTRODUCTION TO NUTRITION Collier Macmillan

Garret, Stephen CHILDREN'S ROOMS Studio Vista

Garvey, Catherine PLAY Fontana/Open Books

Gelson, Hilary CHILDREN ABOUT THE HOUSE Design Centre Books

Gesell, Arnold (ed) THE FIRST FIVE YEARS OF LIFE Methuen

Gesell, A., and Ilg, F. L. INFANT AND CHILD IN THE CULTURE OF TODAY Harper and Row

Gremill-Mathers THE RESPIRATORY SYSTEM Penguin Books

Grey, Jayne PARTY GAMES FOR YOUNG CHILDREN Ward Lock

Griffiths, Ruth A STUDY OF IMAGINATION IN EARLY CHILDHOOD Kegan Paul

Guttmacher, Alan F. PREGNANCY AND BIRTH The New American Library

Gwynne Jones, Eufron CHILDREN GROWING UP Penguin Books

Hadfield, J. A. CHILDHOOD AND ADOLESCENCE Penguin Books

Harvey, David THE BABY BOOK Marshall Cavendish

Hedges, Sid GAMES FOR CHILDREN WHILE TRAVELING Ward Lock

Hostler, Phyllis THE CHILD'S WORLD Penguin Books

Illingworth, R. S. THE DEVELOPMENT OF THE INFANT AND THE YOUNG CHILD Churchill Livingstone

Illingworth, R. S. THE NORMAL CHILD Churchill Livingstone

Illingworth, R. S. THE NORMAL SCHOOL CHILD Heinemann

Jackson, Louise T. JUVENILE COURT STATISTICS US Department of Health, Education, and Welfare

James, Roger UNDERSTANDING MEDICINE Penguin Books

Jolly, Hugh BOOK OF CHILD CARE George Allen and Unwin

Kelley, Clarence M. CRIME IN THE UNITED STATES Federal Bureau of Investigation

Larsson, Lena YOUR CHILD'S ROOM Penguin Books

Leach, Penelope BABYHOOD Penguin Books

Lewis, J. G. THE ENDOCRINE SYSTEM Penguin Books

Llewellyn-Jones, Derek EVERYWOMAN Faber and Faber

Macfarlane, Aidan THE PSYCHOLOGY OF CHILDBIRTH Fontana/Open Books

Matterson, E. M. PLAY WITH A PURPOSE FOR THE UNDER-SEVENS Penguin Books

Miller, Benjamin (ed) THE MODERN ENCYCLOPEDIA OF BABY AND CHILD CARE Golden Press

Mitchell, Ross G. CHILD LIFE AND HEALTH Churchill Livingstone

Nathan, Peter THE NERVOUS SYSTEM Penguin Books

Newsom, John and Elizabeth PATTERNS OF INFANT CARE Penguin Books

Nixon, W. C. W. CHILDBIRTH Penguin Books

Nourse, Alan E. THE BODY Time-Life Books

Rothenberg, Robert FIRST AID Crown Publishers

Reference

Rudinger, Edith (ed) THE NEWBORN BABY Consumers' Association
Ryall, R. J. THE DIGESTIVE SYSTEM Penguin Books
Sandström, C.I. THE PSYCHOLOGY OF CHILDHOOD AND ADOLESCENCE Penguin Books
Saunders, E. J. HUMAN BIOLOGY University Tutorial Press Ltd
Schaffer, Rudolph MOTHERING Fontana/Open Books
Schifferes, Justus J. THE FAMILY MEDICAL ENCYCLOPEDIA Pocket Books
Sheridan, Mary CHILDREN'S DEVELOPMENTAL PROGRESS National Foundation for Educational Research
Smith, Anthony THE BODY Penguin Books
Spock, Benjamin BABY AND CHILD CARE Pocket Books
Tanner, James GROWTH Time-Life Books
Vaughan, Gerald MUMMY, I DON'T FEEL WELL Arcade Publishing
Vincent de Francis, J. D. PROTECTING THE CHILD VICTIM OF SEX CRIMES The American Humane Association
Ward, Brian SEX AND LIFE Macdonald Educational
Weiner, Florence HELP FOR THE HANDICAPPED CHILD McGraw Hill
Wingate, Peter THE PENGUIN MEDICAL ENCYCLOPEDIA Penguin Books
Winnicott, D. W. THE CHILD, THE FAMILY, AND THE OUTSIDE WORLD Penguin Books
Young, Daniel C., and Weller, Barbara F. BABY SURGERY Miller and Medcalf

FAMILY HEALTH GUIDE Reader's Digest Association Ltd
MEDICAL CARE OF NEWBORN BABIES Spastics International Medical Publications
TWO TO TWELVE - THE FORMATIVE YEARS Hamlyn
US FACT BOOK, THE (1976) Grosset and Dunlap
YOUNG CHILDREN AND ACCIDENTS IN THE HOME US Department of Health, Education, and Welfare
YOUR CHILD FROM 1 TO 6 US Department of Health, Education, and Welfare
YOUR CHILD FROM 6 TO 12 US Department of Health, Education, and Welfare

ACKNOWLEDGMENTS

Warm thanks for their assistance are extended to the following manufacturers, organizations, and departments:

Abbatt Toys

Cow and Gate Baby Foods

ESA Creative Learning

Fisher-Price Toys

James Galt and Co.

Gerber Baby Council

Glaxo-Farley Foods

H. J. Heinz Co.

KL Automotive Products

Liga Infant Feeding Service

Little Rock

Milton Products

Newton Aids

Robinson Baby Foods Division

SMA (Wyeth Laboratories)

Sonicaid

American Cancer Society

American Foundation for the Blind Inc.

American Humane Association, Children's Division

Epilepsy Foundation of America

Health Education Council (UK)

National Association for Maternal and Child Welfare (UK)

National Association for Mental Health (UK)

National Association for Mental Health (US)

National Association of the Deaf (US)

National Center for Juvenile Justice (US)

National Children's Bureau (UK)

National Deaf Children's Society (UK)

National Institute of Child Health and Human Development (US)

National Institute of Mental Health (US)

National Society for Autistic Children (UK)

National Society for Autistic Children (US)

National Society for the Prevention of Cruelty to Children (UK)

Royal National Institute for the Blind (UK)

Royal National Institute for the Deaf (UK)

Spastics Society (UK)

United Cerebral Palsy Association Inc. (US)

United States Department of Health, Education, and Welfare

INDEX

Reference

INDEX

Reference